"Ivan Berend brings the sensibility of a leading economic historian whose personal history means he can see the European Union both from the inside and from the outside. He can see its promise yet note its failings. But he also sees that its current 'existential crisis,' as he calls it, means we must choose to either go forward with the bold experiment or slip back into the bad old ways that the EU in its origins was designed to transcend."

— **John Agnew,** *author of* Globalization and Sovereignty: Beyond the Territorial Trap

"I highly recommend reading this book by a world-wide well-known expert author who presents a concise analysis of the given situation of the European Union, surrounded by enemies and attacked by populist-nationalists inside, but still strong enough to reinvent itself and positively influence the future history of Europe and the world."

— **László Valki,** *Professor of International Law, Eötvös Loránd University, Budapest*

"The EU created peace, democracy, and prosperity in a war-torn Europe; yet, it is now troubled. Why? How can it be saved? Students, opinion leaders, and the wider public should read Ivan Berend's elegant, succinct latest book to find answers."

— **Daniel Chirot,** *Herbert J. Ellison Professor of International Studies, University of Washington*

"Populism is a political and ideological challenge to the EU – and potentially an existential threat. This book is a timely summary of its rise and how the EU can reinvent itself without sacrificing its core values."

— **Jonathan Portes,** *Professor of Economics and Public Policy, King's College London*

AGAINST EUROPEAN INTEGRATION

This book gives a complex description and discussion of today's populist attacks against the European Union (EU) following the financial crisis of 2008, which opened the floodgates of dissatisfaction, and the migration crisis which destabilized the traditional solidarity basis of the EU. The problem of Brexit is also explored.

Each chapter presents one of the main elements of the crisis of the EU. These include West European populism, Central European right-wing populism in power, and the exploitation of the EU's mistake during the migration crisis of the mid-2010s. These also include the discovery of Christian ideology against immigration and hidden anti-Semitic propaganda using a hysterical attack against the liberal billionaire philanthropist George Soros, and Brexit. There is a detailed discussion of the failures of the EU to pacify the neighborhood in the South and North, especially in Ukraine, and the rising hostile outside enemies of the EU, including Russia and Turkey; bad relationships with Trump's America; the uncertainty of NATO; and the emergence of a new rival, China, that enters into the Central European edge of the EU.

The author explores strategies for coping with, and emerging from, this existential crisis and ends with the alternative plans and possibilities for the future of the eurozone. This will be an invaluable resource for understanding the crisis of the EU, one of the central questions of contemporary international politics for undergraduate and graduate students, and readers interested in the discussion surrounding an endangered European integration and difficult world politics.

Ivan T. Berend is a Distinguished Research Professor at the University of California, Los Angeles (UCLA), USA. He is a member of the American Academy of Arts and Sciences; the British Academy; the Academy of Europe; and the Austrian, Hungarian, Bulgarian, and Czech Academies of Sciences. He was President of the International Historical Association between 1995 and 2000, and is author of 35 books.

Economics in the Real World

For more information about this series, please visit: www.routledge.com/Economics-in-the-Real-World/book-series/ERW

AGAINST EUROPEAN INTEGRATION

The European Union and its Discontents

Ivan T. Berend

Routledge
Taylor & Francis Group

LONDON AND NEW YORK

First published 2019
by Routledge
2 Park Square, Milton Park, Abingdon, Oxon OX14 4RN

and by Routledge
52 Vanderbilt Avenue, New York, NY 10017

Routledge is an imprint of the Taylor & Francis Group, an informa business

© 2019 Ivan T. Berend

The right of Ivan T. Berend to be identified as author of this work
has been asserted by him in accordance with sections 77 and 78 of the
Copyright, Designs and Patents Act 1988.

British Library Cataloguing-in-Publication Data
A catalogue record for this book is available from the British Library

Library of Congress Cataloging-in-Publication Data
Names: Berend, T. Iván (Tibor Iván), 1930– author.
Title: Against European integration: the EU and its discontents / Ivan T. Berend.
Description: Abingdon, Oxon; New York, NY: Routledge, 2019. |
Series: Economics in the real world | Includes index.
Identifiers: LCCN 2018057074 | ISBN 9780367191078 (hardback) |
ISBN 9780367187880 (pbk.) | ISBN 9780429200458 (ebook)
Subjects: LCSH: European Union—Public opinion. | Populism—
European Union countries. | European Union countries—Emigration
and immigration—Public opinion. | Europe—Economic integration—
Public opinion. | European Union countries—Politics and government. |
European Union countries—Foreign economic relations. |
Global Financial Crisis, 2008–2009—Influence.
Classification: LCC HC240 .B3944 2019 | DDC 341.242/2—dc23
LC record available at https://lccn.loc.gov/2018057074

ISBN: 978-0-367-19107-8 (hbk)
ISBN: 978-0-367-18788-0 (pbk)
ISBN: 978-0-429-20045-8 (ebk)

Typeset in Bembo
by codeMantra
Printed and bound by CPI Group (UK) Ltd, Croydon, CR0 4YY

CONTENTS

INTRODUCTION

The European integration process is the most important and positive development in the history of Europe. It started the process of establishing peace and collaboration between countries that had been warring against each other for roughly half of the last 400 years. It introduced unprecedented economic cooperation, free trade, flow of capital, and labor migration in a single market of 500 million people. According to certain calculations, between 1993 and 2003, the European Single Market has boosted the European Union's (EU's) Gross Domestic Product (GDP) by nearly €900 billion, increasing per household income by €5,700. EU membership increased the per capita GDP of poorer member countries by about 12 percent. According to the European Commission, more than 15 million EU citizens have moved to other EU countries to work or permanently settle after retiring. Further, 1.5 million young people have completed part of their studies in another member state through the EU's Erasmus program.[1]

The relationship between the rich Western and poorer Eastern member countries is not undisturbed and harmonious, but it still provides tremendous economic advantages from integration for both advanced and less-developed member countries. Poorer peripheral countries have received billions of euros from the EU budget as assistance for underdeveloped regions, which have a per capita GDP less than 75 percent of the EU's average. In 2014, for example, 11 Central and Eastern European member countries paid €16.7 billion to the EU budget but received €43.7 billion from it, thus gaining €27 billion. The advanced Western member countries invested in the poorer ones, establishing branches, subsidiaries, and value chains, and exported modern technology to less-developed member countries in order to exploit the possibility of much lower wages. This strategy helped to create modern high tech and semi-high tech sectors in countries previously without those industries and offered increased job possibilities. Workers from poorer regions also moved to find jobs in wealthier countries and sent money home, strengthening consumption. Consequently, several of the less-developed member countries began catching up with the most advanced ones. Spain and Ireland's income levels had previously belonged to the middle-income zone but eventually elevated into the high-income zone, defined as the top 20 percent of incomes from all countries in the world. Ireland emerged as one of the richest countries in Europe. This trend of catching up—which elevated the average income level of the peripheries by 15 percent (from 40 to 65 percent of the average West European level)—characterizes the Baltic and some Central European countries. Meanwhile, the stability of the EU also attracted more investment from outside. Inward investment grew from €23 billion in 1992 to €159 billion by 2005.[2]

The rich Northwestern European member countries also greatly benefited from selling their products on the huge, 500 million strong EU Single Market. Selling in and producing for a large market made it possible to exploit the advantage of scale and scope, decrease the cost of production, and increase productivity and profit. They also profited from providing credit for peripheral countries and building a Europe-wide banking network. Western banks are monopolizing the capital markets of the Eastern member countries, owning 87 percent of the banking sector in those countries. Western countries also benefited from the cheap labor in poorer countries by producing parts of their output in those member countries.

The agricultural sector and the peasant-farmer population in both the advanced and less-advanced member countries gained from the significant subsidies that the EU paid for them. In certain periods, these subsidies constituted about 40 percent of the EU's budget. In 2014, from the budget of €143 billion, agriculture and natural resources received €60 billion; in the budgetary period of 2014–20, these sectors have received 42 percent altogether. It especially helped countries where the agricultural sector was more significant: thus, Poland and Bulgaria gained relatively much more than Germany or Belgium.

According to Andrei A. Levchenko and Jing Zhang's calculations, the main winner from East-West integration is mostly the East.

> For West European countries, the mean welfare gain from trade integration with Eastern Europe is 0.16 percent. For East European countries, the mean gains from trade are 9.23 percent … [but] 20 percent for Estonia. For the West European countries the welfare gains from intra-West European integration are on average 16 times larger than the gains from integration with Eastern Europe. The nearly 8-fold expansion in East European exports between 1990 and 2007 far outpaces the growth of overall world trade. For geographical, historical, and political reasons the share of Eastern Europe in total West European imports from the rest of the world remained stable at about 10 percent from the early 1960s to the early 1990s, but it reached 24 percent by 2007.[3]

Citizens of all member countries, meanwhile, are not burdened by the EU for those impressive political, social, and economic advances. The amount member countries' citizens are paying to the joint budget of the EU is, according to *Politico*'s simple calculations, on average, equivalent to the price of a half cup of cappuccino per day. The citizens of the least developed Central European and Balkan member countries are paying only 15–25 percent of the price of a cup of cappuccino per day.[4]

Nevertheless, in spite of the tremendous advantages, the integration process is a rather difficult historical experience, and the EU has always had discontents. This is quite evident, especially considering European integration started after the climax of nationalist confrontations that had been occurring for more than a century. Although these conflicts culminated in World War II, which, in turn, generated an anti-nationalism reaction after the war, nationalist sentiment evidently did not disappear; indeed, in various countries, it accompanied the entire history of the European Economic Community (later the European Union).

Less than a decade after its foundation, the first major crisis hit the Community in the form of President Charles de Gaulle's "empty chair" policy, boycotting the Community's meetings protecting national sovereignty in protest against the plan to change the voting system, and introducing the weighted majority vote instead of the veto right of each member country. That was the very first significant discontent with supra-nationalization and future federalizing plans. This crisis almost paralyzed further development for nearly two decades.

In the 1980s, Margaret Thatcher, British prime minister, viciously opposed every additional integrating step of the Community, characterizing such efforts as attempts "to create a European superstate exercising a new dominance from Brussels" that ultimately aimed to realize a "utopian goal."[5] When the common currency was introduced at the turn of the millennium, Britain, Denmark, and Sweden opted out, and did not join the eurozone. In the 2010s, David Cameron, then British prime minister, strongly opposed steps toward integrating the member countries' armies and suggested the reorganization of the EU as a simple free trade zone.

In the spring of 2005, the newly created draft Constitution of the EU was voted down by France and the Netherlands. "The rejection," reported the *New York Times*, "could signal an abrupt halt to the expansion and unification of Europe, a process that has been met with growing disillusionment among the wealthier European Union members as needier countries like Bulgaria and Poland have negotiated their entry."[6] The EU's immigration policy met with the harshest possible resistance by Hungary, Poland, and the Czech Republic in 2015–16. These countries flatly rejected obeying the EU's decision.

Discontent accompanied almost every major attempt or step toward further integration or enlargement. Indeed, it actually increased as the scissor of income inequality started opening from the 1980s onward after a half century of the opposite trend. Inequality became rather significant within the member countries, closely following the general trend in the capitalist world from the late twentieth century. Meanwhile, the aggressive enlargement toward the European peripheries dramatically transformed the EU. By the early twenty-first century, the EU, after several waves of enlargements in 1973, 1981, 1986, 1995, 2004, and 2007, already had 27 member countries. (In 2013, the 28th also joined.) The relative homogeneity of the economic and income levels in the six founding member countries already belonged to the past. A "suicidal over-enlargement"[7] has broken the economic and social homogeneity of the EU. Less-developed members often revolted against the rich Western member countries that dominated "Brussels", saying in public speeches that they are "exploitative" and "dictating," even "colonizing."

Nevertheless, sometimes stopping, sometimes slowing down, sometimes dropping certain plans for the future, the EU still continued down the road of integration. The discontents based on the defense of national sovereignty often opposed further integration beyond political alliances and/or free market agreements, and, in some cases, opposed further enlargement. The crises, however, never endangered the existence of the Union.

The 2008 financial crisis opened a new chapter (one might say floodgates) for a continuous wave of devastating opposition and extreme discontent. True, the financial crisis hit the entire Union and spread from the financial sector to the real economy as well. Nevertheless, the impact of the Great Recession was rather different in the Northwestern European core than on the Southern and Eastern peripheries. The latter areas declined into an extremely deep crisis for nearly a decade: they were rendered unable to repay their debts, their banks collapsed, and the countries suffered tragic economic deterioration. Instead of formal equal membership, a sharp divide started separating the Western creditor and Southern and Eastern debtor member countries. This divide shattered the entire integration process and threatened the beginning of disintegration.

Since some of those peripheral countries had already introduced the common currency, their deep crisis endangered the euro as well. For the first time in the history of the EU, the possibility that the common currency, one of the major institutions and the symbol of unification, would collapse and that countries would drop out or deliberately leave the Union became a real possibility. Anti-EU parties in Britain and several other rich countries including France, the Netherlands, and Finland broadly propagated and discussed proposals for either excluding Greece from the eurozone or leaving the Union. As seen with "Grexit," "Brexit," and similar terms coined to denote the possible withdrawal of countries from EU, a new set of anti-EU terms appeared in the global vocabulary and were used in media discussions every day.

In those difficult times, as a consequence, the entire political representation system of Europe was also shattered and undermined. The old center-right and center-left parties started losing large swaths of their members and voters as a substantial number of people felt betrayed and not represented by their old parties. In some countries, the entire old party system collapsed. The center-left parties—government parties for decades that had often cooperated with center-right parties in grand coalitions—lost the most, and started disappearing completely.

The birth of new, sometimes leftist but mostly right-wing, populist opposition parties created a new political representation regime. They revolted against the establishment in their home countries but also strongly revolted against the EU. Its most shocking consequence was the British referendum to leave the EU.

The popularity of and the trust in the EU among the citizens of the member countries gradually hit rock bottom. As the "Eurobarometer 74," the EU's polling institution, reported in 2010, "For the first time in its history, the spring 2010 Eurobarometer (EB73) recorded a situation where distrust in the European Union outweighed trust."[8] While in 2004, 50 percent of the member countries' citizens trusted the EU institutions, and 36 percent did not, from 2009, confidence started changing; by 2010, 47 percent did not, and only 43 percent trusted the EU. Distrust was 64, 60, and 55 percent in Britain, Greece, and Austria, respectively.

By 2015 and 2016, however, a further dramatic decline characterized peoples' view of the Union. Besides years-long economic problems and unemployment, new and crucial crisis factors emerged: the migration crisis combined with Islamist terrorist attacks in several of the countries. These latter factors became the top consideration of the people. Instead of 50 (2004) and then 47 percent (2010), only 34 percent of the citizens of member countries had a positive view, and 35 percent trusted the EU, while 62 percent believed that their voice did not count.[9]

Despite being at the nadir of public opinion on the Union, two-thirds of people still thought of themselves as EU citizens, and half of the population remained optimistic in the future of integration. The decade after the 2008 financial crisis became the darkest decade of alienation from and discontents in the EU.

This time, discontents and hostility against the EU, disturbances, and uncontrollable conflicts emerged in the Southern and Eastern neighborhoods around the EU. In spite of the efforts of the Union to pacify those neighborhoods and assist their development by signing association agreements and making efforts to admit as new members neighboring countries from the Western Balkans, Turkey, and the Eastern neighbors of former Soviet republics such as Ukraine and Moldova, all of those efforts failed. For various reasons, hostile neighbors such as Russia and Turkey appeared at the Eastern and southeastern borders during a time of cooling down in the relationship with the US. Combined with a weakened NATO alliance, this moment marked the first period of endangered security in the EU. China, an elevating new world power, also entered the ring with a huge investment against the EU in its soft Central European and Balkan belly, and attacked the cohesion of the member countries.

After a decade-long crisis, however, the EU emerged from the complex crises in 2017–18. The economy started growing again, the common currency was stabilized and regained its strength, and immigration came under control again. In key countries the most dangerous anti-EU populist parties could not break through in the West, although some became dominant in several of the Mediterranean and Central European member countries. New and more flexible plans were prepared and discussed, and further new integration steps were undertaken within the eurozone. While a new chapter was seemingly opening for the development of the EU, new clouds also gathered on the horizon again. Anti-EU populism did not lose strength; to the contrary, it gained new steam and conquered countries such as Austria and Italy. Anti-Brussels populist groups and governments had a strong grip on Central Europe, penetrated by hostile rivals of Russia and China. While new plans were in the making, conflicts and discontents remained potentially devastating dangers.

Notes

1 Benefits of the European Union, https://econ.economicshelp.org/2007/03/benefits-of-european-union.html, July 3, 2016.
2 Ibid.
3 Andrei A. Levchenko and Jing Zhang, Comparative Advantage and the Welfare Impact of European Integration, National Bureau of Economic Research, Working Paper No. 18061, May 2, 3, 2012.
4 *Politico*, January 16, 2018, "The Capuccino Index".
5 Margaret Thatcher, "Family of the Nations," in *The European Union. Readings on the Theory and Practice of European Integration*, eds. Brent F. Nelsen and Alexander C.-G. Stubb (Boulder, CO: Lynne Rienner, 1998), 49–54.
6 "French Voters Soundly Reject European Union Constitution," *The New York Times*, May 30, 2005.
7 Ivan T. Berend, *The Contemporary Crisis of the European Union: Prospects for the future* (London: Routledge, 2017), 64–87.
8 Standard Eurobarometer 74 Report, Autumn 2010, 43, https://ec.europa.eu/commfrontoffice/publicopinion/archives/eb/eb74/eb74_publ_en.pdf, Autumn 2010.
9 Standard Eurobarometer 85 Report, Spring 2016, https://ec.europa.eu/commfrontoffice/publicopinion/index.cfm/ResultDoc/download/DocumentKy/75902.

1

EXISTENTIAL CRISIS, THE POSSIBILITY OF DISINTEGRATION, AND THE EUROPEAN UNION IN THE 2010s

The rise of an existential crisis: the economic factors

The statement in the title of this chapter—the existential crisis of the European Union (EU) and the ensuing fear of disintegration—was often repeated and broadly believed between 2009 and 2016. Like lightning from blue sky, the 2008 financial crisis stopped more than two decades of high prosperity and aggressive pressure for further integration in Europe. The period around the millennium was probably the most successful time in the half-a-century-long history of the EU. The Single Market project was initiated and realized, the common currency was introduced, and countries around the six founding members lined up before the door to join the EU. Several Southern, Northern, and Central European countries joined, and the number of member countries elevated to 28. Four other rich Western countries—although not members—joined the EU's common market by special treaties, while five others in the Balkans waited for membership. The impressive economic growth promised a relatively rapid catching up of the new, less-developed member countries located at the European peripheries.

In 2008, all of a sudden, everything changed. The international liquidity crisis, caused by the collapse of a major American mortgage bank, Lehman Brothers, froze crediting in the entire world economy. The cheap, credit-fueled prosperity bubble burst in Europe. An unprecedented real estate boom in several peripheral countries, generated by an overenthusiastic feeling of new richness and fueled by cheap credit, stopped. Tens of thousands of newly built homes remained empty; the real estate market collapsed. An EU review registered, "Taking into account the 2007–2012 period, house prices contracted considerably in Ireland (−49.5%, until 2010), Latvia (−35.7%) and Estonia (−30.2%). In Ireland, house prices in 2010 were significantly lower than they had been in 2005. A substantial decrease between 2007 and 2012 was also registered in Spain (−28.0%) and Romania (−26.1%, 2010–2012)."[1] The major banks of Ireland, Spain, Greece, and several other countries became bankrupt. The governments rushed to save the banks by refinancing them, but as a consequence, the countries themselves became unable to pay back their loans. Ireland; Spain; Portugal; Hungary; Romania; Bulgaria; Latvia; and, most of all, Greece declined into an unprecedented financial disaster. The Western banks, especially the major French and German organizations that credited the peripheral countries, were also hit hard.

"The EU economy is facing the biggest global economic downturn since the Second World War," reported the EU Commission in January 2009,

> This will invariably have significant impacts on households, people in (self-)employment, businesses and public finances throughout the Union. The next years will be difficult indeed.... The postponement in investment and consumer purchasing decisions may create a vicious cycle of further falling demand, downsized business plans, reduced innovation activities and labour shedding.... Car sales in the EU have plummeted leading to temporary closures of car manufacturing plants.[2]

The EU rushed to introduce a European Economic Recovery Plan. Its first pillar was

> a major budgetary impulse amounting to €200 billion, or 1.5% of EU GDP to boost demand.... It is made up of a budgetary expansion by Member States of at least €170 billion and EU funding in support of immediate actions in the order of €30 billion. The second pillar outlines a number of short-term actions designed to provide short-term support.[3]

The European saga of recurrent new crises continued as waves followed one another in an endless line. The most disastrous acute crisis was that which devastated Greece. The country continued down a road of irresponsible spending, widespread corruption, tax evasion, and deindustrialization, despite lacking a real modern industrial sector. It became mired in a hopeless situation when the government became unable to repay its debts and sold its bonds because the interest rates skyrocketed (in certain periods surpassing the usury rate of 37 percent).

The Western member countries, also hit by the crisis, were hesitant to act fast and solve the problem of Greece, which unfortunately had already implemented the common currency, the euro, without fulfilling the prerequisites of having a stable financial household behind it. Instead, as the new Greek government announced, the government had reported false figures. Several other insolvent southern countries and Ireland were also eurozone members. Their bankruptcies pushed the common currency to the brink as well. After 2009, all the member countries that were unable to repay their debts were bailed out by the International Monetary Fund (IMF) and the EU. Greece was actually rescued three times.

The deep financial crisis soon spread and undermined the "real economy," industry, and all other sectors as well. The level of national income severely dropped throughout the EU. Economic decline remained the rule for years in several countries. Between 2010 and 2016, 15 member countries suffered Gross Domestic Product (GDP) losses, and three more stagnated. The decline was most severe in the Baltic and Mediterranean regions: the three Baltic countries suffered a 15–18 percent GDP drop; the Mediterranean countries, Greece (more than 15 percent), Portugal (12 percent), and Spain and Italy (both more than 11 percent) also experienced significant losses. Some Central European countries, such as Slovenia and Hungary, also experienced a roughly 11 percent decline. Among the Western countries, the Netherlands's GDP dropped the most, by 10 percent.

It did not help that meanwhile, the GDP increased in ten other member countries: the highest increase occurred in two small countries with strong financial centers, Malta (+18 percent) and Luxembourg (+15 percent). After the decline of the first years, growth soon returned in Ireland, Sweden, and the three Baltic countries (as an average of 11 percent altogether).

The all-around economic crisis in the eurozone naturally undermined the common currency, which lost about one-third of its value. All of a sudden, it became clear that the monetary unification was a mistakenly unfinished construction. It was based on political decisions without the complex financial considerations necessary to create the strong foundation of fiscal unification, much like the construction of a building without a solid base. Throughout history, monetary unification has never happened without fiscal unification. The eurozone countries were not ready to give up central elements of their sovereignty, like national taxation systems and budgetary and crediting independence. Consequently, the euro was tragically endangered during the crisis; its collapse was seemingly near and broadly forecasted.

The unheard-of complexity of the European crisis was crowned by important new elements in the early to mid-2010s. The austerity measures adopted in the crisis-hit countries required cutting state expenditures, including health and educational spending, pensions, and wages. The EU, led by the creditor countries and most of all Germany, forced this policy onto the bankrupt debtor countries in order to help put their financial households in order and save the common currency. These measures were vehemently debated and considered by governments and several experts as counterproductive. I quote one typical statement:

> The medicine could actually kill the patient. The reduction of wages and in public and private spending will in the short run reduce effective demand below the growth potential, and in the long run it will slow down the potential growth rates.... All this makes servicing debt more difficult.

In essence, these individuals argued that EU austerity policy was wrong. In contrast, several experts and politicians did "not shy away from recommending a break-up of the Euro Area.... What is needed is generating economic growth out of which the debt can be serviced."[4]

True, these measures contributed to the decline of the GDP in the austerity countries, which made the relative share of debt compared to the GDP even higher and repayment more difficult. Nevertheless, the EU, in my view, rightly continued forcing the debtor countries to stabilize their finances, eliminate their sometimes huge budgetary deficits, and realize surpluses in order to be able to repay the debts. It was definitely painful, but in the long run, it was the only way to introduce normal financial order and stabilize the common currency in the eurozone. Regardless of the evaluation of austerity policy, it certainly generated mass dissatisfaction, anger, and even revolts in countries forced to apply it. The ensuing confrontation between debtor and creditor countries led to a harsh break in solidarity, the most important building material of the EU.

The social cost of the crisis was tremendous. Wages declined, social benefits were cut, the welfare states were curbed, and huge layers of society lost their jobs. Unemployment increased and, in several countries, elevated above 10 percent, but in some countries that were hit by the crisis especially hard, even to 15–20 percent. Youth unemployment became especially devastating. "At its worst," an EU report noted,

> in February 2013, youth unemployment stood at 23.5% in the euro area versus 12% overall unemployment. As of February 2017, these same figures stood at 19.4% and 9.5%, respectively. These indicators are dramatically more troubling in certain countries, notably Greece and Spain, which respectively showed rates of 47.3% and 44.4% youth unemployment for 2016 – Some 43% of youth aged 15-24 participate in the labour force, versus 85% of people aged 25–54.

There was a "lost generation," especially because youth unemployment also had long-term consequences for later employment and income.[5] Between 2008 and the spring of 2012, during the devastating crisis years, most European households saw a marked deterioration in their financial situation. All income groups were affected. An EU document shows a dramatic picture of the social consequences of the crisis: in some peripheral countries,

> those on low incomes felt the impact [of the crisis] most, especially in Estonia, Greece, Spain, Italy, Cyprus, Latvia, Hungary, Malta, Portugal and Slovakia. Between 2008 and 2011, the proportion of people reporting that their household was only just making ends meet rose sharply (by more than 4 percentage points) in the Baltic States, Cyprus, Greece, Hungary and Ireland. In 2010, 8.5 percent of the working-age individuals were at persistent risk of poverty already in at least three out of the previous four years. Persistent poverty is high, more than 10 percent in Italy, Greece, Portugal, Bulgaria, Romania, Poland and Ireland. The risk of poverty or exclusion among the migrant population remains much higher than among the EU population overall. For people aged 18+ born outside the EU-27,

it stood at 37.8 percent in 2011, compared to 20.8 percent for those born in the country and 22.2 percent for those born in another EU country. Children are generally more at risk of poverty or social exclusion than the overall population, with a rate of 27.1 percent as against 24.2 percent for the population as a whole in the EU in 2011.[6]

An EU policy paper analyzed the news coverage of the crisis, taking one major newspaper from each of the major euro-area countries, such as the German *Süddeutsche Zeitung*, the French *Le Monde*, the Italian *La Stampa*, and the Spanish *El País*. They collected 51,714 news articles on the crisis. It is interesting who was blamed for the crisis by those journals.[7] Most of the articles blamed Greece and the South European region for overindebtedness as a result of fiscal irresponsibility; Germany and the troika for imposing austerity policies; the national governments for mishandling the economy before and during the crisis; the banks' and other financial institutions' practices, which were at the core of the crisis; the exuberant capital markets' mispricing risk, which was leading to vicious spirals; Brussels institutions' not being willing or able to put the right remedies and stricter oversight of national budgets in place; and the European Central Bank (ECB) for being reluctant to act aggressively or for being too aggressive.[8]

Migration crisis and its connection with Europe's demographic crisis

On top of all of those major troubles, in 2015–16, a frightening migration crisis shocked the EU. At that time, nearly three million migrants "flooded" Europe from the Middle East, Africa, and Asia in a chaotic, unorganized way, generating a vicious political crisis.

Before that migration crisis, in 2009, the EU Commission made a demographic analysis and forecasts for the next half a century. The thoroughly calculated demographic facts put the entire migration crisis into a different light. First of all, it pays to recall that in the second half of the twentieth century (between 1950 and 2015), the world population exploded from 2.5 to 7.3 billion. During that time, Europe's demographic trend moved opposite the world's: in Europe, during the last three-quarters of the century, birth rates dramatically declined from 2.5 children/woman in the "baby boom" period of the second half of the 1960s to 1.52 children/woman in 2008, thus dropping below the reproduction level (2.1 children/woman). The share of Europe's population had already halved from about 15 percent of the world population in 1950 to 8 percent in 2000, and, as forecasted, it will shrink to about 5 percent in 2050.

International migration, partly connected to the world's population explosion, accelerated around the turn of the millennium. In the quarter century between 1990 and 2016, the world population increased by 38 percent, but the overall number of migrants increased by 59 percent. The population of Europe, however, in spite of the lack of natural reproduction, still increased by 2 percent as the demographic decline was more than compensated for by the 54 percent increase in immigrants. One-third of the world's migrants moved to Europe.[9] The population of the EU's 28 countries was 380 million in 1950 but 505 million by 2015, and, according to the calculations, it will be 510–520 million by 2030–35. The only source of population growth as well as the labor markets is immigration. From the last decades of the twentieth century, net inflows of immigrants started rising, from over 500,000 people/year in 1998 to more than two million/year in 2003. The Continent definitely needs immigrants because it has suffered from a demographic crisis for decades. The crucial importance of immigrants is clearly demonstrated by the fact that during the one-and-half decades after the turn of the millennium, two-thirds of the EU population growth and—in the past five years—half of employment growth were covered by immigrants.[10] An interesting and convincing case study about the labor supply of the Irish health system reflects that foreign health-care and social care workers represented only 2 percent of the system's labor force in 1998 but already 17 percent by 2006. Their number, however, has to increase four times by 2035 to keep the health system working.[11]

Two detailed EU analyses of the long-term demographic trends maintained that it is a long-term and continuing phenomenon. If the trend does not change, reproduction will not recover but will stay at 1.57 by 2030 and 1.64 by 2060. Consequently, by 2030 and 2060, the labor force will be 10 and 20 percent less, respectively. Life expectancy at birth will increase for men from 76 to 84.5 years and for women from 82.1 to 89 years between 2008 and 2060. In 2008, 84.6 million people were older than 65 years, and among them, almost 22 million were above 80 years old. By 2020, these numbers will increase to 104 and 37 million, respectively. The "oldest-old" (aged 80 years and above) are projected to almost triple from 22 million in 2008 to 61 million in 2060. Europe is experiencing a quite rapid aging. The number of elderly persons (aged 65 or above) already surpassed the number of children (below 15) in 2008. By 2060, there will be more than twice as many elderly people as children. As a result of these unprecedented demographic trends, the old-age dependency ratio—the ratio of people aged 65 or above relative to the working-age population aged 15–64—is projected to more than double in the EU from 25 to nearly 54 percent over the projection period. In other words, instead of four working people, only two are able to cover the sharply increasing health and service expenditures for the elderly population.

Thus, EU Member States cannot rely on a natural increase in labor supply. Besides that, aging badly influences public expenditures. Expenditure on health care is projected to grow from nearly 7 to more than 8 percent of the aggregate GDP between 2007 and 2060. Average public spending on long-term care is projected to double to more than 2 percent of the GDP since the number of disabled elderly people who rely on informal care will nearly double in the EU.

Population and labor force decrease, and the negative consequences of aging could be counterbalanced only, the Commission forecast concluded, by the immigration of 59 million people to the EU over the entire projection period until 2060. Only net immigration could keep the ratio of working-age-to-total population constant at its 2008 level. According to these calculations, a significant net immigration—over 25 million additional inflows over the period from 2008 to 2020—was needed beyond the nearly 44 million immigrants already incorporated, who represented 9 percent of the population in 2008.

The contrast between the political reaction to and consequences of the migration crisis of 2015–16, and the continuous demographic crisis of Europe and the need of immigrants is extremely sharp and conflicting. Immigrant labor is the only solution for continuous labor supply, but the political impact of the immigration crisis is undermining the solution.[12]

In the 2010s, the world's migration situation became tragic. By the end of 2015, more than 65 million people were forcibly displaced from their homes, of which more than 20 million had crossed international borders. This marked the largest displacement since World War II. A great number of refugees targeted Europe for settlement. In those years, millions of migrants from civil war-torn Syria, Afghanistan, and Niger joined people uprooted by dramatic climate change and hunger in the regions from sub-Saharan Africa to Pakistan who were migrating to Europe. In an endless, frighteningly unorganized, and chaotic flow, migrants crossed the Mediterranean Sea, walked through the Balkans, and arrived from Turkish camps with the help of human traffickers. The so-called Dublin System, supposed to regulate responsibilities for the reception and processing of asylum applications, collapsed. The countries in which refugees first entered the EU became unable to cope with the challenges. In both 2015 and 2016, about 1.2 million first-time asylum applications were registered in the EU. From January 2015 to September 2017, their numbers were 2.9 million, far above the 2008–11 annual average of 265,000.

Since the spring of 2015, parallel with the refugee surge, as an EU document reflects, the share of people identifying immigration as the most important issue facing the EU has sharply increased. Immigration concerns tracked by Eurobarometer peaked in November 2015. The immigration problem became a central issue, but the *perception* of immigration was strongly exaggerated. An IPSOS Group S.A. survey found that in all countries where the question was asked, people perceived that there were many more migrants than there actually were. Among the EU countries, the largest gaps between perceived and actual shares of immigrants in the total population are found in Italy, Belgium, France, the UK, Hungary, and Poland.

Angela Merkel seemed confident that she could resume her role as Europe's leader, as was the case during the euro-crisis, when her decisions were largely imposed on the other countries. At the advent of the refugee crisis, Merkel assumed a leading role once more. Her famous claim "We can do it," addressed to the German public, was actually predicated on consent from other countries that she had taken for granted. She did not bother to consult, not to mention coordinate, with the area's other leaders. This time, however, she failed and became powerless, unable to tackle what had become her biggest challenge.[13]

The same happened to the European Commission, which issued a European Migration Agenda containing proposals for resolving the refugee crisis. At the heart of this was the distribution and reception of refugees by the member countries using a quota system. The aim to establish a coherent migration policy was not new. It has repeatedly been formulated since 2005 and has laid down key objectives such as better organization of legal migration and mobility, prevention and combating of irregular migration, and eradication of human trafficking. These attempts have always failed. The Commission proposal met the bitter resistance of some Member States. Although twenty Member States voted for the Commission proposal, the Czech Republic, Hungary, Poland, Romania, and Slovakia voted against it, with Finland abstaining (the UK, Ireland, and Denmark chose an opt out).

The Hungarian Viktor Orbán government rejected solidarity with the EU; reacted with harsh restrictive measures; and built razor wire fence along its southern borders to stop migrants entering the country, spending €800 million. (Meanwhile, Orbán requested that the EU pay half of the price "in solidarity," which was swiftly rejected by the European Commission.) The Hungarian government treated the refugees with a harshness that infringed their human rights, with the clear aim of diverting routes for asylum seekers away from Hungary.[14] This had a domino effect, and the trademark Schengen Agreement on "borderless Europe" collapsed. In April 2016, it was estimated that European countries had built or started 1,200 km of fencing to stop migrants. Several other countries reintroduced border control. Between mid-2016 and December 2017, a total of ten Schengen States, among them France, Germany, Italy, Sweden, Portugal, Poland, Spain, Greece, and Bulgaria, had internal border controls in their territories. The crisis reached its zenith. The new great migration shocked Europe and generated an often harsh overreaction against immigration.[15]

Terror attacks

As one cannot understand the migration problem of Europe without its close connection to the demographic crisis of the Continent, the political consequences of the migration crisis are not understandable without the "coincidence" that the migration crisis was accompanied by a horrifying series of terrorist attacks that killed and injured thousands of people throughout Europe. This significantly deepened the crisis of the EU. Terrorism was not a new phenomenon in Europe. It had accompanied fascist and Nazi atrocities in the interwar decades and the war years. During the peaceful postwar half century, violent terrorist attacks were launched in Italy and Germany by the so-called Red Brigades and Red Army Faction. Spain experienced decades-long waves of Basque terrorism; in Britain, the endless violence of the Irish Republican Army (IRA) was an everyday danger. (In the US, mass murderers killed children in schools and audiences in movie theaters and concert halls; according to the Federal Bureau of Investigation (FBI), between 1980 and the early 2000s, 94 percent of the terror attacks were carried out by white Americans.) Nevertheless, the decade of the 2000s opened a new chapter of global terrorism, Jihadist Muslim terrorism, starting with the attacks against the US on 9/11 of 2001; amplified by President Bush's "war against terror"; and sustained in the rapid succession in 2004 and 2005 of the Madrid and London bombings, the Van Gogh murder, and the Beslan school siege in Russia.[16]

Terrorism in the early twenty-first century generated tremendous reverberations and angry Islamophobia in the Western world. Succeeding the earlier trend of hijacking airplanes and executing occasional sporadic terror actions, the well-planned 9/11, 2001, Al-Qaeda terror attacks at the World Trade Center in New York and the Pentagon in Washington, D.C., opened a new chapter in terrorism and intensified what had previously been a somewhat hysterical anti-Muslim atmosphere in the US and Europe. Several Muslim terrorist organizations emerged. In 2015, four Islamic extremist groups were responsible for three-quarters of terrorist killings: Islamic State of Iraq and Syria (ISIS), Boko Haram, the Taliban, and Al-Qaeda. The majority of victims were killed in Iraq, Afghanistan, Nigeria, Pakistan, and Syria. Terrorist attacks also mushroomed in America and Europe. One of the ISIS leaders, Abu Muhammad al-Adnani, called upon Muslims to murder Europeans: "Smash his head with a rock, or slaughter him with a knife, or run him over with your car."[17] After the dramatic 2001 attack, in the next decade and a half, Islamist extremists committed 23 attacks in the US. Young Muslims, often second-generation individuals from immigrant families who were born in the US and Europe, were recruited by terrorist organizations to wage Jihadist war. An EU analysis found in 2017 that 73 percent of the attacks in Europe and North America over the past three years had been committed by homegrown terrorists, and another 14 percent involved citizens from neighboring countries. By contrast to foreign terrorist fighters, homegrown terrorists are more often "lone wolves" labeled as "amateurs."[18] An estimated 7,000 European Muslims (among them a few converted whites) went to Iraq and Syria to fight for the Islamic Caliphate. According to collected information on 600 ISIS fighters, more than half were recruited from Belgium, Britain, France, and Sweden. About one-third of the volunteers, after a couple of years, returned to Europe.[19]

It was easy to mobilize frustrated, desperate young Muslims who were unable to integrate and who lived in poverty. Joblessness was rather high among them. As various investigations reflected, a great many who joined terrorist organizations had committed various (sometimes only small) criminal actions before. Generally, they were not even religious, and their joining ISIS had nothing to do with religious Islam (killing is a sin in Islam, as in all other religions). Instead, terrorists had simply found a "heroic cause" that gave a new motivation to their lives. These radicalized people, as a group of analysts maintained, were not really interested in the Middle East or Islam as a faith but rather were interested in radical anti-imperialist struggles, not much different from Che Guevara or the Baader Meinhof group several decades ago. Other groups follow fundamentalist

Islam theology and doctrine but abstain from politics and violence, but this often serves as the breeding ground for individuals to pass in due course into violent action of the jihadist type. Most of the terrorists were young people.[20] In the August 2017 Barcelona attack, the terrorist was 22 years old, and the men responsible for the twin attack in Cambrils were 17 and 24 years old, respectively. In the Finland knife attack (also in August 2017), the perpetrator was an 18-year-old Moroccan man; in the May 2017 Manchester Arena attack, the terrorist was 22 years old. Two of the so-called 7/7 bombers from the July 2005 London bombings were under 20.

A few major attacks happened in 2003, such as two terrible attacks in Istanbul in a synagogue and a suicide bombing that killed 400 people. In November 2004 in Amsterdam, the assassination of filmmaker Theo Van Gogh in retaliation for his film about Muslim women produced tremendous reverberations. Also, in 2004, a commuter train bombing in Madrid killed more than 400 people, inspiring a terrible series of murderous attacks that culminated between 2015 and 2017. The carnage was launched by the Charlie Hebdo killing in Paris in January 2015; in November of the same year, a synchronized series of attacks killed 130 people in Paris. France saw eight attacks between December 2014 and July 2016. An attack of three coordinated suicide bombings occurred in Brussels in March 2016. The Nice Bastille Day car attack on July 14, 2016, which left 86 dead, was followed by similar car attacks in Berlin, Stockholm, and London within one year. In Germany, the 2016 New Year's Eve celebrations were accompanied by atrocities in the center of Köln, where mass sexual assaults, 24 rapes, and numerous thefts shocked Germany. In the same week, similar incidents occurred at public celebrations in Hamburg, Dortmund, Düsseldorf, and Stuttgart. This sexual terrorism was followed by five violent nonsexual attacks in July 2016 and culminated in the 2016 Berlin Christmas Market attack. In January and June 2016, and January 2017, three major attacks shocked Istanbul again. An EU expert declared in 2016 that "the terrorist threat remained critical in Western Europe throughout 2017 and continued to be dominated by jihadi terrorism. 16 attacks struck eight different countries, while more than 30 plots were foiled."[21]

Populist attacks against the EU

This desperate situation, which frightened Europe and alienated millions of people from immigrant minorities, was successfully exploited by emerging populist parties throughout Europe. Immigration, terror, and increasing crime were closely connected in the public view. This was actually measured in America. According to a Gallup poll in 2017, half of the American population believes there is a correlation between these two phenomena; statistical analysis, however, proves the opposite. Between 1980 and 2016, the number of immigrants in the US increased by 137 percent, while crimes committed decreased by 12 percent, and violent crimes decreased by 36 percent. In metro areas, the population grew by 109 percent, but assaults, robberies, and murders declined by 13, 42, and 40 percent, respectively.[22]

Populist parties attacked the "welcome culture" and multiculturalism preached by their governments and, in general, criticized the "treacherous elite," the "German dictate," and the entire EU. In some countries, for the first time in the history of European integration, debates started about the prospect of leaving the EU. Anti-EU parties were established and openly talked about and supported this possibility. Moreover, the British government of David Cameron held a referendum in the summer of 2016, and a small majority of the voters voted to leave the EU (discussed in Chapter 4). That was the first time that a country had left the EU. The possibility that other countries would follow became an everyday topic of discussion. The German finance minister suggested that Greece should leave the eurozone and probably even the EU. In some of the rich countries, such as Finland and France, anti-EU parties argued for exit from the Union. "Grexit" and "Brexit" became household terms. After long decades of integration and enlargements, the beginnings of disintegration appeared on the horizon and were often discussed in the media.

In that disparate atmosphere of mass dissatisfaction, popular acceptance of the EU sharply declined. Only about one-third of the population of the member countries felt that the EU was advantageous for them. Right- and left-wing populists launched harsh political attacks against the integration in Britain, France, the Netherlands, and throughout Central Europe. Euroscepticism, moreover, outright hostility against the EU, became the dominant zeitgeists.

In a statement typical of this time, Professor Otmar Issing, a former chief economist of the ECB, "predicted in 2016 that Brussels' [*sic*.] dream of a European superstate will finally be buried," as a report phrased it, "amongst the rubble of the crumbling single currency he designed." The respected economist launched a withering attack on Eurocrats and German leader Angela Merkel, accusing them of betraying the principles of the euro and demonstrating scandalous incompetence over its management. And he savaged the whole idea of a United States of Europe, saying that the attempt to push through federalization via the back door had churned the ground the currency was built on into a quagmire of patchwork legislation, into which it was fast sinking... One day, - Issing prophesized -

> the house of cards will collapse. Realistically, it will be a case of muddling through, struggling from one crisis to the next. ... It is difficult to forecast how long this will continue for, but it cannot go on endlessly.[23]

Recognition of the existential crisis

These kinds of forecasts mushroomed. The first Vice President of the European Commission, the Dutch social democrat Frans Timmermans, said, "for the first time, I fear that the European project can fail." Enrico Letta, former Italian prime minister, joined: "With the unresolved economic crisis, the Brexit, terrorism, the refugee crisis, we are living an unprecedented situation that calls into question the European project itself." Mario Monti, former European Commissioner and Italian prime minister, stated, "the mechanism has broken down, crises no longer provide new energies as on previous occasions."[24] And the President of the European Parliament Martin Schultz denounced the lack of political will on the part of the governments of the Member States to deepen EU integration.

Others concluded that the central problem was produced not only by the current complex crisis but by a deeper one as well: the exhaustion of the central driving force—the possibility of eliminating new European wars—that had previously pushed integration ahead with strong public support.

> What were those *raisons d'être*, those driving forces that have promoted European integration with the more or less explicit consent of the citizens? In the past those reasons were clear, but to a great extent they have lost their cogency and their mobilizing force because the objectives to be reached have already been achieved.[25]

There were not only private statements about the existential crisis any longer. The new President of the European Commission Jean-Claud Juncker, a federalist of the old guard, stated in his annual State of the Union address to the European Parliament, "The European Union is facing an existential crisis."[26] Martin Schulz, then head of the European Parliament, stressed another aspect of the crisis, noting that some governments of member countries were cherry-picking by accepting generous EU funding for poorer regions while ignoring member rules they did not like. "If countries continued [doing so]," Schulz professed, "this would end in destroying the European Union."

This chorus became dominant after the British referendum to leave the EU in June 2016.

An entire international chorus emphasized the presence of an existential crisis. The influential *Washington Post*, in a long article entitled "An existential crisis for an integrated Europe after Brexit vote," reported,

> Britain's historic vote to leave the EU plunges the 28-nations bloc into an existential crisis, dealing the dream of an integrated Europe its greatest blow since the march toward unity began in the aftermath of World War II. … The question is whether Britain's move to become the first nation to exit the union will mark the start of a cascade of similar referendums that could threaten the bloc's very survival. … Most experts predict at least a freezing if not a serious rollback of decades of strides toward regional integration.[27]

George Soros, the multibillionaire American philanthropist and friend of the EU, repeatedly spoke about frightening dangers, even in the summer of 2017: "The EU is in an existential crisis and needs to be reinvented in the face of growing threat." In addition to Brexit, which he stated would be "an immensely damaging process, harmful to both sides," Soros also named Russia, Turkey,

Egypt, and Trump's US as hostile outside enemies to the EU. Experts such as Stevan Blockmans of the Center for European Policy Studies underscored the negative probable impact of Brexit, suggesting that it was "likely to provoke a crisis of tremendous proportions, one beyond any that we have known so far."[28]

Hundreds of similar forecasts and statements were made—and could be cited—between 2009 and 2017. They were quite understandable. The combined economic, currency, and political crises, and the slow, hesitant, and always partial response of the EU naturally generated those frightened or triumphant statements. Moreover, several experts recognized that the EU itself was responsible for the crisis for reasons including its unfinished and in many ways dysfunctional institutional system, its "democratic deficit," its overly complicated and thus very slow decision-making process, and often its lack of strong leadership.

Brexit, which marked the first country's decision to leave the Union, seemed to be the start of disintegration, especially because it was enthusiastically welcomed in France and the Netherlands by Marine Le Pen and Geert Wilders, and by populists in other countries, including politicians aligned with the Alternative for Germany Party. They all attacked the EU, wanted to gain the majority after the 2017 national elections, and hoped to withdraw their countries from the eurozone.

The outside factor: loosening alliances and hostile neighbors

The crisis of the EU was basically a "domestic" issue, caused by factors within the Union. Nevertheless, inner tensions within the Union intensified and became more dangerous because they were also compounded by outside factors. For the first time in the history of European integration after the Cold War, outside dangers emerged again. In this subchapter, I am going to list but not deliberate those dangers; Chapter 9 is given to its detailed discussion. One of the most novel dangers was the crisis surrounding the alliance with the US, in terms of both the military alliance and economic cooperation. North Atlantic Treaty Organization (NATO) was undermined by the new American policy, and the first trade war emerged on the horizon in 2017–18 during the early years of Donald J. Trump's presidency. After Trump's announcement declaring the introduction of tariffs for steel and aluminum imports in March 2018 sparked fears over the possibility of new tariffs for European car export, Mario Draghi, the President of the ECB, stated that "if you put tariffs against your allies one wonders who the enemies are."[29] However, sometime later, the US transitorily excluded the EU from the tariffs. Was it only a bluff? Since the Trump administration took office, the EU could not count on its most traditional ally any longer.

This new state of affairs became even more frightening because the geographic surroundings of the Union turned increasingly hostile. Russia under President Vladimir V. Putin emerged as the main enemy of the EU, posing both economic and military danger in its strong attempt to undermine integration by building a hostile rival enemy bloc at the borders of the EU (and even *within* Eastern and

Southern member countries). Russia successfully counterbalanced the EU's attempts to build an alliance system around the Union by accepting countries that were not members but wanted to join in the West Balkans and at the Eastern borders of the EU. It built a close alliance with Turkey, which also turned against the Union, despite having been a candidate to join since the 1990s.

A new but alarming danger, faraway China—the rising new superpower under the leadership of Xi Jinping, whose autocratic grip was strengthened and whose attempts to gain more international influence were made easier due to the withdrawal of Trump's America from the world stage—also entered the ring against the EU. China started building strong economic ties with the Balkans and Central and Eastern Europe based on huge investment and credit invasion. The creation of the "Balkan Silk Road" and increasing trade connections between China and eleven EU member countries definitely undermined the economic base of the Union and strengthened the "war for sovereignty" in several Central European and Balkan Member States of the EU. These outside dangers accompanied the emergence of inner troubles and conflicts, and strengthened them in the period when the EU, at last, mostly coped with the deepest economic crises and began consolidating itself.

Deep crisis is over, but are new ones coming?

In contrast to the oft-mentioned danger that the British step of leaving the Union would generate similar steps in other countries, thus catalyzing the start of disintegration, nothing similar happened. There was no appetite in other countries for following in Britain's footsteps. The populist-nationalist political forces that enthusiastically welcomed Brexit in France, the Netherlands, and Germany, and advocated for following it, were unable to break through. Three major anti-EU parties were defeated during the 2017 national elections. In the Netherlands and Germany, they both received only 13 percent of the votes. Instead of the anti-EU French Front National of Marine Le Pen, the strongly pro-integrationist Emmanuel Macron was elected as president of the country, and his newly formed party gained a shocking majority in the parliament.

Instead of disintegration, the EU became strong again in 2017 and 2018. The common currency, the euro (saved in 2013), became stable again and regained its international position in the emerging multicurrency era. In February 2018, it was again at 1.240 level against the US dollar in contrast to the 1.062 level a year before. Austerity measures, strongly blamed as counterproductive, worked in Ireland, Spain, Portugal, and even Greece. As governments in crisis-hit countries put their financial households in order, budgetary deficits were replaced by surpluses, and economic growth returned, equaling the US's growth rate of 2.2 percent, and even increasing to 2.5 percent in 2018. The immigration crisis was essentially ameliorated. Quite a few countries—Estonia, Latvia, Lithuania, and Slovakia—joined the eurozone during the crisis years. Further integration, especially in banking and fiscal unionization, was (at least within the eurozone) on its way. The eurozone's 19 member countries formed a strong core for the EU, which included more than 337 million inhabitants and boasted an average per capita GDP of more than $39,000. On the basis of these metrics, after the crisis, the zone belonged to the upper 20 percent of the countries of the world. If the eurozone would only continue to promote further integration, it would become the most important economic force in Europe, if not the world.

The decade—after the decade of crisis following 2008—opened with new worldwide prosperity. According to the latest forecasts by the IMF, global GDP growth is set to accelerate to 3.7 percent, the highest rate since 2010. The European Commission and the Organization for Economic Co-operation and Development (OECD) also project a similar pickup in global growth. "Yet, there is a good chance," as the European Council of Foreign Relations commented, "that these already rosy forecasts still underestimate the momentum. For the first time since 2011, all major country groups are set for a robust, simultaneous upswing, with economic growth rates of at least around 2 percent."[30] This new world economic environment is highly advantageous for the EU.

Europe definitely survived its deepest and most complex crisis to date in the 2010s. Nevertheless, the dangers did not disappear. Populist movements and parties were still strong and dominant in several Central European and Mediterranean countries, led by Hungary and Poland but also Slovakia and the Czech Republic; these organizations actually took over Austria and Italy, the EU's third-largest economic power. The possibility of further breaks cannot be excluded. The geographical region surrounding the EU was still politically very unstable and partly hostile. Russia and China initiated dangerous political, military, and economic plans to divide Europe. The American ally was more than uncertain and unpredictable, as shown by its initiation of a tariff war against the EU in early 2018. Germany's political establishment, the de facto leader of the Union during recent times, was weakened and unable to play its previous role. The EU survived the existential crisis but remains very fragile and may face new crises.

This fragility is especially dangerous because European societies will likely have to face unavoidable new challenges in the near future. Several experts warn about the further impact of the endlessly running technological revolution as well as the consequences of the rapid spread of driverless cars, the robotization of industrial production, and the application of artificial intelligence that will eliminate millions of jobs. In five years, self-driving trucks themselves will eliminate hundreds of thousands, or perhaps even millions, of jobs. Similar developments will destroy customer service representative, assembler, and fabricator jobs. Although calculations are varying and often change, Oxford University experts recently calculated that 47 percent of existing jobs in the US are susceptible to automation.[31] This danger may be quite similar for Europe.

On the other hand, new technology also creates new jobs. Over the past five years, the demand for data analysts has grown by 372 percent, and within that field, the demand for data-visualization skills has shot up by 2,574 percent.[32]

Unfortunately, workers who lost or are currently losing their jobs in shrinking old sectors cannot shift and go to work in newly opened fields. For ideological gender reasons, a great many men in blue-collar jobs refuse to take less "masculine" roles in services or fast-growing areas such as health care. Moreover, they are unable to go into new high tech fields like data analysis. Jobs in these sectors require information technology (IT) literacy that older workers lack: in more developed OECD countries, one in four adults has zero or limited knowledge in those areas. This requires new institutionalized training and retraining regimes or so-called "lifelong learning." "Lifelong learning," *The Economist* analyzed,

> starts at school … education should not be narrowly vocational. The curriculum needs to teach children how to study and think. … But the bigger change is to make adult learning routinely accessible to all. One way is for citizens to receive vouchers that they can use to pay for training. Singapore has such 'individual learning accounts'; it has given money to everyone over 25 to spend on any of 500 approved courses.[33]

This proposed solution constitutes the more difficult road. Populist parties and their demagogue leaders offer an easier and more popular "solution," from reopening closed coal mines and steel mills to reestablishing eliminated jobs by pushing out imports from other countries. This approach, of course, goes against the modern trend of development and may not be a lasting solution. Nevertheless, it remains more popular among blue-collar workers. "This could provide decades' worth of fuel to the revolt against the global elites. … The populist wave … may be here to stay."[34] In other words, in spite of the new emerging, robust prosperity in the world and Europe, populism can still survive.

Will the EU be able to reinvent itself, reestablish popularity, and restore trust in member countries' citizens? Only strong French–German tandem leadership, assisted by further strengthened EU institutions and steadfast policy to rebuild solidarity and cooperation, will rebuild Europe. The resulting organization will probably be slimmer in form and lead to badly needed further integration. The strong French leadership is ready to act: Emmanuel Macron, the new French president, put exact plans on the table that proposed further integration to push the eurozone at least toward federalization. Whether they will be realized or not depends on the efficacy of German–French tandem leadership after the German coalition government gained its final form in mid-March 2018. The new German "grand coalition" government, however, is seemingly too weak to be a European leader in the same way as before or even an equal partner with Macron. The 177-page-long coalition agreement leaves "plenty of leeway for disagreements over competing priorities. Pensions, healthcare, Europe and asylum and migration policy are all areas where there are explosives built into the coalition agreement," as the deputy EU spokesman for Merkel's conservative bloc told Reuters. The agreement also has a clause stipulating that in two years, the parties will review the fulfillment of the agreement. The door for a split remains open.[35]

Escaping forward?

The weakness of renewed French-German tandem leadership strongly calls into question the reality of the idealistic plans that evidently surfaced during the crisis years, including the return to further integration, supranationalization, and even the federalist solution. The European Parliament has adopted three resolutions exploring the future development of the EU. One of the rapporteurs, Guy Verhofstadt, explained the urgency of in-depth reform, given the challenges the EU faces. As the old *raison d'être*, the peace in Europe, has been achieved, a new *raison d'être* for European integration is needed. Could that give new life force to a project that runs the risk of dying out slowly? Positioning a strong EU as the answer to future global challenges might be the ground upon which to build the new European narrative.

> Member States have always feared an in-depth reform of the Union. But let's face the reality: they're all with their back against the wall. So, it's now the moment to reform the European Union, to make it a real Union and not a loose confederation of Nation States still based on unanimity rule, always acting too little, too late. You cannot govern a continent like Europe, if you still need the approval of all 28 Member States. ... A smaller, less bureaucratic real European government, not a Commission of 28.... And then also a European Defense Union, because there is a threat from outside the Union. ... We need also a European Border and Coast Guard to really manage the migration flows. I think that there is no other solution for Europe than to do these in-depth reforms.... And if we, if not all of the current member-States [but] at least a small but determined number of them, are not able to do so, within 30 years the EU may have died or fallen into insignificance.[36]

Martin Schulz formulated an even more explicitly federalist view in his speech at the Social Democratic Party of Germany's conference in Berlin before negotiations started about the German grand coalition. He explicitly called for the creation of a "United States of Europe" by 2025 as well as a more robust social security net and a phasing out of coal power. He wanted EU Member States to sign off on a new constitutional treaty that committed the bloc to take steps toward a federal Europe.

> Such a constitutional treaty has to be written by a convention that includes civil society and the people. This constitutional treaty will then have to be put to the member states and those that don't approve it will automatically have to leave the EU.[37]

Nevertheless, Martin Schulz resigned from his party leadership in February 2018 and will not be a member of the grand coalition government.

In early 2018, the future of the EU looked somewhat more promising, at least because the rising economic prosperity eliminated some of the basic troubles that weakened the EU and fueled its discontent. But the realization of the ambitious plans for further integration is still more than questionable. Anti-European forces are still strong and present, and, moreover, dominate quite a few countries within the EU and around it. The EU has had to travel down a long and very bumpy road, and still faces many dangers ahead.

Notes

1 *Archive of European Integration.* The regional and urban dimension of the crisis. Eighth progress report on economic, social and territorial cohesion. Commission staff working document accompanying the report. SWD (2013) 232 final, 26 June 2013.

2 *Archive of European Integration, Draft joint employment report. Implementation of the Lisbon Strategy structural reforms in the context of the European economic recovery plan – a more detailed overview of progress across the EU in the specific macro- and micro-economic as well as the employment areas. COM (2009) 34 final, Vol. II, 28 January 2009.* [EU Commission–COM Document].

3 Ibid.

4 Stefan Collignon, "Taking European Integration Seriously: Competitiveness, Imbalances, and Economic Stability in the Euro Area," in *Competitiveness in the European Economy*, eds. Stefan Collingnon and Piero Esposito (London: Routledge, 2014), 24, 37, 38.

5 "With respect to earnings, those who are unemployed for 26 months before age 22 earn $1,400 to $1,650 less than their peers at age 26 and $1,050 to $1,150 less at age 30. This 'wage scar' has been found in other studies too. One finds that if a young person spends a year unemployed before the age of 23, they will earn 23 percent or 16 percent lower wages ten years later for men and women, respectively." *Archive of European Integration*, Blame it on my youth! Policy recommendations for re-evaluating and reducing youth unemployment. CEPS Research Report No. 2018/01, January 2018.

6 *Archive of European Integration, Evidence on demographic and social trends. Social policies' contribution to inclusion, employment and the economy. Social investment package. Commission staff working document. SWD (2013) 38 final/I, 20 February 2013.* [EU Commission–SEC Document].

7 16,486 articles from the *Süddeutsche Zeitung*, 9,566 from *Le Monde*, 6,416 from *La Stampa*, and 19,246 from *El País*.

8 *Archive of European Integration*, Bruegel Policy Contribution Issue n°03, February 2018. [Policy Paper], Müller, Henrik and Porcaro, Giuseppe, and von Nordheim, Gerret, "Tales from a Crisis: Diverging Narratives of the Euro Area."

9 Anna Flagg, "The Myth of the Criminal Immigrant," *The New York Times*, March 30, 2018, sec. The Upshot. https://goo.gl/JWUoh1.

10 *Archive of European Integration, Evidence on demographic and social trends. Social policies' contribution to inclusion, employment and the economy. Social investment package. Commission staff working document. SWD (2013) 38 final/I, 20 February 2013.* [EU Commission–SEC Document].

11 *Archive of European Integration*, Alan Barrett and Anna Rust, "Projecting the Future Numbers of Migrant Workers in the Health and Social Care Sectors in Ireland." ESRI WP275. January 2009. [Working Paper] Due to the lack of Irish nursing graduates, 90 percent of new nurses came from India and the Philippines. Calculating the demographic changes, including aging, Ireland needed, as the 2009 calculations concluded, a net inflow of about 30,000 nurses per annum up to 2016, 20,000 per annum between 2016 and 2026, and 15,000 per annum thereafter. The analysis added that

almost every European country is experiencing a shortage of registered nurses. For example, Britain had 57,000 fewer nurses than needed to staff the National Health Service in 2001.

12 *Archive of European Integration*, The 2009 Ageing report: Economic and budgetary projections for the EU-27 Member States (2008–2060). European Economy No. 2/2009, [EU Commission–Working Document]; *Archive of European Integration*, Long-term care in ageing societies–Challenges and policy options. Social investment package. Commission staff working document. SWD (2013) 41 final, 20 February 2013.

13 *Archive of European Integration*, Think Tank Review Issue 34, April 2016, LUISS School of European Political Economy, Carlo Bastasin, "The migration Crisis—A Case for a 'Merzi' Leadership," March 17, 2016.

14 *Archive of European Integration*, Think Tank Review Issue 34, April 2016, Friedrich-Ebert-Stiftung, Petra Bendel, "Refugee Policy in the European Union: Protect Human Rights!" March 2016.

15 *Archive of European Integration*, March 2018, Sergio Carrera and Marco Stefan, "The Future of the Schengen Area: Latest Developments and Challenges in the Schengen Governance Framework since 2016," [Policy Paper].

16 See the editor's introduction to the volume: Michael Emerson, ed., Ethno-Religious Conflict in Europe: Typologies of Radicalisation in Europe's Muslim Communities (Brussels: CEPS Paperbacks, 2009).

17 *Independent*, September 22, 2014, https://www.independent.co.uk › News › World › Middle East.

18 *Archive of European Integration*, Egmont Security Policy Brief No. 89 July 2017, Thomas Renard, "Europe's "new" jihad: Homegrown, leaderless, virtua," [Policy Paper].

19 *Archive of European Integration*, *Think Tank Review Issue 34, April 2016*, New America Foundation, Albert Ford, Alyssa Gabrielle Sims, David Sterman, and Peter Bergen, "ISIS in the West - The Western Militant Flow to Syria and Iraq," March 25, 2016.

20 Michael Emerson, ed., Op. Cit, 2009.

21 *Archive of European Integration*, EU Global Strategy – Expert Opinion No. 4. Egmont Commentary, 22 January 2016.

22 *The New York Times*, March 30, 2018, sec. The Upshot. https://goo.gl/JWUoh1.

23 Nick Gutteridge, "'The Euro Is Finished.' Currency's Creator Says It Will Soon Collapse and Destroy the EU," *Express*, October 17, 2016, https://goo.gl/AJZuU5.

24 *Federalist Debate*, March 2017, No. 1, "A New Ambition to Overcome the Existential Crisis of the European Project," www.federalist-debate.org.

25 *The Federalist Debate*, March 2017, No. 1, Op. Cit. https://goo.gl/h5x7QM.

26 Jennifer Rankin, "EU Is Facing Existential Crisis, Says Jean-Claude Juncker," *The Guardian*, September 14, 2016, https://goo.gl/2FpneC.

27 Anthony Faiola and Michael Birnbaum. "British Exit from the E.U. Sets Up a European Crisis of Diminished Power," *Washington Post*, June 24, 2016, sec. Europe. https://goo.gl/VDCJnB.

28 Ibid.

29 Jack Ewing, "E.C.B. Shifts Guidance, as Europe Moves toward Normalcy," *The New York Times*, March 7, 2018, sec. Economy, https://goo.gl/VcUJGz.

30 Policy Brief. European Council on Foreign Relations, January 5, 2018, Hackenbroich, Jonathan, and Jeremy Shapiro. "Opportunities Amid Disorder: Europe and the World in 2018," https://goo.gl/vvad3M.

31 University of Oxford: Oxford Martin Programme on Technology and Employment, September 17, 2013. Carl Benedikt Frey and Michael Osborne. "The Future of Employment: How Susceptible Are Jobs to Computerization?" https://goo.gl/d43NCm.

32 "Lifelong Learning Is Becoming an Economic Imperative." *The Economist*, January 12, 2017, https://goo.gl/7BPQSM.

33 Ibid.
34 Eduardo Porter, "Is the Populist Revolt Over? Not If Robots Have Their Way." *The New York Times*, January 30, 2018, sec. Economy. https://goo.gl/mr93XQ.
35 Paul Carrel, "Tensions Build in New, 'Explosive' German Coalition," *Reuters*, March 9, 2018, https://goo.gl/ugf6FC.
36 "The Future of Europe: Europe 'Is Undergoing an Existential Crisis,'" Web Video. EuroparlTV, accessed April 2, 2018, https://goo.gl/2oYzAR.
37 Philip Oltermann, "Martin Schulz Wants 'United States of Europe' within Eight Years," *The Guardian*, December 7, 2017, https://goo.gl/UESDzB.

2

INEQUALITIES WITHIN AND AMONG MEMBER COUNTRIES UNDERMINED HOMOGENIZATION AND BECAME A SOURCE OF DISCONTENTS

Capitalism and inequality

Rising inequality became a central problem around the turn of the millennium. After nearly half a century of decrease and moderation after World War II, beginning in the 1980s, inequality started to return. For the first time since globalization transformed capitalism, the scissors of income difference significantly opened. Thomas Piketty, the author of the 700-page economics bestseller *Capital in the Twenty-First Century* (2013), presented a large-scale statistical investigation that convincingly proves that the Kuznets curve, the celebrated postwar theory developed by the American Nobel laureate economist Simon Kuznets, is incorrect. Kuznets's broadly accepted theory, expressed by a bell curve, maintains that large-scale inequality increased during early capitalism (the first half of his bell curve) but significantly decreased as capitalism entered its advanced industrialized stage (the second half of the curve).

Piketty positions the Kuznets curve as a flawed Cold War theory, arguing instead that

> the process by which wealth is accumulated and distributed contains powerful forces pushing toward divergence … toward an extremely high level of inequality. Forces of convergence also exist, and in certain countries at certain times, these may prevail, but the forces of divergence can at any point regain the upper hand, as seems to be happening now, at the beginning of the twenty-first century.[1]

In other words, decreased inequality was not caused by the advancement of capitalism, but by outside political factors, the requirement of solidarity during the war, and the competition between capitalism and socialism during the Cold War decades. These latter factors, however, evaporated by the 1980s, and the inherent rule of capitalism, growing inequality, became dominant again.

Increasing inequality within the EU countries

The most broadly used measurement of inequality, the Gini coefficient,[2] clearly reflects this trend. This index measures equality on a scale between 0 and 1, where "0" would mean that every citizen would have the same income, and "1" would signify an extreme case where one person would possess all of a country's income. In other words, the lower the index, the more egalitarian a country is. In the mid-1980s, most of the European countries had a rather equal income distribution. Most countries had a very low Gini coefficient, between 0.20 and 0.25; in a few less egalitarian countries such as Britain and Italy, Gini coefficients were about 0.30. In socialist Eastern Europe, the average number was also about 0.25.

By 2014–15, the inequality scissors opened significantly. In the Organization for Economic Co-operation and Development (OECD) countries, in general, Gini coefficients increased from 0.29 in the mid-1980s to 0.31 by the mid-2010s. In the Baltic countries, formerly pretty egalitarian Soviet republics, the Gini index range became 0.34–0.38. In former socialist countries, including Bulgaria, Croatia, Poland, and Bosnia, the index increased from 0.30 to 0.37. In Greece and Italy, the average number increased to 0.34; in France, Germany, Austria, and Ireland, from 0.30 to 0.32. In Britain, it increased to 0.34, and in Spain, it increased to 0.36. Only in a few former socialist countries and in Scandinavia—specifically Slovenia, Slovakia, the Czech Republic, Romania, Sweden, Denmark, Finland, and Belgium—the Gini coefficient remained in the lower range of 0.25–0.28.

True, Europe was still more egalitarian than Russia (which had been very egalitarian in the Soviet times): in 2016, Russia's Gini index number was higher than that of any European country, at 0.41. And both were still much more egalitarian than the US, where the Gini index, unique in advanced countries, was 0.47 (thus ranking it alongside countries from Latin America and Africa, not other advanced countries). In the third world countries, the Gini index was between 0.42 (Argentina, Ghana) and around 0.60 (Zambia, Haiti, and Namibia). Overall, inequality significantly increased in the European Union (EU), although it remained lower than in the US, Russia, or third world countries.[3]

Inequality has a special connection with the change of family structures and, connected with this, gender-inequality.

> Changes in values, opportunities and increasing mobility have led and continue to lead - an EU document reflects - to changing family structures. Since 1970, there have been fewer marriages, falling from eight to five a year per thousand people, while the number of divorces has risen from one to two per thousand. This has probably increased the number of single-parent and recomposed families. More children, now over a third, are born

outside marriage…. Overall, the male breadwinner model, on which much family policy has been grounded, is no longer predominant. [Meanwhile], women's activity rate is still 12.7 percentage points below that of men (64.9% against 77.6% for the 15–64 age bracket in 2011). A higher proportion of women works part-time, which means that on average women work 17% less hours than men. Finally, the gender pay gap of 17% (in average hourly gross wage) is partly due to women earning lower pay for work of equal value, and partly due to women being concentrated in jobs that pay less. As a result, women's annual gross labor market earnings can be estimated to be 42% below those of men on average.[4]

Growing inequality after a half century of decrease became one of the main sources of dissatisfaction throughout Europe. This fact offered fuel for populists who positioned themselves as defenders of average, "forgotten" people, blue-collar workers, the agricultural population, and the unemployed.

The economic growth that returned in Europe from 2017 to 2018 and, after a long stagnation, reached a 2.5 percent annual growth rate probably offers the possibility of curing inequality and stopping its increase within the core countries. One of the tangible positive consequences is the increase in job possibilities. As one commentator noted, "More EU citizens work than ever recorded. Twelve million moved into work in just the past four years [2014–18]. That is more than the total population of Belgium or Greece."[5] Nevertheless, it still did not significantly change the situation of Europe's poor. According to the latest report, some 119 million or almost 24 percent of the EU population are still at risk of poverty or social exclusion.[6]

Inequality among member countries of the EU

Beside inequality within countries, inequality among core and peripheral EU member countries represents a ticking time bomb. During the 2010s, it became one of the central issues for the EU. Inequality is a worldwide phenomenon, although since the globalization of the 1970–80s, inequality between countries has decreased, even as inequality within countries has increased. As a United Nations University analysis stated in 2016: inequality among nations

> has declined steadily over the past few decades, from 0.739 in 1975 to 0.631 in 2010, driven primarily by countries arising by their extraordinary economic growth, especially in fast developing China, India and some other Asian countries. This trend has been achieved despite an increasing trend in inequality within countries.[7]

Some of the formerly less-developed countries, mostly in East Asia, led by China, are gradually catching up with the advanced West. However, worldwide backwardness still remained an explosive issue. The famous umbrella organization Oxfam International,[8] a confederation of 20 organizations that works in 90 countries to fight inequality, published its report on global inequality, as usual, to coincide with the annual Davos meeting of representatives of big businesses and governments in January 2018. According to the shocking report, 82 percent of the wealth produced in the world in 2017 went into the pockets of the wealthiest 1 percent. The 3.7 billion lower-income people, 50 percent of the world's population, did not receive a cent from the increased wealth. The wealth of billionaires increased by 13 percent, six times more than the income of the average worker, which has increased by only 2 percent since 2010. According to the calculations, the CEOs of the top fashion companies earn as much money in four days as a worker in a Bangladesh apparel company makes in her whole life.

While inequality is much lower in EU member countries than worldwide, this phenomenon still became a central problem there. In a recent study, Thomas Piketty maintained that three major forms of inequality challenge the EU: growing inequality within the member countries, inequality between the North and the South, and the East-West divide. The Northwestern member countries have profited from crediting to and investing in the Southern and Eastern countries of the EU, thus exploiting them.[9]

Regarding the East-West divide, Piketty quotes the calculations of Filip Novokmet's doctoral dissertation (which was directed by Piketty at the *École des hautes études en sciences sociales* in Paris):

> In Paris, Berlin or Brussels, people cannot understand the lack of gratitude on the part of countries which have benefited from huge public transfers. But in Warsaw or in Prague, events are interpreted quite differently. They point out that the rate of return on the private investment from the West was high and that the flows of profits paid today to the owners of the firms far exceeds the European transfers going in the other direction. In fact, if we examine the figures, they do have a case.[10]

Western, and first of all German, investors have gradually become the owners of a considerable proportion of the capital after the collapse of communism of the former communist countries of Eastern Europe. Western investments represent roughly a quarter of the stock of fixed capital (including housing) in Eastern Europe, and over half of the ownership of firms in the region is in Western hands.

"Between 2010 and 2016," relates Piketty (quoting Novokmet's figures),

> the annual outflow of profits and incomes from property (net of the corresponding inflows) thus represented on average 4.7% of the gross domestic product in Poland, 7.2% in Hungary, 7.6% in the Czech Republic and 4.2% in Slovakia, reducing commensurately the national income of these countries. By comparison, over the same period, the annual net transfers from the European Union, that is, the difference between the totality of expenditure received and the contributions paid to the EU budget, were appreciably lower: 2.7% of the GDP in Poland, 4.0% in Hungary, 1.9% in the Czech Republic and 2.2% in Slovakia.[11]

These calculations, surprisingly enough, are senseless. First of all, they compare two rather different and incomparable amounts. Capital income from foreign direct investments (FDI) has nothing to do with EU budgetary payments. One can compare capital income with capital investments, but not with EU assistance. Second, the figures are totally wrong. Gábor Oláh, a Hungarian economist, recalculated these figures regarding Hungary. Instead of the 7.2 percent of the GDP profit outflow from Hungary, it turned out that 2.2 percent of capital outflow is debt interest repayment and not profit withdrawal. The profit outflow would thus be only 4.8 percent of the GDP. Furthermore, another 1.6 percent of the profit from FDI was reinvested in Hungary, and the real net capital outflow from the profit of foreign investments was only 3.2 percent of the GDP. It also pays to note that the amount of profit transfer from Hungary does not only go to EU countries, but to the US, Japan, and South Korea as well. Profit outflow to EU member countries is not higher than 2.9 percent of the GDP. This amount is 1.1 percent less than the inflow of EU assistance.[12] In other words, Novokmet's calculation, surprisingly published on Piketty's blog, is full of mistakes and entirely wrong.

Nevertheless, the calculations published on Piketty's blog were enthusiastically welcomed by right-wing populist leaders of Central European countries, who revolted against and attacked the EU while pocketing billions of euros from the EU budget in the form of assistance for less-developed areas. According to the European Commission, since Hungary joined the EU in 2004, the country had paid €12 billion in membership fees to the EU's budget but had received back €48 billion in aid between 2004 and 2016. Thus, for every €1 the country paid in membership, it received €4.5 back. If we add the years during which Hungary received EU assistance before gaining official membership, then between 2000 and 2016, the EU paid five times more to Hungary than the country paid to the EU.[13]

However, the populist government often maintained that the EU money was not a gift, but repayment for part of the huge profit Western countries earn and transfer to the West from their countries. Viktor Orbán stated that the inflow of EU funds for the country's "economic or social development ... do not come as a gift – as I said we are entitled to them."[14] Poland's Jarosław Kaczyński, echoing Orbán, also insists that the EU money is not a gift but an entitlement. The fact is, however, that Poland is the largest beneficiary of EU assistance for less-developed Member States. Poland has received one-and-a-half times more aid from the EU than the 16 countries who received the legendary Marshall Plan assistance over a four-year period after World War II combined. Between 2008 and 2020, Poland, a country with a GDP of €418.7 billion in 2013, will receive €257.1 billion of EU assistance. While each recipient country of the Marshall Plan received an annual average of $2.5 billion over four years, Poland currently receives €21.5 billion per year and will continue to do so through 2020. This lavish assistance adds an additional 5–7 percent to the country's GDP. Infrastructural investments in Poland and Hungary were covered by 61 and 55 percent by EU aids to these two countries, respectively.

The Poles have also been the biggest winners of the EU's Schengen Agreement allowing the free movement of people within the EU. Some two million Poles are working in other EU countries. This opportunity significantly lowers unemployment in the country; moreover, workers abroad regularly send money home to their families. Hungary also profits from the free flow of labor, as about 600,000 Hungarians—four times more than the number of emigrants after the defeat of the 1956 revolution in the country—are working in Western member countries.

Most of all, FDIs and technology exports from the Western member countries established modern sectors, including high tech companies, improved infrastructure, and increased productivity. In other words, this support became the main driver of development and the spread of knowledge in the former communist countries. That is the key for catching up with the more advanced countries. Piketty strongly underlines this factor when he states in his aforementioned book,

> historical experience suggests that the principal mechanism for convergence at the international ... level is the diffusion of knowledge. In other words, the poor catch up with the rich to the extent that they achieve the same level of technological know-how, skill and education.

He adds, "Internationally, it [capital ownership inequality] is almost impossible to sustain without a colonial type of political domination."[15]

Nevertheless, neglecting these facts and Piketty's statement in his blog that "one might reasonably argue that Western investment [in peripheral countries] enabled the productivity of the economies concerned to increase and therefore everyone benefited,"[16] the lieutenants of Viktor Orbán triumphantly welcomed the Piketty blog's statement about capital outflow from Hungary. Repeating his boss's argument, one such individual claimed, "It is not true that Hungary receives huge aids from the Union. ... Much more money is going out from the country than the inflow of aid from the Union." According to this argument, the outflow of a significant portion of capital income also caused lower wages in the Central European countries.[17] This statement was also false.

The wage gap between the West and the East is also traditional, stemming from the much lower productivity level in the latter region. As a basic economic rule, the lower the productivity, the lower the wages. In the early 1990s, the created value in an hour of work in France, Germany, and the Netherlands was equal to 100 percent (this was virtually also equal to the US), whereas Portugal and Greece produced only a half (48 and 59 percent), and Hungary and Poland only a fifth to a quarter (21–25 percent) of it.[18] Furthermore, lower wages are also connected to the lower price level in those countries, which makes wages relatively higher in purchasing power parity than exchange rate calculations. Poland's per capita income in 2014 was equivalent to only 26 percent of the US level, but in purchasing power parity, it reached almost 46 percent of it.[19]

The wage gap is not the consequence of Western exploitation. In reality, when foreign-owned companies settled in the region from the 1990s, they paid wages that were over twice as high as those of local companies, thereby starting to increase the wage level. The wage gap is thus an inherited characteristic connected with lower development and productivity levels. When communism collapsed, the wage level in the former communist countries stood at 5–7 percent of the Western level based on exchange rate parity. Within a few years, it increased to 15 percent and was growing. For local workers in Slovakia and neighboring countries, Volkswagen paid only 15 percent of the wages and benefits it paid in Germany, but that was still much higher than the average wage level in the region. Investment, in other words, led to an increase in wages and living standards.

Inequality within the EU is not created by the Western exploitation of the peripheral countries. Actually, they became richer and started to catch up with the West after joining and beginning to profit from EU membership. Between 1992 and 2014, four major Central European countries—the Czech Republic, Hungary, Poland, and Romania—increased their per capita income level by 2.7 times, while France, Germany, Belgium, and Austria, as an average, increased theirs by 2.3 times. In 1992, the four former communist countries' average per capita income levels were only 27 percent of the aforementioned four Western countries' levels[20], but by 2014, they were already at 33 percent.[21]

Inequalities within the EU were not created by the exploitative connections between the EU's core and peripheral member countries but inherited from diverse previous development that was implanted in the EU as a result of enlargement toward the peripheries. Inequality among founding member countries was not a problem faced by the integrating European Community. The European Steel and Coal Community (1951) that was transformed into the European Economic Community (1957), the predecessor of the EU (1993), was founded by six West European countries: France, Belgium, the Netherlands, Luxembourg, Germany, and Italy. (The latter was actually a southern country, but its most developed northern region belonged to Western Europe.) The founding countries were rather homogenous in terms of their economic and income levels. They were all industrialized, strongly urbanized modern countries with similar sociopolitical structures and characteristics. Excepting Luxembourg, the smallest and richest country, the other member countries were on a similar income level. The income level of the richest (Germany) was only 7 percent higher than the average income of the founding member countries, and that of the poorest (Italy) was only 15 percent lower.

Nowadays, using the 2016 income figures, the core countries of the EU are also on a quite similar stage as their average per capita income level ranks in the top 20 percent of all countries of the world, between $38,000 and $50,000. (Small Luxembourg is an exception: it is the richest with a per capita income of more than $100,000.) Italy, although a high-income country, is the least rich (with about $30,000 per capita GDP) due to its less-developed southern region. The country's per capita income is about 19 percent less than France's and 27 percent less than Germany's.

Some Nordic countries, such as Denmark, Sweden, and Finland, and the Central European Austria, joined later (Denmark in 1973, the others in 1995) but actually have somewhat higher income levels (between $43,000 and $52,000) than those of the founding countries. Thus, these nine countries all belong to the high-income zone and form a relatively homogenous group, which aids close co-operation. Ireland, which was considered a peripheral country when it joined in 1973 with hardly more than half of the income level of the Northwest European core, achieved the greatest economic success of catching up. Nowadays, with its more than $62,000 per capita income, Ireland is one of the richest members of the EU and has become the European core's tenth country.

The enlargement of the community in the 1980s and 2000s, however, led to the incorporation of 16 countries with much lower economic standards, including standard income levels that were roughly half or significantly less than half of the Northwestern members' standard income levels. When the Mediterranean countries joined in the 1980s, their combined average income level was only about 61 percent of the nine Northwestern countries' combined average level. Some of those countries made great progress but could not reach faster growth than that of the Western core. As such, all of them still represent a lower level of economic development, and as of 2016, their combined average income level was still equivalent to only 61 percent of the nine Northwestern member countries' combined average income level. Even the best among them, Spain, has hardly more than half the economic level of Denmark and two-thirds of that of Germany (with $27,000 per capita GDP).

When the former communist Central European countries were accepted in 2004, their per capita income level was just one-third of the member countries' average. Similarly, when the two Balkan countries were accepted in 2007, their combined average income level was only 14 percent of the EU average. Inequality among member countries became substantial after those enlargements.

The development range in the early twenty-first century (in 2016) is bookended by Luxembourg, with its more than $100,000 per capita income, and Bulgaria, with hardly more than $7,000. The eleven Central European, Baltic, and Balkan former communist countries have an average income level of $11,000, which is only about 22 percent of the Northwestern core and 35 percent of the Mediterranean member countries' combined average level. Instead of the original homogenous community, the enlarged EU nowadays has an advanced, high-income core and a much less-developed middle- (and in some cases even low-) income periphery.

"Large income per-capita gaps," reported the EU Commission in January 2009,

> remain across countries and the gap between most EU Member States and the best performing Member States is still large. For instance, in 2008 the average per capita GDP of the EU as a whole was still 34% below that of the

five best EU performers. Moreover, over the last three-year period, while some impressive income catch-up has been achieved by the 12 Member States which joined in 2004 and 2007, the per-capita GDP gap has widened in some [Mediterranean] former EU15 Member States.... Data highlight the diversity of the EU. The Global Competitiveness index ranking ranges between 3 and 4 (Denmark and Sweden) to 67 and 68 (Greece and Romania) while the World Bank business regulatory environment ranges between ranks 5, 6 and 7 (Denmark, the UK and Ireland) to ranks 75, 76 and 96 (the Czech Republic, Poland and Greece).[22]

These differences, however, are far bigger and deeper than what can be expressed in terms of income. Behind the per capita income differences, a huge spectrum of social and cultural differences also separates the European core from the peripheries. These factors are strongly contributing to the preservation of relative backwardness. Lower per capita income also means lower living standards, lower educational levels, and different cultural and behavioral attitudes; moreover, it entails significantly different political traditions and tendencies. These differences are deeply rooted in history and are thus rather stable characteristics since they have entirely different millennial development narratives behind them. The huge economic and social gap that exists in the early twenty-first century was basically the same as that a century before. Only two or three countries have changed places: Finland, Ireland, and Italy have elevated from the middle- to the high-income category; otherwise, the gap between advanced and less-developed countries has increased during the twentieth century.

The income gap, indeed, is very broad. Is this phenomenon the consequence of exploitative East-West economic connections within the Union? Answering this question, we have to repeat the fact that the existing gap was inherited. The greatest part of now-peripheral countries such as those in Central and Eastern Europe started their European historical journey half a millennium later than the Western countries and joined the Christian cultural sphere only in the tenth and eleventh centuries. Most of them lost independence and were incorporated for several centuries into huge empires, namely the Habsburg, Russian, or Ottoman Empires. None of them participated in the Protestant revolution, the Enlightenment, and the two Industrial Revolutions during the nineteenth century.

Different histories generated diverse cultural patterns. Living 400 years under occupation and/or predatory states that robbed their own people led to an attitude of hostility against alien and robber states and their institutions. Cheating the state and not paying taxes became a cultural virtue. Institutions in the oppressive, backward states of the Russian or Ottoman Empires, indeed, did not serve the people and mostly did not work efficiently either. People learned not to turn to those institutions for support and arrangements, but to instead rely upon traditional social networks composed of kin, friends, and influential protectors. Corruption also became the rule and came to exist as the culturally accepted catalyst for procuring institutional support when necessary.

Combined with this culture of corruption, endemic poverty produced a cultural attitude that viewed labor as work that always enriched others; thus it was considered to be a burden. People developed different relations to money, preferring mutual assistance. These habits are still alive and virulent. Guided in part by their inherited cultural distrust of authorities and state institutions, people in Mediterranean, Central European, and Balkan countries were easily swayed and mobilized by populist leaders against the "self-serving bureaucrats of Brussels," which they positioned as new oppressive "colonizers." Beginning in the early nineteenth century, these countries often revolted against foreign powers and developed passionate nationalism. Their borders were never really safe, changed relatively often, and had neighbors who were mostly enemies. During the two World Wars soldiers in the armies were taught to die and kill for the nation. Nationalist sentiments were alive and thus easily revitalized and manipulated by skillful demagogues.

Avoiding official institutions and cheating the state remained common practices in the peripheral countries. These phenomena are partly connected with the inefficiency and bad work of the institutions in those areas. Italy, which has already emerged from a former peripheral state, still preserves this legacy. Due to institutional inefficiency, the country currently stands in 77th place worldwide in terms of the ease of starting a new business, and in 87th place for doing business. Regarding the quality and functionality of institutions, Italy occupies the 92nd place. As a comparison, Hungary ranks 97th for institutional quality and 99th for business ethics. These rankings of the 70s and 90s places fall well below the normative range of European standards since Europe has only 50 countries from the world's roughly 190–200.

As corruption "helps" the function of institutions in these countries by catalyzing activity, consequently, it penetrates every sphere of everyday life. There are tacit "fixed" prices to arrange many common tasks. For example, to get a driver's license in Greece one has to pay the official €1,400. The EU average on the so-called Corruption Perception Index, which measures corruption on a scale of 0–100 (100 signifying a total lack of corruption), is 66. The Scandinavian countries' average is between 89 and 91. At the end of the scale, the five most corrupt countries of the EU are Romania, Bulgaria, Greece, Italy, and Hungary. In terms of world ranking, Greece occupies the 80th place, and Italy occupies the 61st, placing these countries equal to or behind Senegal and South Africa.

Corruption is closely connected to tax evasion. According to various calculations, tax evasion consumes billions of euros, equal to 4–5 percent of the GDP in certain countries. In Italy, in the 1980s, 45 percent of value-added tax (VAT) was not paid; in Greece, one-third was not. Shopkeepers asked shoppers if they needed a receipt; if not, the business was not reported, and the parties did not have to pay taxes on the goods. As a former finance minister of Greece announced, there would have been no debt crisis in the country if taxes had been properly paid.

Similarly, in several industries such as those involving repair work (for example, car repair), buying and selling are realized on the so-called black market or shadow economy, where business transactions occur without parties officially reporting them and paying taxes. According to official evaluations, the value of business transactions happening on the black market is equal to 25–33 percent of the GDP in the Balkans and the Mediterranean countries of the EU. This is somewhat above the Latin American level of 24–26 percent but definitely below the African, Thai, and Philippine levels of 68–76 percent. In contrast, in the 35 most advanced countries of the OECD, this portion is 17 percent; in the North European countries, it constitutes only 9–15 percent of the GDP.

Histories of development also created different work ethics in the core versus peripheries. In the latter area, work always served others interests and thus was considered a burden or a forced task for lower class people. The upper classes, the nobility and gentry, looked down upon work as vulgar and shameful. In most of these areas Protestantism did not gain ground and consequently the Protestant work ethic was not dominant. At the EU's periphery, work ethics differed from the North-Western countries' traditions. Comparing core and peripheral countries within the EU, this legacy is still present. This cultural distinction is clearly manifested in the fact that the labor market participation is much lower in the latter set of counties. The EU's average employment rate of people between 20 and 64 years in the mid-2010s was 71 percent, but in Sweden it was more than 81 percent, while in Greece it was only 60 percent; in Croatia, Romania, and Bulgaria, it was only 51–53 percent, and female participation was only at 27 percent. The big difference stems partly from the older generation's (54–64) massive early retirement, and partly from the much lower percentage of female participation. Before the 2008 crisis, in Greece, the average life expectancy was nearing 80 while the retirement age was 58 years, and in some fields 48 years. Poland just reduced the compulsory retirement age to 60 years. While the gender gap in Sweden is less than 4 percent, meaning that the percentage of working women is nearly equal to that of men, in the peripheries, this gap is huge: in the Czech Republic, it is 16 percent, but in the Balkans, it is much bigger.

Major cultural and behavioral differences are slowing down the catching-up process in peripheral EU countries and making them much weaker. This is the main factor behind their preserved relative backwardness. Western investments and crediting actually helped their development by generating technology imports to the region and creating modern economic sectors that did not exist before, including virtually the entire export sectors of these countries. Foreign investments were the main engine of growth in these regions. The fact that the banking sector of Central Europe is virtually owned by Western countries (87 percent) and led to a flood of loans into the region created a consumption and construction boom around the turn of the millennium. After the 2008 financial crisis, the EU arranged an agreement with the Western banks (the Vienna Consensus) whereby they consented to continue crediting the region. This agreement helped the countries by saving them from the burden of refinancing their banks. In Spain and Ireland, the collapse of the banks after 2008 forced the governments to refinance their banking sector, which led to state insolvencies that required bailouts by the International Monetary Fund (IMF) and the EU.

Regardless of the causes of income differences between the Western and Eastern member countries of the EU, this phenomenon definitely weakens solidarity and harmonization within the Union. Especially after the 2008 financial-economic crisis, it became a source of conflict among member countries and particularly increased discontents in the less-developed ones. Indeed, instead of formally equal membership, after the 2008 crisis, the Union had Western creditor countries versus peripheral debtor countries. After the former forced the latter to introduce austerity measures to put their financial households in order, they were easily painted as oppressive and exploitative.

While in the West, only people belonging to the lowest 15–25 percent of the population felt "forgotten" and "left behind," at times, two-thirds of the population in the peripheral countries expressed these feelings. The disappointed population gathered behind demagogues who delivered "revolutionary" speeches by naming the enemies and became the rulers of the countries. It was easy to mobilize desperate people to back populist governments to fight for "regaining freedom" from "colonizing Brussels." Inequality within and among the member countries of the EU prepared the soil for discontent and populist parties to grow rapidly.

There is not much hope that inequality will be significantly decreased by the work of internal features of neoliberal contemporary capitalism in the near future. Nevertheless, newly emerging economic prosperity as a result of returning economic growth may have a positive outcome. If the EU leadership learns from the existential crisis of the 2010s and copes with the major elements of the crisis, continued attention to these problems may lead to a clear recognition of the need to lower the level of inequality. History teaches that the only force that may counterbalance the internal mechanism of capitalism and decrease inequality is the clear recognition of the need for social solidarity and the mobilization of political forces to generate a trend of moderation. World War II and the Cold War decades taught this lesson, and Europe learned it accordingly. The recent existential crisis and sharp discontents are a new historical situation that may teach this lesson again, leading the EU to get rid of neoliberal deregulation and return to the control and regulation of capitalism's inner mechanisms through these processes. It worked in the second half of the twentieth century and may work again in the first half of the twenty-first century.

Notes

1 Thomas Piketty, *Capital in the Twenty-First Century*, trans. Arthur Goldhammer (Cambridge, MA: The Belknap Press of Harvard University Press, 2017), 35.
2 "Gini Coefficient," *World Bank*, accessed April 8, 2018, http://go.worldbank.org/3SLY UTVY00.
3 Sergio Vieira, "Inequality on the Rise?" *World Economic and Social Survey (WESS) 2013 background document* (United Nations, December 2012), https://goo.gl/r4FbKk, "GINI Index (World Bank Estimate) | Data," *World Bank*, accessed April 8, 2018, https://data.worldbank.org/indicator/SI.POV.GINI.
4 *Archive of European Integration*, Evidence on demographic and social trends. Social policies' contribution to inclusion, employment and the economy. Social investment

package. Commission staff working document. SWD (2013) 38 final/I, 20 February 2013. [EU Commission–SEC Document].

5 Ive Marx, "Europe's Poor Need More Than Jobs," *Social Europe*, March 2, 2018, https://goo.gl/oDHKMu.

6 "Europe 2020 Indicators–Poverty and Social Exclusion," *Europe 2020 Strategy Report* (Eurostat), accessed April 9, 2018, https://goo.gl/hQZEf8.

7 "Global Income Inequality Has Declined in Relative Terms, But Gone Up Substantially in Absolute Amounts," *Press Release* (United Nations University), accessed April 9, 2018, https://goo.gl/27cX4L.

8 "Oxfam International," accessed April 9, 2018, www.oxfam.org/en/about.

9 Thomas Piketty, "2018, l'année de l'Europe," *Le Monde* (blog), January 16, 2018, http://piketty.blog.lemonde.fr/2018/01/16/2018-lannee-de-leurope/.

10 Ibid.

11 Ibid.

12 Gábor Oblath, "Nem Fosztogatnak, Hanem Osztogatnak–Magyarország Kizsákmányolásáról," *Portfolio*, January 31, 2018, https://goo.gl/FjCZvS.

13 *Millenium Intezet*, Budapest, Hungary, Newsletter, February 10, 2018.

14 Csaba Tóth, "Full Text of Viktor Orbán's Speech at Băile Tuşnad (Tusnádfürdő) of 26 July 2014," *The Budapest Beacon*, July 29, 2014, https://goo.gl/9JCgDN.

15 Piketty, *Capital*, 90–91.

16 Piketty, *Le Monde* blog.

17 Kasnyik Márton, "A davosi elit szerint is baj, hogy egyre gazdagabb a davosi elit," trans. Ivan Berend, *G7*, January 22, 2018, https://goo.gl/AQkYXS.

18 Angus Maddison, *Monitoring the World Economy, 1820–1992* (Paris: Development Centre of the Organisation for Economic Co-operation and Development, 1995), 47.

19 *The Economist, Pocket World in Figures 2017* (London: Profile Books, 2016), 192, 230.

20 Calculated based on data in Angus Maddison, *Monitoring the World Economy*.

21 Calculated based on data in *The Economist, Pocket World in Figures 2017*.

22 *Archive of European Integration*, Draft joint employment report. Implementation of the Lisbon Strategy structural reforms in the context of the European economic recovery plan – a more detailed overview of progress across the EU in the specific macro- and micro-economic as well as the employment areas. COM (2009) 34 final, Vol. II, 28 January 2009. [EU Commission–COM Document].

3

THE POLITICAL REPRESENTATION OF DISCONTENT

Disappearing traditional political parties and rising populism

From class to national parties

During the 1970–80s, something radically changed within European politics. The postwar sociopolitical arrangement seemed to be exhausted: the widespread postwar feeling of solidarity and the optimistic views on development and social engineering efforts—which had generated both economic growth and more social justice—evaporated. In those difficult decades of two oil crises, high inflation, and economic stagnation, a new chapter marked by a distinct cultural and political setting opened in Europe. The ideas and practices of welfare policy financed by high taxation, general trade unionization, and the regulatory state were replaced by a new zeitgeist of neoliberal ideology and concomitant policies, including defending the undisturbed market from state intervention, decreasing taxes, and even neoliberal suggestions to privatize health care and schooling.

In this new atmosphere, the dominant postwar mass parties that had represented the diverse interests of major social groups or layers declined into crisis. Most of the mass parties dropped class representation and became "statal" (or state) parties representing the general interests of the entire nation-state. Party membership generally deteriorated: in the 1990s, party membership in Italy, Sweden, and Denmark dropped to one-quarter of its previous levels; in Britain, to one-fifth. Political apathy decimated the active electorate. In the postwar decades, on average, 88 percent of the electorate participated in elections. By contrast, in Britain, Portugal, and Ireland, between 1997 and 2002, 30–40 percent of them remained at home.[1]

Old mass parties are disappearing

Several of the big mass parties disappeared. The deep crisis and then collapse of Soviet communism disqualified the communist parties. Almost all of them disappeared in Central and Eastern Europe from the 1990s on or changed their names and ideologies, and rebranded themselves as Western-style social democratic parties. The strongest Western communist parties in France and Italy also disappeared or transformed. The Italian Communist Party, which had 1.8 million members, was replaced by several groups and parties; the most important one became the *Democratici di Sinistra*, or Democratic Party of the Left, with 600,000 members. Some ruling right-wing Cold War parties shared this destiny. The most extreme case was Italy, where all the previously dominant parties disappeared, including the Christian Democratic Party, which formed most of the governments in the country until the 1990s. In France, during the 2017 elections, "the two parties that have dominated French politics for decades are fighting for their lives."[2] At the second stage of the presidential elections, they did not even have candidates. In the parliamentary elections, they occupied only 142 of the 350 seats. Instead, the newly established party of Emmanuel Macron, *La République En Marche!*, gained the overwhelming majority. These figures reflect a dramatic change since 2007 and 2012, when the two traditional leading parties gained 57 and then 56 percent of the vote.

The British Conservative Party, although still relatively strong, had only 400,000 members in 1997; by 2013, membership declined to 100,000. This trend is especially striking when one compares the party's 1952 membership of 2.8 million.[3]

Melting down of the social democratic parties

One of the most important changes in political representation was the dramatic melting down of the social democratic parties. From the late nineteenth century onward, these parties emerged as the political representation of the industrial working class. In some cases, they were closely connected with the trade unions. Longtime opposition underdogs, they fought against the ruling bourgeois parties for workers' interests. A kind of turning point in their history occurred when the Swedish Social Democratic Party won the election in 1932, formed the government, and introduced Europe's first welfare state.

After World War II, social democratic parties formed the governments in several European countries. In 2000, social democratic parties governed in 10 of the European Union's (EU's) 15 countries. At that time, however, they dropped their old identities of representing the working class, often modified their programs accordingly, and became so-called "catch-all" parties that declared they represented the interests of the entire nation. This change was clearly expressed by the German Social Democratic Party's ratification of the Bad Godesberg Program in the autumn of 1959. This program transformed Germany's oldest socialist party, which was founded as the General German Workers' Association in 1863 and had been a longtime Marxist party. That naturally meant a political shift from the left to the center. The formerly sometimes-sharp difference among left-wing and right-wing parties paled, making the dominant parties pretty similar in certain aspects. Several times the former arch-enemies formed "grand coalitions" and governed together, as in Germany after 1966 and for quite long during the 2010s. As Yascha Mounk of Harvard University remarked in 2016, in recent years, Europe's center-left and center-right parties had tended to work together, either unofficially or in grand coalition, in what was viewed as high-minded and sensible, an important bulwark against the rise of the far right.... [Nevertheless,] those 'ideologically weird' coalitions tend to alienate voters by implying there were little real differences between establishment right and left.[4]

Unquestionably, those changes elevated former opposition parties to governing parties with national importance. However, the traditional workers' base of these parties developed the feeling that "their party" no longer represented their special interests. In quite a few cases, they considered their party leaders traitors, as was the case with Gerhard Schröder in Germany or Tony Blair in Britain. As German Chancellor in the early twenty-first century, Schröder created a more flexible labor market by relaxing labor market rules to enable the easy dismissal of workers. These changes also essentially forced the unemployed to accept any (even badly paid) jobs after a certain period of unemployment, because unemployment benefits were curbed and expired after a short time. These reforms helped create an impressive economic boom in the country, but it badly hurt workers' interests. When the French socialist president François Holland tried to follow this program, he failed due to strong workers' resistance.

Tony Blair wanted to find a "Third Way,"[5] and governed as the representative of traditional British capitalism and great power interests. Blair followed the American president George W. Bush and enthusiastically joined his wars in Iraq and Afghanistan. As with European social democrats in other governments, Blair espoused neoliberal economic ideologies and policies, and argued that the deregulation that served big corporate interests equaled the national economic interest.

"Agreements between the center-left and the center-right have long been seen as a fundamental building block of European stability. But now ... the popularity of mainstream parties is falling fast, with the center-left's support collapsing particularly quickly."[6] Indeed, the traditional workers' base was alienated from the social democratic parties. They did not feel those parties represented their interests any longer. In February 2018, the *New York Times* published a long interview with a third-generation Ruhr coalminer, Guido Reil, who joined the trade union at the age of 18 and the German Social Democratic Party at the age of 20. He worked in six mines during his lifetime, but when all of them (together with 2,500 others) were closed, he took an early retirement at the age of 48. In the 2010s, he left the Social Democratic Party; in 2017, he voted for the populist *Alternative für Deutschland* (AfD, Alternative for Germany). He plans to join the new workers' movement, the Alternative Union of that right-wing party. Expressing sentiments shared by many other workers, he stated his belief that open borders and a welfare state cannot successfully coexist, and that old trade unions had colluded with the bosses.[7]

The case of the German miner Guido Reil represents a Europe-wide phenomenon. The old base of the social democratic parties is melting down. This trend is strengthened by the structural changes in the advanced European economy. As a consequence of globalization (which shifted industrial jobs to low-wage Third World countries) and, most importantly, technological changes that dramatically increased automation and robotization, industrial employment drastically dropped from 40–50 percent of the European population to 15–25 percent. More industrial products are now being produced with a much smaller workforce. This trend was accelerated by environmental considerations. To decrease pollution and global warming, most of the coal mines were closed in Western Europe, even in Belgium, where the coal industry was a leading export sector. The industrial working class was decimated, and their trade unions became insignificant.

The 2008 crisis, characterized by skyrocketing unemployment and austerity cuts to welfare expenditures, wages, and pensions, was the final major factor that produced the crisis of the social democracy. These parties lost a great part of their membership and voters. In 1998, the German Social Democratic Party of Schröder gained 40 percent of the votes; in the fall of 2017, the party under Schulz received 20.5 percent. Before the formation of the German grand coalition, the Social Democratic Party's popularity had slid even further. The *Deutsche Welle* reported in late February 2018 that "The populist Alternative for Germany (AfD) has overtaken the Social Democrats (SPD) in a national opinion poll for the first time." The AfD's 16 percent support was a half-percent more than the support of the SPD. "The figures released by the INSA polling institute show the SPD in free fall."[8]

In the French presidential elections of 2017, the social democratic candidate got 6 percent of the vote altogether. The same phenomenon happened in the Netherlands and the Czech Republic, where social democratic parties received only single-digit electoral votes. In several Central and Eastern European countries, social democracy virtually disappeared or transformed into populist parties, as in Slovakia.

A great part of the former socialist base began to vote for extreme populist parties, either as punishment for their old parties' perceived desertion or in order to find new representation. In some cases, these voters supported new leftist-populist parties such as the Greek *Syriza* or the Spanish *Podemos* parties, but in general, they favored right-wing populists. These parties dramatically gained ground all over Europe. They vowed to represent the "left behind" and "forgotten" people's interests. They were strongly against immigration and promised to defend "white workers' interests." They were antiestablishment and rejected the old parties, often calling them corrupt. Most of them flatly denied the continued existence of the left and the right; indeed, they mixed the programs of the old left and right (the Italian populist Five Star Movement most explicitly). They espoused racist views against non-Europeans and were often authoritarian but also advocated for workers' interests; they supported anti-technological-development programs, including reopening the coal mines and the reintroduction of old industrial jobs. They also rejected European integration and the free flow of goods, capital, and labor.

These ideas and programs were actually partly advanced by the traditional mainstream conservative parties as well. They wanted to compete with populist parties "by co-opting some of their largest issues, particularly in regards of immigration. So far that strategy has proven mostly successful" in the Netherlands, Denmark, Austria, and Britain.[9]

Rising populist parties

In the early twenty-first century, populism emerged as a mainstream political force, and newly established populist parties mushroomed. Some of them, however, were established somewhat earlier, like the *Freiheitliche Partei Österreichs* (Austrian Freedom Party). This party was established by former Nazi officers in 1955 and taken over by Jörg Haider, the son of a former Nazi couple. Similarly, the French *Front National* was established by the neo-Nazi *Ordre Nouveau* (New Order) group and Jean-Marie Le Pen in 1972. One of the leading right-wing populist parties in Central Europe, the Hungarian *Fiatal Demokraták Szövetsége* (FIDESz), on the other hand, was established as a liberal democratic anti-communist party in 1988.

Later, in the 1980s–90s, however, these political organizations transformed into modern right-wing populist parties. Haider himself transformed his party, as did Viktor Orbán, one of the strong-man founders of FIDESz; the Front National made this change when Marine Le Pen took over the party from her father.

In Hungary, the transformation of a similar postcommunist racist party, *Magyar Igazság és Élet Pártja* (Hungarian Justice and Life Party or MIÉP, founded in 1993), into the openly anti-Roma and anti-Semitic *Jobbik* (*Jobboldali Ifjúsági Közösség*) Party, which was only established in 2002, provides yet another example of transformation. Jobbik also started transforming in 2014 under the new leadership of Gábor Vona, when it dropped its far-right ideology to become an acceptable modern populist party.

The mostly newly founded populist parties of the 1990s and 2000s constitute a long list, including the Dutch Geert Wilders' *Partij voor de Vrijheid* (Party of Freedom), founded in 2005; the Belgian *Vlaams Belang* (Flemish Interest Party), established in 2004; the Bulgarian *IMRO* – Bulgarian National Movement (1991) and *Attack* (2005); the *Dansk Folkeparti* (Danish People's Party), established in 1995; the *Perussuomalaiset* (True Finns Party), founded in 1995; the Greek *Syriza* (2004) and *Laïkós Sýndesmos* – *Chrysí Avgí* (Golden Dawn) (1993); the Spanish *Podemos* (2014); the Lithuanian Order and Justice (founded as the Liberal Democratic Party in 2002); the *Prawo i Sprawiedliwość* (Polish Law and Justice) (2001); the Slovak Kotleba – People's Party – Our Slovakia (2010); the *Sverigedemokraterna* (Sweden Democrats), established in 1988; the British UK Independence Party, founded in 1993; the *Adalet ve Kalkınma Partisi* (Turkish

Justice and Development Party) (2001); the *Eesti Konservatiivne Rahvaerakond* (Conservative People's Party of Estonia) (2012); the *Alternative für Deutschland* (Alternative for Germany), founded in 2013; and several others, some of them without parliamentary representation.

Some of these parties are left-wing, but most of them are right-wing or—most often—have a mixture of right- and left-wing programs with strong anti-immigration, and extremely nationalistic positions. All have a part of the population behind them. Hungary probably represents one of the most extreme cases because both the government and the biggest opposition parties—FIDESz and Jobbik—are populist right-wing nationalist parties that together had nearly 50 percent electorate backing (and 70 percent from the seats in the parliament) in April 2018. Italy is also an extreme example because the entire traditional party system collapsed, and the newly created party system almost entirely consists of right-wing populist parties, such as the *Lega Nord* (which dropped "Nord," or "North," from its name to become nationwide),[10] Gianfranco Fini's originally extreme right-wing *Alleanza Nazionale*, the *Movimento Cinque Stelle* (Five Star Movement) led by Beppe Grillo, and Berlusconi's *Forza Italia*. Together, these parties boasted a 75 percent backing by the population in the elections in March 2018. Clearly, this state of affairs represents the new normal rather than an extreme anomaly.

Although most of the dominant populist parties are newly founded, populism is hardly a new phenomenon in Europe. John Abromeit reminds us that the progressive populism of the French Revolution transformed in the mid-nineteenth century as a result of Pierre-Joseph Proudhon's progressive socialist populism. Moreover, the later nineteenth-century Russian and Balkan "peasantism" could be considered the beginning of the populist trend in European politics.[11]

Progressive populism, however, was transformed in the twentieth century. Beside the populist workers' movement, Soviet-style Stalinism dominated most of the European communist parties, and "fascism was able effectively to place itself within" populism by offering an alternative to both capitalism and communism. The originally middle-class fascist movement, via its populist agenda, conquered a great part of the working class.[12]

After World War II and especially from the 1960s onward, populism flourished in Latin America and in the newly established Third World countries in Africa but hardly existed in Europe. Populism reemerged on the European continent during the last decades of the twentieth century and boomed during the early twenty-first century. Populist parties became the home for disappointed middle-class people, who felt that they had gradually begun to lag behind and that their accustomed environments and lifestyles were endangered by growing crime and immigrants with alien customs and habits. Populist parties also attracted masses of people from the less-developed agricultural countryside and large numbers of industrial workers, whose wages had stagnated, many of whom had lost their jobs in huge masses due (as they believed) to "unfair" competition with immigrants and low-wage countries in Asia, which they felt were stealing their jobs.

Cas Mudde, one of the best experts of populism, defines the populist ideological phenomenon in his edited work *The Populist Radical Right* (2017) as a combination of three features: (1) nationalist xenophobia (ethnic, religious, and racial prejudices, such as Islamophobia, and policies that are anti-minority, anti-immigrant, and sometimes anti-Semitic and anti-Roma as well as anti-neighbor); (2) authoritarianism (strict conservative "law and order" policies, especially against "immigrant crime"); and (3) the populist concept of a unified, exploited people whose *volonté générale* (general will) should be realized instead of the corrupt, self-serving elite; the political class; and the media. They, together with their "political correctness," have to be eliminated. The populists, left or right, want to mobilize the people.

Populism, however, is "unrelated to the left-right distinction"; it is not a coherent but rather a fluid political trend with a "thin-centered ideology ... [that] almost always appears attached to other ideological elements, which ... are appealing to a broader public. ... This means that populism can take very different shapes."[13]

This means that populism might merge with communist, anti-capitalist ideology as well as extreme right-wing concepts (ethno-populism); it may appear as anti-European nationalism but may even be combined with neoliberalism, as was the case with the Forza Italia and the UK Independence Party.

Tony Blair, the former Labor Party British Prime Minister, explained populism in the following way:

> Rightist populism ... [is] a new coalition, comprising formerly left-leaning supporters in working-class communities who feel left behind by globalization and traditionally right-leaning supporters who hate liberalism. Both constituencies believe that traditional culture is at risk from immigration and 'political correctness'. ... Both feel let down by the so-called elites and think that the solution is an authoritarian figure who dismisses what a biased establishment thinks. ... The modus operandi of this populism is not to reason but to roar. ... Its supporters welcome the outrage their leaders provoke, so that even when they are in government, they act as if they were excluded from it....[14]

People who join populist parties, indeed, feel "let down" by established parties and the political elite. Let me add, quite often with good reason. Established parties and politicians are often self-serving, even corrupt, and easily make compromises. Disappointed people look for those who offer solutions. Populists do so; moreover, they present their ideas in an easily understandable, simple way. They present difficult problems in an oversimplified form, ignoring the complexity of problems and the validity of competing arguments; they invariably approach serious issues in a one-dimensional manner and seek to address those issues by offering instant solutions. Oversimplification is closely connected and at times overlaps with the use of half-truths. That makes populist argumentation seem more realistic and rooted in real facts, allowing people to more easily identify certain claims with their own experience.

Populist politicians are mostly exclusionists. They always name an enemy, inside and/or outside the country, and scapegoat them as the cause of the nation's problems.

Enemies are often the "others," a foreign power, "Brussels" (the EU), a segment of the society, the very rich upper 1 percent, an ethnic or religious minority, Jews, immigrants, Muslims, or representatives of a certain political ideology. Some of the main perpetual enemies are liberalism, liberal democracy, the political (and/or business) establishment, and established parties and politicians. They portray the latter as corrupt, self-serving quislings in the service of special interests. They routinely cast their adversaries and rivals as "enemies of the nation" serving alien interests.

Populist parties in several cases are gathering behind strong, charismatic leaders who are often great orators, using the language of the average people around the kitchen table. These leaders are popular, and able to deftly mobilize the crowd by inflating their passions. Keith Spencer Felton points to "an elevated use of language [that] can magnify meaning, and motivate beyond the facile measure. ... The influence of language upon history is ineluctable. ... Exemplary oratory buoys civilization over its perennial perils."[15]

Populism opened the age of "post-truth politics." This is in part the consequence of the growth of social media, which spreads uncontrolled rumors at an extraordinary speed. Members of shared online networks trust each other more than the "fake" mainstream media and accept this biased news as truth.

The solid populist base is composed of less-informed rural people, uneducated and less-educated individuals who are generally somewhat older, and desperate people. Several of them are right-wing conservatives. Nevertheless, former left-wing workers also joined *en masse*. The populist base exhibits the phenomenon that mass psychologist Gustave Le Bon recognized a century ago: crowds, especially mass rallies and demonstrations, inflame passions and destroy rationality. The intensified emotions of the crowd are "contagious," and the old "herd" instinct takes over.

Central political issues for populists

This topic was discussed in detail in the introduction and requires only a very short summary here. In the name of the people, populist parties are exploiting the dissatisfaction of large layers of societies, which developed as a result of several new phenomena in Europe around the turn of the millennium. Growing inequality (discussed in Chapter 2) was one of the issues. Lagging wages and, especially after 2008, rising unemployment (in many cases 10–12 percent; in some, even more than 20 percent) led to widespread discontents. Even more devastatingly, in some countries, such as Spain and Greece, the youth unemployment rate hit 50 percent, and this downturn was weaponized by populist leaders. All these factors offered the opportunity for them to pose as defenders of the "lost people." Populists may be especially effective among desperate people in crisis situations, such as after national disasters, and also in times of radical change. Even if the change is historically positive, it destroys the accustomed environment, requiring new adjustments and causing uncertainty about the future. As the changes and painful difficulties in Europe at the turn of the millennium were connected to immigration, that became the central concern for huge swaths of the population. Due to the collapse of colonialism during the first few decades after World War II, millions of people—partly from former colonies in Indonesia, India, North Africa, Algeria, and Morocco, and from sub-Saharan Africa—arrived and settled in Europe. This influx of people generated hostile reactions in certain Western European population groups.

Poor people in Spain, Portugal, and Italy also migrated to rich Western neighboring countries for work in the late 1950–60s. Millions of Yugoslavs and Turks joined. After the collapse of communism in Central and Eastern Europe in 1989–91, about 15–20 million people moved to the West from that region as well. The "Polish Plumber" became a household term. The demographic crisis of the West European countries, where the decreasing and aging population required labor input in those countries, enabled immigrants to easily fill the jobs that were not popular among the natives. The Turkish garbage collector became a stock character in German literature.

The new immigrants and their children, however, often remained in ghettos without real integration into society. Differences in language, culture, diet, behavior, and even clothing separated them. Local communities were not always welcoming. Unemployment among the immigrants was much higher, and educational level was much lower than the average in those countries. Crimes were more often committed by them. In turn, French, Spanish, and other movies often presented immigrants as part of criminal gangs.

From the 1970–80s, a new chapter opened in the sharpening social conflicts between the local and immigrant populations in Europe. Beginning with the Palestinian militant movement and continuing with the Al-Qaeda terrorist organization, terrorist groups mobilized nonintegrated Muslim young immigrants, including some who were born in Europe but felt more at home in those circles. People easily generalized their feelings into vitriolic stereotypes about Muslims and started to fear and even hate immigrants.

That problem significantly intensified after the September 11 terror attack at the World Trade Center in New York City in 2001, an event followed by the American population's demand for retribution, which led to wars in Iraq and Afghanistan. The Islamist (Jihadist) militant movement that emerged recruited thousands of young Muslims from Europe to participate in civil wars in the Middle East.

In the mid-2010s, fatal Islamist terror attacks shocked Paris, Nice, London, Köln, Berlin, and Madrid. Anti-Muslim sentiment strengthened. Meanwhile, tragic climate change, hunger, and bloody civil wars in Africa, the Middle East, and some parts of Asia created a new, major migration crisis. Millions of migrants flooded Europe, from Niger, Morocco, and Syria to Afghanistan and Bangladesh. It culminated in a chaotic, unorganized, and uncontrolled migration to the European continent in 2015–16.

The German-led "open arms" policy to accept the immigrants into the EU generated the greatest crisis of the integration process and sparked a revolt against the official policy of the EU regarding immigration. Racist sentiments definitely played a role in this backlash, but it would be a mistake to label the immigration-fatigue reaction in several countries as motivated only by racism. Their otherness, combined with the huge, ever-increasing percentage of nonintegrated immigrants, caused some uncomfortable feelings and rejection among local populations.

Foreign-born subpopulations already reached 5–6 percent of the total populations in Hungary and Finland; this number reached more than 12 percent in France, 13 percent in Britain, 15 percent in Germany, and 18 percent in both Austria and Sweden. Ireland, Belgium, Estonia, and Latvia also had foreign-born populations that amounted to more than 10 percent of the total population.[16] This huge percentage of immigrants was mostly a new phenomenon in Europe. It was so unusual in several countries that it shattered the everyday lives of individuals in many local communities. Quite a lot of people did not like white East Europeans, nor Near Eastern, African, or Asian neighbors of color. Some just felt uncomfortable because of increasing crime, while others shared hatred against aliens. One should not forget that generation after generation of people in war-ridden European countries was educated and indoctrinated to hate other nationalities: for the French, the Germans; for the Germans, the Slavs; for the Hungarians, the Romanians. In some cases, people were even taught to hate other "ethnic" peoples in the same country: for the Flemish, the Walloons; for the English, the Irish; for the Croats, the Serbs.

All these prepared the soil for the populist rejection of immigration. In the West, South, and East, this revolt closely merged with rising "Euroscepticism" and even harsh anti-European Unionism, especially after 2015 when the EU decided to allow the new wave of mass immigration. Populists accused the EU's liberal standing, multiculturalism, and acceptance of migrants. They also blamed the EU for the free movement of people within the Union, which allowed millions—first from Central and Eastern Europe and later from all over the world—to go and take jobs in the West. Populist nationalism attacked the EU under the banner of regaining national sovereignty, defending the borders, and rejecting the "bureaucratic and anti-democratic rule of Brussels." The EU's decision to distribute part of the new immigrants led to a flat denial in several Central European member countries. This repudiation marked a dramatic change in the attitude toward integration, compared with the postwar (in Central and Eastern Europe the postcommunist) enthusiasm for it.

Anti-EU revolt became strong in Britain, the Netherlands, Spain, Italy, and even France and Germany, the traditional twin engines of integration. In 2015–16, anti-EU populists engaged in frontal attacks against the EU, frightening the organization with breakthroughs in several countries. They talked about the straitjacket of the common currency and argued for the elimination of it. They even supported the full dissolution of the EU. The election of Donald J. Trump as president of the US in 2016 gave this trend significant impetus and electrified the European populists. Trump embraced a similarly populist, anti-immigration, and nationalist "America First" program to defend the national borders and eliminate the "unfair advantage" of allies in trade. Populism became a widespread political representation of discontents throughout the world.

Because of their common anti-EU anger, the nationalist populists have sympathy and a kind of cooperation with each other. Sometimes they participate in the campaigns of other populist parties; they all feel they have a lot in common with Donald Trump, for whom they have strong sympathy. His former strategist,

Steven Bannon, even tried to form a kind of "Populist International" with a "think tank that weaponized populist economic and social ideas," accompanied by a website that spread this ideology in national languages. He traveled and lectured throughout Europe "about the grand vision for a global populist vision" in 2018. He also plans to teach and "train an army of populist foot soldiers." Bannon has also prophesized a major international clash of white Western civilization with the other ancient civilizations of China, Turkey, and Iran (Persia). "Elites can't fight because people have to buy into it."[17] Populism is on the offensive.

Bannon also participated in the party congress of the French Front National in Lille in March 2018 and tried to encourage the demoralized party, which suffered bad defeats in both the presidential and parliamentary elections in 2017. The party even wants to change its discredited name. Bannon told them:

> Let them—the media, the running dogs of the global elite—call you racist. Let them call you xenophobes. Let them call you nativist. Wear it as a badge of honor. You are a part of a worldwide movement. History is on our side.[18]

However, the next day, Marine Le Pen announced a name change to get rid of the stigma of the past: the new name was *Rassemblement Nation* (National Rally or Gathering). She added, "I have thought and consulted long and hard on the name. It must carry a political message and clearly indicate our political project for France. It must imperatively include the word 'national,'" she told the party's conference.[19] (What a surprisingly bad choice! *Le Rassemblement National Populaire* [RNP], founded in February 1941 by Marcel Déat, was a fascist party that collaborated with the Nazi occupants during the war.[20])

Populism is on the rise but still may be defeated. Several recent elections in some of the West European countries, especially in France, clearly reflect this possibility. Established and newly founded political parties alike have to unmask populist oversimplifications and half-truths, and instead offer real solutions to real problems. They have to return to an efficient social policy agenda, like the kind that worked after World War II. They have to offer sufficient controls on immigration and defense of the European borders, as well as control global capitalism by returning to regulations that subordinate the market to society.

Notes

1 Gianfranco Bettin and Ettore Recchi, eds., *Comparing European Societies: Towards a Sociology of the EU* (Bologna: Monduzzi, 2005), 229, 244–247; Michael Saward, "Making Representations: Modes and Strategies of Political Parties," *European Review* 16, no. 3 (July 2008): 271–286, doi:10.1017/S1062798708000252. 3, 16.
2 Pierre Briançon, "France's Two Big Parties Face Long-Term Decline," *Politico*, April 20, 2017, www.politico.eu/article/frances-two-big-parties-face-decline-conservatives-socialists/.
3 John Strafford, "The Decline and Fall of the Conservative Party," *Open Democracy*, August 16, 2013, www.opendemocracy.net/ourkingdom/john-e-strafford/decline-and-fall-of-conservative-party.

4 Amanda Taub, "Paving over Differences, Europe's Centrists Risk Rougher Ride," *The New York Times*, February 12, 2018, Print edition, sec. Europe.
5 David Walker, "The Third Way: Tony's Ology for Sceptics," *The Guardian*, September 22, 1998, www.theguardian.com/politics/1998/sep/22/labour.comment.
6 Taub, "Paving over Differences."
7 Katrin Bennhold, "Germany's Far-Right Party Sees Labor Unions as a Path to Gains," *The New York Times*, February 6, 2018, Print edition, sec. Europe, https://goo.gl/3dK5Eb.
8 "Germany's Far-Right AfD Overtakes Social Democrats in Poll," *Deutsche Welle*, February 19, 2018, http://p.dw.com/p/2swwW.
9 Rick Noack, "Europe's Far Right Is Rising, But Mainstream Conservatives Are the Real Winners So Far," *Washington Post*, May 9, 2017, sec. WorldViews, https://goo.gl/mT6QDi.
10 Jason Horowitz, "Why Italy's Insular Election Is More Important than It Looks," *The New York Times*, March 2, 2018, sec. Europe, https://goo.gl/Ds8Bu6.
11 John Abromeit, "Transformation of Producerist Populism in Western Europe," in *Transformations of Populism in Europe and the Americas: History and Recent Tendencies*, eds. John Abromeit, Bridget Maria Chesterton, Gary Marotta, and York Norman (London: Bloomsbury Publishing, 2015), 236, 239, 254. See also the three studies in this volume about Russian and Balkan peasantist populism (51–104).
12 Ghiţa Ionescu and Ernest Gellner, eds., *Populism: Its Meaning and National Characteristics* (London: Macmillan, 1969), x.
13 Cas Mudde and Rovira Kaltwasse, "Populism and Political Leadership," *The Oxford Handbook of Political Leadership*, May 1, 2014, https://goo.gl/3trXiK.
    Cas Mudde and Cristobal Rovira Kaltwasser, *Populism: A Very Short Introduction* (Oxford: Oxford University Press, 2017), 2. Cas Mudde, "The Populist Zeitgeist," *Government and Opposition* 39, no. 4 (September 1, 2004), 541–563, 543; Cas Mudde, ed., *The Populist Radical Right: A Reader* (London: Routledge, 2016), 4–5.
14 Tony Blair, "Tony Blair: Against Populism, the Center Must Hold," *The New York Times*, March 20, 2018, Print edition, sec. Opinion, www.nytimes.com/2017/03/03/opinion/tony-blair-against-populism-the-center-must-hold.html.
15 Keith Spencer Felton, *Warriors' Words: A Consideration of Language and Leadership* (Westport, CT: Praeger, 1995), xv.
16 "Migration and Migrant Population Statistics," Eurostat–Statistics Explained (European Commission, March 2018), https://goo.gl/nw2rbz.
    Phillip Connor and Jens Manuel Krogstad, "Immigrant Share of Population Jumps in Some European Countries," June 15, 2016, https://goo.gl/Jas2d7.
17 Jason Horowitz, "Bannon Takes on Europe, with Populist Toolbox in Hand," *The New York Times*, March 10, 2018, sec. Europe, https://goo.gl/4tx1vM.
18 "Quotation of the Day: 'Let Them Call You Racists,' Bannon Tells Anti-Immigrant Party in France," *The New York Times*, March 10, 2018, sec. Today's Paper, https://goo.gl/1cMTuk.
19 Kim Willsher, "Marine Le Pen Marks Front National Leadership Win with Rebrand Proposal," *The Guardian*, March 11, 2018, https://goo.gl/dccR5T.
20 Critics immediately noted that Front National leaders had suffered collective historical amnesia in choosing the name of a Nazi-supporting party. Others recalled that it was a deliberate use of the name of Charles de Gaulle's party, *Rassemblement du Peuple Français* (RPF), which was founded in 1947, or of Jacques Chirac's *Rassemblement pour la République* (RPR) party, which was created in 1976. Nicolas Sarkozy renamed his party *Le Rassemblement* in 2014.

4

BREXIT AND ITS POSSIBLE IMPACT

Joining late—leaving early

One of the strongest signs of discontent among member countries of the European Union (EU) was the British decision—the very first one in history—to leave the EU. David Cameron's government decided to hold a referendum in 2016 about leaving the EU to cope with his own opposition within the Tory Party. It was an irresponsible tactical step, as the referendum was not a widespread popular demand. The referendum did not have a binding role for the government or parliament. It is important to note that only somewhat more than half of the electorate participated in the vote: 18.1 million people were not registered, and 12.9 million did not go to vote. From the 33.5 million who voted, 16.1 million voted for remaining in the EU, and 17.4 million supported the "Leave" bloc; thus, those who voted in favor of leaving the Union, called Brexit, actually represented only 27 percent of the population. The outcome of the referendum was a 48 versus 52 percent majority for leaving.[1] To evaluate the impact of this crucial step that, for many, tolled the death knell of European integration, let's have a closer look at Brexit.

It is a well-known truth that Britain was never enthusiastic about integration. Winston Churchill, the most influential British politician of the twentieth century, was the first to come up with the idea after World War II, in a speech in Zurich in 1946, to form a United States of Europe. But he also clearly expressed the British view: "we are with Europe, but not of it … we are interested and associated but not absorbed"; Britain will assist integration from outside. The dominant British interest, he added in 1950, is "the Empire and Commonwealth," followed by "the fraternal association of the English speaking world" (especially with the US).[2] The US, Britain's main ally, and its presidents after the war, tried to push Britain to lead and, later, at last, to join in forming the European Economic Community during the entire 1950s. The British government resisted. Moreover, in 1960, it initiated the foundation of a rival free trade bloc, the European Free Trade Association (EFTA), with its old trading partners.

Britain, however, soon experienced a sharp decline in its power: its huge co-lonial empire collapsed by 1960. Britain's centuries-long, successful "gun-boat diplomacy" also ended in a fiasco after a humiliating troop withdrawal during the Suez Crisis in 1956. The British pound was not the world money any longer. Politically and economically, Britain became a relatively small country and by far not the strongest in Europe any longer. This painful awakening, together with the clear recognition that the European Community was much more successful than EFTA, led Britain at last to revise its policy and ask for membership in the Community during the 1960s. After two rejections due to French vetoes by Charles de Gaulle, Britain, at last, joined in 1973.

Nevertheless, the only attraction for them was the huge advantage of the large free trade market. Britain never accepted the founding fathers' idea of an "ever closer union." It always played the role of the brake, obstructing the in-troduction of supranational institutions and further integration. It opposed the common currency and several times blocked closer military cooperation. Britain did not join the common currency when it was introduced and opted out from the Schengen Agreement of a borderless Europe. To achieve its goal of avoiding further integration, Britain always advocated and assisted further enlargement, in order to make the Union less homogenous and less able to go ahead with fur-ther supranationalization toward federalization. Britain was always more Atlantic than European, having never given up its "Atlantic policy," nor its close and spe-cial connection with the US. On that basis, Britain was a roadblock for further integration.

A great part of Britain's population, especially its elite, was still living under the delusion that Britain held the status of a great power. They never got rid of their "island mentality" and were concerned about the Continent as a potential rival and even an enemy. All these attitudes were represented in an extreme way by a large section of the governing Tory Party and the United Kingdom Independence Party (UKIP), founded in 2000 by the so-called ultra-Tories. These forces—led, among others, by the overambitious London Mayor Boris Johnson and UKIP leader Nigel Farage—launched a propaganda war that char-acterized Brexit as a move to regain sovereignty, push out East European immi-grants from Britain, and save a tremendous amount of money paid as membership fee to the EU in order to invest it at home to fix the declining health-care system. They talked about reestablishing British global power. Prime Minister Theresa May, who followed Cameron after the referendum, declared that Brexit "should make us think of global Britain, a country with self-confidence and the freedom to look beyond the continent of Europe and the economic and diplomatic op-portunities of the wider world." *The Economist* that quoted May added, "Talk of 'global Britain' fosters dangerous illusions."[3]

Most of the Brexiters' argumentation was based on delusion or lies. While they argued against the free movement of labor within the EU, Britain badly needed an immigrant workforce. When they talked about the heavy financial burden of EU membership, they always mentioned the amount the country paid as a membership fee, but "forgot" to deduct from it the EU money that was flowing back to assist British agriculture, scientific research, and the former industrial strongholds that had become rust-belt zones in the heart of the country. They spread the view that Britain, by stepping out, would not lose anything and instead gain a lot.

Long after the truth became evident, and even after some of the Brexiters went so far as to apologize during the negotiation talks with the EU, some members of that group repeated the same claims again in 2018. British demands endangered the so-called two-year-long transition period when Britain would remain in the Single Market, although a transition period was crucially important for the British economy to adjust to the new situation. Nevertheless, Jacob Rees-Mogg, chair of the pro-hard Brexit ERG group, said: 'I would be happy to move to WTO [World Trade Organization] terms without a transition and save £39bn that could be spent on the NHS [National Health Service]. It is rather feeble as threats go.'[4]

David Davis, the chief British negotiator, also lied when he "confirmed *The Guardian*'s report that under the draft withdrawal agreement Northern Ireland would effectively stay in the single market and customs union."[5] This statement was not true at all, although it would be in Britain's definite interest if it wanted to avoid a new Northern Irish political explosion. Northern Ireland, although part of Britain, wanted to keep free trade with the Irish Republic. Michel Barnier, the EU's chief negotiator, immediately clarified that "there was no possibility of a trade deal that could avoid barriers to trade, and that the UK had not yet offered any 'specific solutions' to avoid a hard border."[6]

The irresponsible, baseless statements and beliefs of the Brexiters merely repeated what Boris Johnson had often stated before the referendum: essentially, as he repeatedly boasted, "our policy is having our cake and eating it."[7] He repeated several times that free trade with the EU's Single Market was not endangered and thus that the country would continuously enjoy free trade with the EU after Brexit, while Britain would again ascend to become the preeminent sovereign global power.

The less-educated people in the countryside and the older generations believed in those lies and voted to leave. The bulk of the more educated urban population, the younger generation, Scots (who voted 62 to 38 to remain), Northern Irish people (who voted 56 to 44 to remain), the population of Gibraltar, and the industrial and banking business sectors all voted to stay in the EU; however, they remained in the minority.

The Theresa May Tory government that took over after the referendum lost its majority in the earlier elections in parliament and had a rather weak position at the Brexit talks in Brussels. Moreover, it was unable to work out and represent a consistent government policy to follow. Will Britain want a "hard landing" (leaving the common market) or a "soft" one (remaining in the Single Market)? In the latter case, the country has to accept all the EU rules and pay a membership fee but loses its ability to form the EU's policy.

"Hard" or "soft" landing? The Chequers plan

The hard core of the Tory Party and Prime Minister Theresa May declared several times that "Brexit is Brexit," and targeted a "hard landing." Nevertheless, very soon frightening signs signaled danger for Britain. The EU's Single Market is the most important market for Britain to sell its products. The country also buys a great quantity of product parts from value chains on the Continent; the bulk of the country's food supply comes from there as well. Major industrial companies and banks have expressed their intention to leave Britain if the country leaves the common European market. Boris Johnson and several others have disregarded these industry signals and continue to advocate for a "hard landing," in which Britain will leave both the EU and its common market. Theresa May, however, at last recognized the danger and suggested a new solution. On July 9, 2018, she gathered her cabinet at Chequers, the private residence of the prime minister, and offered a new program, the so-called "Chequers deal."

According to this plan, Britain would leave the EU at the given deadline, March 29, 2019, ending free movement and taking back control of its borders. EU citizens will no longer be able to come and go as they please, and Britain will no longer send vast sums of money each year to the EU. A new, business-friendly customs model will be introduced with the freedom to strike new trade deals around the world. Britain will also not officially be part of the customs union anymore. But Theresa May does want the UK to be treated like an EU country—namely, she wants Britain to be able to trade with EU countries without extra taxes. Her plan calls for the establishment of a UK–EU free trade area for industrial goods and agricultural products only, which will be governed mostly by EU regulations. The UK will not be regulated by European law, and the European courts will not be able to govern in Britain, but the EU will still set the central guidelines for the trading partnership, which the UK wants to continue participating in fully. Unlike before, however, the British Parliament can challenge the EU rules if it sees fit and has the last word on them. Nevertheless, Britain would remain part of the common pricing for agricultural goods and would still be able to access the EU market on favorable terms. Although Britain would no longer be part of the common market, there would be no hard border between Ireland and Northern Ireland (which remains part of the United Kingdom).[8] May's government has also shown sympathy toward selective integration for the UK in certain industries, as well as participation in EU-wide security arrangements, such as sharing crime databases. This type of selective cooperation with the EU would suggest that where possible, Britain will cooperate as long as it proves economically or politically beneficial.

In other words, after leaving both the EU and the common market, Britain will require a unique, special status. The country will not be a member, but it will not be an associate member like Norway or Iceland. Small wonder that the EU leadership has rejected the British suggestions and called the Chequers program an attempt to "cherry-pick" the major advantages of EU membership while avoiding the accompanying responsibilities. Any country with free access to the European Single Market, including associate members, like Norway and Iceland, has to accept the basic principle of the EU, the so-called "four freedoms": the free movement of goods, services, capital, and labor.

All in all, the British government was unable to offer an acceptable plan to the EU during the negotiation period of more than two years after the referendum. The UK government consistently said that it would aim for the "best possible deal" but that "no deal is better than a bad deal." This position was restated in the Conservative and Unionist Party Manifesto for the 2017 general election.[9]

After the rejection of Theresa May's Chequers plan by the EU, she presented a plan of extended transition to the British Parliament, but it was voted down by a huge margin of 432 to 202, "the biggest parliamentary defeat on record for a ruling party," as *The Economist* stated. Perhaps it will have another plan and another vote? Perhaps a second referendum? Perhaps Britian will drop out from the EU without any agreement? As *The Economist* summed up, this is "the mother of all messes."[10] Everything is chaotic. Sylvie Kauffmann, former editor of *Le Monde,* has written vitriolic remarks on the madness of Brexit and views it as falling apart, quoting the joking remark of French legislator Jean-Louis Bourlanges: "The British always had one foot in the EU and one foot out; now with Brexit they want the opposite," and then concluded: "From across the Channel, it seems the British may have lost their mind."[11]

The consequences of Brexit

Britain's inability to compromise may lead to the worst possible outcome: leaving the EU without any kind of agreement. In October 2018, Theresa May asked to extend the deadline by a year, and the EU seemed ready to grant it. While extending the transition period would delay the most deleterious consequences, unless significant developments are made, Britain will still eventually have to sign a statement formally leaving the Union and accept all the negative consequences, including the reestablishment of the hard border with Ireland. In the late fall of 2018, close to the deadline, the consequences of Brexit are frightening.

Brexit poses a severe challenge for the EU as well. According to the IMF, a "no-deal Brexit" could create economic pain across Europe with no winners. Ireland could lose 4 percent of its GDP; the Netherlands, Denmark, and Belgium could lose 1 percent.[12] More importantly, the EU would lose political strength, necessary budget funds, and the prestige associated with an alliance with one of the strongest countries in Europe (and the world).

On the other hand, the real loser of such an outcome would be Britain. The British pound lost 12 percent of its value against the euro compared to what it was just before the EU referendum. According to initial estimates by the British government, leaving the advantages of EU membership behind would cost the UK's businesses about £65.5 billion per year (or $82 billion). Over a 15-year period, this would lower the country's GDP by 5.4–9.5 percent. Analysts also believe that the UK would find it difficult to replace the lost trade revenue from the EU, which has a consumer market of around 500 million people and a GDP of around €12 trillion. About 44 percent (or £220 billion of £510 billion) of the UK's exports currently go to EU countries. Export trade with the EU accounts for about 12.5 percent of UK's GDP, while the EU's trade with Britain amounts to only about 3 percent of the EU's GDP.[13]

Exhibiting typical Brexiter delusions, both UKIP and several influential members of the Tory Party have called for a Commonwealth Free Trade Agreement that would replace EU trade by expanding trade within the Commonwealth and the broader Anglosphere. The *Financial Times* warned about the "British illusion of Commonwealth trade after Brexit. Deals with disparate economies cannot replace the EU single market."[14] In reality, countries closest to Britain such as Australia take only 1.6 percent of UK exports; the 53 countries with a combined population of 2.4 billion that compose the Commonwealth only receive 9.5 percent of the UK's exports altogether. The UK's entire export volume to the Commonwealth is roughly equivalent to its exports to Germany.[15] Besides, the EU has trade agreements with several Commonwealth countries, and Britain might find it difficult to match the negotiating power of the EU. With more than 50 partners around the globe, the Union has more free trade agreements than any other single nation or trading bloc.

Furthermore, according to some estimates, the limitation of access to Europe's financial markets could cost Britain as much as £38 billion in business, £10 billion in tax revenue, and more than 70,000 jobs. Several international banks and companies are already packing up in preparation for moves to Ireland or other EU countries. International investors may also hesitate to invest in Britain, instead seeking countries that do have access to the huge EU Single Market. Britain has to face several years of difficult trade negotiations with numberless countries to rebuild its international economic connections.

All these considerations genuinely lead to the question: did Brexit contribute to and become a major factor in the EU's existential crisis, as is often broadly stated? Without question, the departure of an important and strong West European country will weaken the EU. Nevertheless, in my view, the answer to the previous question is still an evident "no." First of all, the tremendous pain of leaving the EU is a big warning to other countries and anti-EU forces. Furthermore, Britain has always been a hesitant, uncommitted member. It always wanted to be a kind of "outside insider." After leaving the Union, Britain will no longer be able to oppose steps leading to further integration. Thus, Brexit marks the disappearance of an important impediment that formerly blocked the progress of further integration. Paradoxically, Britain's removal may actually make the members of the Union more united.

Notes

1 "EU Referendum Results." *The Electoral Commission*, accessed April 2, 2018. https://goo.gl/K9WTq2.
2 *"Winston Churchill's* speech in the House of Commons on 27 June, 1950," In *In the Balance. Speeches 1949 and 1950 by Winston Churchill*, eds. Randolf S. Churchill (London: Cassel, 1952), 299.
3 Adrian Wooldridge, "Global Britain or Globaloney," *The Economist*, March 15, 2018, sec. Bagehot Column, https://goo.gl/8sjy9U.
4 Daniel Boffey and Jennifer Rankin, "Barnier and Davis Wage War of Words over Brexit Transition Claims," *The Guardian*, February 9, 2018, https://goo.gl/VZnq9k.
5 "Brexit Transition Deal Breaks Seven Promises," *The Guardian*, March 19, 2018.
6 Tom Newton Dunn, "Boris Johnson Declares Support for 'Hard' Brexit." *The Sun*, September 30, 2016, https://www.thesun.co.uk/news/1889723/.
7 "Boris Johnson Joins Forces with Liam Fox and Claims Brexit Will Let Britain," *The Sun,* October 1, 2016.
8 Alex Barker, "The Soft-Brexit Chequers Deal: What It Means," *Financial Times*, July 8, 2018, www.ft.com/content/aeb53c82-82ac-11e8-96dd-fa565ec55929.
9 "Forward, Together: Our Plan for a Stronger Britain and a Prosperous Future," *The Conservative and Unionist Party*, 2017, www.conservatives.com/manifesto, 35–36.
10 The Economist, January 19, 2019. "The mother of all messes" and "Brexit and Parliament. The Noes have it."
11 Sylvie Kauffmann, "Watching Brexit fall apart," *The New York Times*, January 23, 2019.
12 Richard Partington, "No-Deal Brexit Would Harm EU Countries as Well as UK, Warns IMF," *The Guardian*, July 19, 2018, sec. Business, www.theguardian.com/business/2018/jul/19/no-deal-brexit-would-harm-all-european-countries-warns-imf.
13 See among others: "The economic consequences of Brexit." https://ukandeu.ac.uk/research-papers/the-economic-consequences-of-brexit/, November 27, 2018; *Financial Times*, June 23, 2018, "What are the economic effects of Brexit so far?"
14 Editorial Staff, "A British Illusion of Commonwealth Trade after Brexit," *Financial Times*, April 18, 2018, sec. Opinion, www.ft.com/content/2761fc62-42eb-11e8-93cf-67ac3a6482fd.
15 Matthew Ward, "Statistics on UK Trade with the Commonwealth," *House of Common Briefing Report* (House of Commons Library, April 12, 2018), https://researchbriefings.parliament.uk/ResearchBriefing/Summary/CBP-8282.

5

ANTI-EUROPEAN UNION POPULISM IN WESTERN AND SOUTHERN EUROPE

Liberal democracy and its multiethnic culture

Populism was on the rise in highly developed and rich Western Europe and the Mediterranean South, which had made significant economic progress and had started to catch up with the West beginning in the late twentieth century. In the mid-2010s, Western Europe, with its average of $37,000–$50,000 per capita income level (which neared the US's roughly $57,000 per capita income figure), was one of the richest areas in the world. Mediterranean Europe and Ireland, areas that were traditionally on the periphery of the continent and were relatively backward (with a per capita income approaching only 55–60 percent of the West's), have elevated to the world's top 20 percent of rich countries. These countries boasted an average per capita income level of more than $30,000, which neared more than two-thirds of Western Europe's average amount.

Nevertheless, antiestablishment populism gained significant ground in both advanced regions of Europe. "The specter of populism is haunting Europe," stated Jacquis Rupnik at the end of 2017.

> Whether the AfD in Germany, the National Front in France, Bepe Grillo's Movimento Cinque Stelle in Italy, the FPÖ in Austria or Geert Wilders in Holland, all are different incarnations of nativist populist political forces that are challenging liberal democracies. They are reshaping the political landscape of the member-states of the European Union and threatening the EU with paralysis or even disintegration.[1]

Populism built its strength on the shortcomings of the Western economic system of neoliberal capitalism. It profited from growing income inequalities within and among countries (discussed in Chapter 3). The returning economic crisis was strongly generated by neoliberal deregulation, which had devastating social effects during the 2010s, including the high unemployment (especially among the youth) that created a major hotbed of populism. Huge layers of the societies, especially in the relatively backward countryside areas and certain old industrial regions, became rustbelts that felt left behind (discussed in Chapter 1) and joined populist parties. One of the most mobilizing factors of social dissatisfaction, however, was the immigration crisis of the 2010s. Immigration to Europe, previously a region of emigration, started gradually in the 1950–60s. This trend was partly connected to the decimation of the European population during the war. That was followed by a marked demographic change of sharply decreasing birth rate to sub-replacement fertility rate. Europe's population, consequently, rapidly aged during the postwar period. Due to its rapidly aging population, Europe needed a new labor force, which made immigration important and possible (discussed in Chapter 1).

This demographic change paralleled a sociopolitical change. In reaction to the two devastating World Wars and the interwar decades of burning nationalism in Europe, postwar liberal democracies turned against nationalism and started preaching tolerance and multiculturalism, and accepted other ethnic and religious groups as part of their national communities. That was the natural conclusion drawn from living through the wars, fascism, and murderous Nazi intolerance. It was admirable to see how Germany gradually but strongly—in conjunction with a generational change—turned against its past. Indeed, during a news conference with the visiting Turkish prime minister in 2015, Chancellor Angela Merkel made this point clear, explicitly stating (as Reuters reported) that she was the chancellor of all people of her country, and that "Islam [also] belongs to Germany."[2] Two years later while campaigning for the presidency at a mass rally in Marseille, Emmanuel Macron stated:

> To be a patriot is to want a strong France, open to Europe, and faced toward the world. And when I look at Marseille, I see a French city, marked by 2,000 years of history, of immigration, of Europe. … I see Armenians, Italians, Algerians, Moroccans, Tunisians, Malians. … But what do I really see? I see the people of Marseille. I see the people of France.[3]

These courageous statements in 2015 and 2017—in the midst of anti-immigration sentiments—well represent the position of liberal democracy. But this standpoint was not shared by a huge faction of Germans, French, Italians, Poles, Hungarians, and many others. Those who did not accept immigrants as members of their traditional communities were often labeled racist and xenophobic in political debates and literature. However, not everyone who joined and followed anti-immigration politics was necessarily racist. When one examines the current moment in relation to the past (even as recently as two or three generations back), these individuals' difficulty in apprehending and accepting these kinds of changes becomes perhaps more understandable. "The attempt to turn countries with mono-ethnic identities," said the German-born Yasha Mounk of Harvard University, "into truly multiethnic nations is a historically unique experiment, and so it should hardly come as a surprise that it has encountered some fierce resistance."[4] Anti-immigration sentiments were also generated by the difficulties of immigrants' integration into Western societies. The integration of immigrants into the labor force might take decades. More recently arrived refugees and family members have a rather low employment rate of about 30 percent, while the employment rate of refugees and family members who arrived 20 years ago or even earlier is about 65 percent. The EU's unemployment rate of the non-EU born population in 2016 was twice as high as the rate for the native-born population.[5]

Furthermore, a great part of immigrants in Europe are Muslims and that makes their integration into the native societies much more difficult. An EU analysis in 2009 offers a convincing picture of Muslims in Europe. Their inflow started during the postwar reconstruction period when they arrived from former European colonies to work. Immigrants included Turks to Germany; Pakistanis and Bangladeshis to Britain; Algerians to France; and Moroccans to France, the Netherlands, and Spain. Many of these immigrants chose to stay permanently and had children who developed a Muslim-European identity. In the early twenty-first century, Muslim communities in various European countries ranged between 2.3 and 9.6 percent of the population. Nevertheless, they mostly remained separated from the native societies. Spanish, German, and British Muslims, as polls reflect, think of themselves as "Muslims first" and then as members of their respective countries. This phenomenon was clearly recognized by the native population. Approximately two-thirds of Britons and Spaniards and three-fourths of Germans believe that Muslims want to be separate from society. In 2008, half of the Germans and Spaniards held unfavorable views toward Muslims. People in most of the European countries view growing Islamic identity as "bad," especially in Spain (82 percent), Germany (83 percent), and France (87 percent). Xenophobia is on the rise. In Britain, for example, in 2001–02, the police reported almost 15,000 anti-Muslim incidents, but in 2007–08, they reported 26,500, an increase of 77 percent over six years.

Besides identity differences, Muslim integration is strongly hindered by their marginal position in Europe. In Germany, the public earns more than twice as much as Muslims in the highest bracket; in Spain, more than four times. Although income disparity is most striking in Germany and Spain, it also exists in France and Britain. Approximately 20 percent more Muslims in France and Britain fall into the lowest income bracket compared to their respective publics. Disparities in income levels seem to highlight the difference between Muslims and the public in Europe.

Parallel with economic integration, social and cultural integration also exhibits major difficulties. While the UK has achieved success in socioeconomic integration, it has mostly failed in the field of cultural and value integration. The opposite was true for France, but the Netherlands has failed at both. Across all ages, Muslims have fewer educational qualifications than the general public. The differences are striking. One-third of Muslims between the age of 25 and 34 have no educational qualifications. This is three times as large as the general public in the same age range; 47 percent of Muslims between 35 and 49 have no qualifications, compared to only 22 percent in the general public. These figures clearly indicate that the Muslim communities do not have the same opportunity for education that the general public does. Only half of Muslim males between 16 and 24 are economically active in relation to 68 percent of the wider society. Discrepancy is even much bigger regarding Muslim women. "Overall," the analysis concludes, "the immigrant Muslims of Western Europe have remained poorer, less educated, and more socially marginalized."[6]

Anti-immigrant sentiments are also generated by the fact that immigrants and crime are closely connected in peoples' minds in several Western countries. For example, in Stockholm, the capital city of peaceful and flourishing Sweden, gang wars, and the use of hand grenades in certain suburbs such as Varby Gard became a common phenomenon (as the media reported in early 2018). In this settlement, populated mostly by migrants, about 100 grenade attacks or confiscation of grenades happened every year between 2014 and 2017, as the police reported. The weapons were smuggled from Bosnia and Serbia via a diasporic network in Sweden. The price of a hand grenade on the black market was $12.50. One of the police officers, Peter Springare, reported that many of the criminals in violent crimes he investigated were Iraqis, Turkish, Syrians, Somalians, and Afghans. According to Swedish police reports, about three-quarters of the members of violent gangs were either nonintegrated immigrants or their Swedish-born sons (this latter group made up more than 40 percent of that amount). Even if only a relatively small segment of immigrants were criminals, they had a relatively huge role in crimes. These facts were broadly popularized by films and crime series, especially those in French, Spanish, and other non-English European languages. Reporting on the situation in 2017, the *New York Times* concluded that alongside the traditional debates over education and health care, "crime and immigration are certain to be key issues in September's general election" in Sweden.[7] Populist parties and politicians exaggerated and masterfully exploited the connection between immigration and crime, often lashing up passionate anti-immigration sentiments among voters.

Although many of the people of Europe consider the connection between immigration and crime to be "common knowledge," this connection is still questionable in spite of several genuine, high-profile cases. Police statistics in Germany reflect a sharp decline (almost 10 percent) in crimes during 2017, a couple of years after the country accepted 1.1 million immigrants. This was the sharpest drop in crime the country experienced since 1993, over 25 years before. While murders and drug offenses did increase somewhat, overall violent crime declined by 2.4 percent, and other categories of crime sharply decreased: theft offenses declined by almost 12 percent, and shoplifting decreased by nearly

7 percent. The number of stolen cars and bicycles has decreased by almost 9 and 10 percent, respectively. Most surprisingly, the number of non-German suspects fell sharply to 736,265 cases, or almost 23 percent![8]

It is admirable that in most Northwestern European countries, "fierce resistance" against immigration represented only a minority of the population. The situation is different in Southeastern Europe, due in part to different histories and socioeconomic situations. For example, in Italy (especially in its southern region), Hungary, and Poland, the majority of the people voted for nationalist, populist, anti-immigration parties. These are the countries where nationalist-populism made breakthroughs in the 2010s. Strangely enough, Britain—virtually alone among the most advanced West European countries—also belongs to the group of countries where populism became triumphant. A closer look may explain the reasons.

Why populism became triumphant in Britain

Britain was the only Western country in which anti-European populism was able to achieve a breakthrough. Britain, however, represents a unique case. The country was always ambivalent regarding European integration. Brexit was already discussed in Chapter 1, but it needs some further analysis. Britain joined the EU rather late in 1973, opted out of introducing the common currency, consistently opposed every attempt of further integration that introduced supranational institutions, and wanted virtually nothing besides an all-European free market. The British elite lived in the memory of the great Empire, which was the first in the world to industrialize, and subordinated and colonized a great part of the world. At its peak, Britain controlled nearly one-quarter of the landed area of the globe and ruled nearly half a billion subjects. The Brits, in their island country, always shared an "island mentality," a feeling of independence outside Europe. For centuries, British politics worked against any kind of continental unification and tried to keep the balance of power in Europe. After the collapse of colonialism, Britain built its modern Commonwealth, mostly of former colonies—from Australia and Canada to India and South Africa—with 52 member countries and a collective population of 2.4 billion, nearly one-third of the world's population. During a critical and dangerous time, Winston Churchill, one of the country's most influential mid-twentieth century politicians, famously spoke of the "special relationship"[9] between English-speaking nations, especially between Britain and the US. In spite of collective British memories of imperial decline, the former power of the British Empire, the formation of the Commonwealth, and the political connection with the US preserved the British people's collective feeling that Britain was still a great power, especially at a time when most of the world's map was pink.

That was the proper soil for the breakthrough of anti-EU populism during the 2016 referendum, which decided whether Britain should leave or remain in the EU. A faction of the governing Tory Party led by Boris Johnson, the former Mayor of London, along with the United Kingdom Independence Party (UKIP, established for the specific goal of convincing Britain to leave the EU) under Nigel Farage, influenced receptive layers of the society. Johnson portrayed the EU as a self-serving, useless bureaucracy. Although Britain pocketed huge profits from the membership—which made the British banking industry (known as "The City") the main banker of Europe, and channeled more than half of British trade to other member countries—anti-EU politicians have spoken about the "huge losses" the country suffered because it supposedly paid a high membership fee but received "nothing" in return. Although it is commonplace for free trade to occur smoothly on the common market in 28 countries with 500 million people involved (an economic situation that has been very favorable for Britain), uniform standards that enable products to be salable throughout the community are indispensable. Boris Johnson, however, deployed a few extreme examples to voice mockery about standardization as an empty bureaucratic play. "After five months' study," he stated, "the European Economic Community (EEC) Commission has decided snails should be categorized as fish, not meat."[10] All Member States "have agreed that an unstretched condom should be 16 centimeters long. However, the EC has dismissed Italian plans for a maximum condom width of 54 millimeters.... This is a very serious business."[11] Actually, standardization was a very serious business, and the small EU bureaucracy would not have been able to work out the standard without significant contributions from interested industrial organizations which rushed to contribute.

Nigel Farage went even further when he accused the EU of "colonialism," which he characterized, bizarrely enough, as "entirely contrary to the British tradition": he repeatedly descried "pointless regulations ... [a] one-size-fits-all colonialism—entirely contrary to the British tradition—and driven by ... the bureaucrat's desire for homogeneity and tidiness."[12] Boris Johnson never tired of spreading the view that the EU had become obsolete. He emphasized that the reasons which had led to its foundation were no longer present:

> There will be no war between France and Germany, and the Soviet threat is a busted flush. That leaves no urgent necessity to create a tightly unified Little Europe, except in the hearts of those who are so anti-American that they would abandon national independence ... [to] creating a rival superstate.[13]

He characterized the desire for unification as an artificial, "Procrustean squeezing or chopping of national interests."[14] "Why is Europe so feeble? The answer is that Europe is not a natural political unit."[15]

Johnson's main argument was that the tremendous advantage of regaining independence would make Britain a global power again. When the national veto right was replaced by qualified majority vote, he compared the situation to the Battle of Hastings in 1066, a catastrophe for England, wherein the nation was attacked, defeated, and conquered by the Normans. He employed a quote by eleventh-century English historian William of Malmesbury to describe the contemporary situation: "England today is the home of foreigners and the domain of aliens...." In the twenty-first century as in the eleventh, he suggested, Britain was ruled by the French: "The European Community ... is ruled by France ... [They] are dressing up French national interests as the European dream...." Johnson portrayed the French-dominated European Commission as unabashedly anti-British and decried its "semi-ritual humiliation of the British Government."[16] "Think of what we can achieve if we vote Leave. We can take back control of huge sums of money—£10.6 billion net per year."[17]

> We already know the official bill for our membership is due to rise to £20.65 billion per year by 2020–2021.... A vote to stay is a vote to keep sending more and more money to a dysfunctional bureaucracy ... estimate[d] payouts could be as high as £43 billion by 2021, a huge sum of money that would be better spent on schools and hospitals.[18]

His figures were wrong since he did not deduct the money that flowed back to Britain as assistance for rustbelt and agricultural areas, and for research. After the referendum, the Brexiters had to confess that they were "mistaken."

Johnson played the migration card as well:

> The Eurozone's economic crisis is fueling the rise in migration. Millions of people in southern Europe ... disproportionately come to Britain.... We are tying ourselves to a broken Eurozone economy while simultaneously accepting unlimited migration of people trying to escape that broken economy. The only way to restore democratic control of immigration policy is to vote to leave on 23 June.[19]

"We must begin now with what I call ... the re-Britannification of Britain."[20]

In a similar way, Nigel Farage was also an ardent advocate of the British nation-state and democracy that nationalist-populists wanted to "reestablish" outside of the EU. He, unlike Johnson, loved to insult EU officials in vulgar language and created scandalous scenes at the European Parliament. Once, when the new president of the European Council, former Belgian Prime Minister Herman Van Rompuy, delivered an introductory speech at the EU Parliament, Farage insulted him by comparing his charisma to a "damp rag": "Your intention is to be the quiet assassin of European democracy and of European nation states.... Perhaps that's because you come from Belgium which, after all, is pretty much a non-country."[21]

All this rhetoric and these arguments stemmed from the traditional British way of thinking and its attitude toward Europe and the world. British self-identification, which exploited the existing difficulties of the 2010s, worked well. The 27 percent of the British population that ultimately had the decisive votes believed that they would be better off outside the EU, and voted to leave.

Wilders, Le Pen, and others

A similar rhetoric characterized Geert Wilders, the Dutch anti-EU populist as well. Ambitious and self-interested, he established his own party, first named after him (*Groep Wilders*, or Wilders's Group); he later changed its name to *Partij voor de Vrijheid* or PVV (Party for Freedom). From that time on, he held sway as a crusader against the "Islamization of the Netherlands" and the EU.

"The Netherlands back to us!" he stated in his party's program.

> Millions of Dutchmen are fed up with the Islamization of our country. Fed up with mass-immigration, asylum, terror, violence and insecurity. Instead of financing the whole world, and people that we don't want here, we will spend our money on regular Dutchman.... The Netherlands will be sovereign again. So we must leave the European Union.[22]

Instead of the EU, he suggested the refounding of the European Free Trade Association (EFTA), the former British-founded counter organization to the EU, which was established in 1960 and subsequently failed; as is well known, soon afterward, Britain applied for EU membership three times. Wilders, however, maintained, "There is a perfectly good alternative to the European Union—it is called the European Free Trade Association, founded in 1960 .... Leaving the European Union would ... be beneficial for the Netherlands."[23]

The French right-wing populist Jean-Marie Le Pen—an admirer of far-right French writers and politicians, and a former fighter for French colonialism—established his Front National Party in the 1970s and advocated for a nationalist "France First!" approach. After the Maastricht Treaty in 1992, he became an ardent enemy of the EU. "Our frontiers have disappeared.... The Schengen convention deprives our country of one of the essential aspects of sovereignty: the control of frontiers. [Europe became] the Europe of immigration, of drugs and of organized crime."[24]

His daughter, Marine Le Pen, a loyal follower of her father for decades who later took over the Front National, repeated her father's views: "Europe of Schengen is equal to Europe of thieves.... We must reestablish national borders; borders that protect, borders that separate. Schengen's Europe is also the Europe of terrorism."[25] She wanted France to leave the common currency, and even exit the EU itself:

> The EU does not live up to the utopia they have sold us.... I want to destroy the European Union, not Europe! I believe in a Europe of nation-states.... I don't want this European Soviet Union. ... The EU is deeply harmful, it is an anti-democratic monster.... Today, we are simply allowing our right to self-determination to be stolen from us....

Like Boris Johnson, she also argued that the EU served foreign interests; but in contrast to Johnson, who talked about the EU serving French interests, she said, "These treaties promote German interests…. The French want to regain control of their own country."[26]

When the Brits voted to leave the European Union, Le Pen became triumphant:

> The European Union has become a prison of peoples. Each of the 28 countries … has slowly lost its democratic prerogatives…. In the name of ideology, different economies are forced to adopt the same currency…. [The European Parliament is] based on a lie: the pretense that there is a homogenous European people…. [Brexit is] the people's first real victory. … The People's Spring is now inevitable![27]

She celebrated the beginning of the EU's dissolution and wanted to guide France to follow in Britain's footsteps: addressing supporters of a unified Europe who believed "that the European Union is irreversible," she lauded Britain's decision to leave. She argued that the EU was "built on the backs of ordinary people" and approvingly noted that "The United Kingdom has committed the heresy of breaking the chains of the EU. … It is a slap in the face to the European system which was increasingly based on fear, blackmail and lies."[28]

The British, Dutch, and French populist anti-EU movements and parties that revolted against the EU led in part to the rise of right- or left-wing populist movements in virtually all of the West European countries. In addition to the established populist parties in France and the Netherlands, rising populist parties emerged in two other vital EU member countries: Germany and Italy. In strong and stable Germany, the two leading parties—the Christian Democratic Party and the Social Democratic Party—that had dominated the entire half-century after the war were suddenly challenged and lost a great part of their voters to the populist *Alternative für Deutschland* (AfD, or Alternative for Germany) Party. The AfD gained 13 percent of the votes during the 2017 national elections, a relative success that significantly shifted the traditional political landscape. This party was founded in 2013 to protest the EU bailout of Greece and some other insolvent member countries, which were funded using taxpayer money from rich member countries including Germany. They also blamed the common currency that was in circulation in countries of solid and stable financial households (like Germany), and highly indebted countries with irresponsible finances (like Greece). The solution that the AfD offered was to leave the eurozone and reestablish the Deutschmark, the successful and independent German currency.

During the migration crisis that started almost immediately after the establishment of the AfD, their campaign also focused on Islam and migration. They exploited the mistake of Angela Merkel's "open-arms" policy, which they characterized as an uncontrolled invasion of migrants into Germany. The anti-immigration program gradually occupied the center of the party's politics.

AfD sees Islam as alien to German society, and some of their rhetoric (an extremely sensitive topic in Germany) has been tinged with Nazi overtones.

The mistake of the Merkel government regarding immigration in 2015–16 offered a major weapon for the opposition. Two years after the peak of the immigration wave (in which more than one million people came to Germany), more than 80 percent of refugees are still jobless—in a country where the unemployment rate is at 5.5 percent. The fact is that a great part of the refugees does not fit the requirements of the German labor market. Like the opposition, the newly formed grand coalition is also ambivalent about this issue. A couple of days after the formation of the new government, Interior Minister Horst Seehofer—who belongs to the "sister party" of Merkel's Christlich-Demokratische Union (CDU), Bavaria's Christian Social Union (CSU)—stated in an interview that "Islam is not a part of Germany. Germany has been influenced by Christianity.... However, the Muslims living in Germany obviously do belong to Germany." [29] His statement conflicted with the position of Chancellor Merkel.

It is true that the AfD is not at all homogenous. It has a well-distinguished, relatively moderate wing previously led by Frauke Petry. After the elections when Petry resigned, that faction of the party was led by the 38-year-old economist Alice Weidel; a more radical ethnic nationalist wing was led by Alexander Gauland, a 76-year-old lawyer and journalist who had previously been a member of the CDU for 40 years.[30] In the case of the AfD, one could speak about the "radicalization of the center." The party has attracted its 23,000–25,000 members from the two leading parties. According to polls, almost a million of its new voters have come from the center-right faction of the CDU, and half a million have come from the center-left Social Democratic Party (SPD). Their brand of nationalism, however, started to involve far-right groups. The party was especially strong in the former East Germany, where a great part of the people felt "forgotten" and left behind.[31]

Another populist party that also became significant in Europe, the Italian *Movimento Cinque Stelle* (Five Star Movement), was founded by the talented former comedian Beppe Grillo in 2009. It attracted voters from the entire political spectrum as well. This party is now led by 30-year-old rising political star Luigi Di Maio. Many of the party's newly elected parliamentary representatives are barely older than 25 years of age, the minimum limit to be a parliamentarian. This trend clearly illustrates the revolt against older, established politicians. Indeed, Grillo announced, "We've started a war of generations ... [The older politicians are] all losers, they've been there for 25–30 years and they've led this country to catastrophe."[32]

The party's program is a mixture of right- and left-wing radicalism. Just eight years after its founding, it won more than a quarter of the votes in the 2013 general election, making it Italy's biggest opposition party. At the European Parliament elections in 2014, it became the second-largest party. Since that time, it has won municipal elections in Rome, Turin, and Livorno; and several smaller places, especially in the South.[33] At the 2018 parliamentary elections, the Five Star Party became the biggest party of the country.

As in Italy, populism became dominant in other Mediterranean countries. One of the most outstanding examples is Greece. In October 2009, the socialist PASOK Party led by George Papandreu, which had played a leading role in post-dictatorial Greece after 1974, won the elections and formed the government. In December of that year, Papandreu publicly announced that the previous government had lied about the country's financial situation. As a result, Greece had an almost 13 percent budgetary deficit and €300 billion debt, or 110 percent of the GDP. By 2010–11, as Papandreu stated, the "Greek economy [became] a sinking ship."[34] Government bonds automatically dropped to "junk rate" level, and the country had to pay more than 26 percent interest in the summer of 2011. Greece became unable to repay the huge debts and became insolvent; it was then bailed out three times by the International Monetary Fund (IMF) and the EU. The EU lenders forced severe austerity measures upon Greece in order to normalize the country's financial household. The consequences were extremely painful: wages were cut by 15–40 percent and pensions by 35 percent; unemployment, especially among youth (50 percent), became tragic.

In this critical situation, the old party structure collapsed. In the 2015 elections, the two leading center-right and center-left establishment parties, New Democracy and PASOK, together hardly gained more than a quarter of the votes, while the antiestablishment far-left and far-right parties attracted more than 45 percent. The extreme right-wing Golden Dawn Party had more votes than the socialist PASOK (7 percent), reflecting the Europe-wide disappearance of social democratic parties. The winner of the landslide populist breakthrough became the Coalition of the Radical Left (*Synaspismós Rizospastikís Aristerás*). Syriza, as it called by abbreviation, is a left-wing populist party that was founded in 2004; in 2015, it gained nearly two million votes (about 36 percent) and formed the government. Its chairman, Alexis Tsipras, became prime minister in January 2015. Syriza, Tsipras, and Finance Minister Yanis Varoufakis launched vicious attacks against the neoliberal capitalist West, especially Germany and the EU. They demanded €278.7 billion compensation from Germany, which they said had a "moral obligation" to compensate Greece for Nazi atrocities during the war (an amount somewhat larger than Greece's debt to Germany). Journals published fake photos of Angela Merkel in a Nazi uniform and Hitler mustache. They also said that "the IMF has criminal responsibility for the situation of the country." They tried to play the Russian card: Tsipras visited President Putin in Moscow, called for and won a referendum to reject the terms of the EU bailout, and demanded the power to write off the greatest part of Greece's debts. Tsipras blamed the Western countries of the EU, or the "core": guided by neoliberal doctrine, he argued, they "set tough rules regarding austerity" that subordinated and exploited the other countries.[35]

Nevertheless, Syriza's left-wing attacks against the Western core of the EU and neoliberal capitalism failed. At the end of the day, they had to accept the terms that were offered and introduced the austerity measures, which constituted the requirement for the bailout as dictated by the EU and IMF. The left-wing populist government did not resign but remained in power and carried on.

Populist, mostly right-wing nationalist, parties mushroomed during the financial-economic crisis; several of them became leading political forces during the 2010s. During that decade, several far-right populist parties were actually already participating in governments in Austria, Croatia, Estonia, Finland, Italy, Latvia, the Netherlands, Poland, Serbia, Slovakia, and Switzerland; they had supported minority governments in Bulgaria, Denmark, and Norway. The relative success of the Danish People's Party in the rich and politically stable Scandinavian country expresses a crisis of confidence in the EU.[36]

In some of the countries, extreme right-wing parties, such the Greek Golden Dawn and the Hungarian *Jobbik*, with its typical paramilitary forces, were also present in politics.[37] The latter became the second biggest party in Hungary. Extreme left-wing parties also gained importance in Spain. Founded in 2014, the Spanish *Podemos* gained only 8 percent of the votes; in December 2015, it received 21 percent of the votes in the national parliamentary elections and emerged as the third-largest party in the country. *Unidos Podemos*-supported platforms hold power in most of Spain's large cities, including Madrid, Barcelona, Valencia, A Coruña, Palma, and Cádiz. They have 90 deputies among the 350 parliamentarians.

In 2016—after the Brexit vote in Britain and then the election of Donald J. Trump in the US—the potential for populist, anti-EU Party breakthroughs became frighteningly feasible in several key countries in Western Europe, including France and Germany, which both had upcoming national elections in 2017.

Populist defeats and victories, 2017–18

Nevertheless, the major populist parties suffered defeat in the Netherlands, France, and Germany in 2017. That eliminated the immediate danger of a series of referenda for leaving the EU. Moreover, in the two key countries, France and Germany, strong pro-EU parties gained the majority. In France, Emmanuel Macron had a landslide victory against Marine Le Pen. Geert Wilders got only 13 percent of the vote in the Netherlands. The AfD received the same percentage, while the two strongly pro-EU Christian Democratic and Social Democratic parties together gained 54 percent of the vote. That was a significant victory for the EU.

One should not forget, however, that while Geert Wilders lost the elections, the rival government party won by shifting toward the more extreme right by adopting several of Wilders's programs. In France, still at least one-quarter of the population remained behind Le Pen. The winner, Emmanuel Macron, also borrowed a much stricter immigration policy in the early spring of 2018 to take the wind out of Front National. Populism is still alive and dangerous in the West. Moreover, anti-EU populism not only failed to disappear: in two countries, Austria and Italy, populist parties achieved breakthroughs at the end of 2017 and early 2018. On December 18, 2017, a new Austrian coalition government took office, consisting of the conservative People's Party (ÖVP)—which had borrowed several right-wing elements from former Nazi sympathizer Jörg Haider's Freedom Party. The ÖVP won 31.4 percent of the vote and formed the coalition with the far-right populist Freedom Party, which received 27.4 percent. (The Social Democrats got only 26.7 percent.) Although they were not the leading parties, right-wing populism had found its way into the Austrian government again. The Social Democratic Chancellor Kern admitted that Austria has seen a "massive slide to the right."[38] One of the central issues, as everywhere, was immigration. The number of people who wanted a radically changed immigration policy as the top requirement more than tripled, from 24 percent in 2015 to 77 percent in 2017.[39]

In Italy's March 2018 election, a right-wing populist coalition composed of *Lega Nord* (Northern League, the party that dropped "Nord" from its name to become a nationwide party), Berlusconi's *Forza Italia*, and another far-right party gained 37 percent of the votes (with Lega receiving the biggest share). The rising populist Five Star Movement emerged from the elections as the single strongest party, with more than 32 percent of the votes. It particularly dominated in the South, where it received half the votes. The populist parties thus gained more than 70 percent of the votes. Nevertheless, none of the populist parties or coalitions could form the government alone, as according to new electoral laws it required 40 percent of the votes.

During the euro-crisis, the Five Star Movement advocated leaving the eurozone. Di Maio has said, "The euro as it is today does not work." He proposed either a return to the Lira or the introduction of a separate "Euro 2," a common currency only for the richer Northwestern EU member nations.[40] They also pledged to introduce deep tax cuts and to eliminate austerity measures, as well as to fight corruption. The party also advocated for environmental protection, a good public water supply, and sustainable transport. It is against military interventions in other countries and would like to distance Italy from the US. The party's founding principle was direct democracy, with candidates and policies chosen through online voting. Although they revolted against Brussels, the party does not support calling a referendum on EU membership. Its views on immigration, refugees, and improved relations with Russia resemble those of Marine Le Pen.[41] What makes the situation in Italy even worse for the EU, however, is that the other big winner was the strongly anti-immigration and anti-EU Lega; it received 17.4 percent of the votes, a six-fold increase compared to previous elections. The Lega is in the coalition with Berlusconi's Forza Italia, which gained only 14 percent of the votes.

The biggest loser was the only traditional establishment party, Italy's center-left coalition, which mustered only about 23 percent of the vote. It is likely to end up as the third-largest group in parliament, behind the right-wing coalition and the Five Star Movement. The outcome of the election, including what kind of coalition will be formed, is not yet clear as of spring 2018. What is clear, however, is that a shocking populist breakthrough occurred in the country. The two domi-nant, strongly Eurosceptic or explicit anti-EU parties—the Five Star Movement, with its combined left- and right-wing program, and the right-wing Lega—together received 54 percent of the votes and thus may determine Italy's poli-tics. This is a tremendous danger for the EU because Italy—with its 60 million inhabitants—has the third-largest and third-strongest economy in the EU, with more than $2 trillion GDP. The country is the largest wine producer and the eighth-largest exporter in the world. Even if Italy does not leave the eurozone or the EU, the new government definitely will oppose any further integration steps, which will weaken the EU. Italy was taken over by the populists.

If one considers that populist, highly anti-EU parties are ruling Hungary, Poland, Slovakia, and the Czech Republic, and are strong in several other coun-tries in Central Europe, populism is more than alive.

Notes

1 Jacques Rupnik, "Evolving or Revolving? Central Europe since 1989," *Eurozine*, December 15, 2017, www.eurozine.com/evolving-or-revolving-central-europe-since-1989/.
2 Andreas Rinke, "Merkel Says Islam 'Belongs to Germany' ahead of Dresden Rally," *Reuters*, January 12, 2015, https://goo.gl/FpCrVM.
3 Yascha Mounk, "A Primer on the French Election," *Slate*, April 18, 2017, https://goo.gl/18u5Zg.
4 Yascha Mounk, "How Liberals Can Reclaim Nationalism," *The New York Times*, March 4, 2018, Print edition, sec. Opinion.
5 *Archive of European Integration, Bruegel Blueprint Series 28, 22 January 2018*. [Policy Pa-per], Uuriintuya Batsaikhan, Zsolt Darvas, and Inês Goncalves Raposo, *People on the move: migration and mobility in the European Union*.
6 *Archive of European Integration,* Bruegel Blueprint Series 28, 22 January 2018. [Policy Paper], Brandon M. Boylan, *"Integrating Muslims into Western Societies: Transatlantic Policies and Perspectives,"* 2009.
7 Ellen Barry and Christina Anderson, "Hand Grenades and Gang Violence Rattle Sweden's Middle Class," *The New York Times*, March 4, 2018, Print edition, sec. Europe.
8 "Crime in Germany Drops 10 Percent in 2017, Report Shows," *Deutsche Welle*, April 22, 2018, https://goo.gl/SmVuNA.
9 Winston Churchill, "The Sinews of Peace: A Speech to Westminster College" (Fulton, MO, March 5, 1946). New York, Halcyon-Commonwealth Foundation, 1965.
10 Boris Johnson, *Lend Me Your Ears* (London: Harper Perennial, 2004), 29.
11 Ibid., 7, 37–38, 203, 204.
12 Nigel Farage, *Flying Free* (London: Biteback Publishing, 2011), 56–58.
13 Boris Johnson, *Have I Got Views for You* (London: Harper Perennial, 2006), 8, 203–204.
14 Boris Johnson, *Friends, Voters, Countrymen: Jottings from the Stump* (London: Harper Collins, 2002), 178–181.
15 Johnson, *Lend*, 43–45.
16 Ibid., 179, 43, 48.
17 Boris Johnson, *Facebook Post*, June 20, 2016, accessed May 1, 2018, https://goo.gl/SmhWnn.
18 Boris Johnson and Michael Gove, "Getting the Facts Clear on the Economic Risks of Remaining in the EU - Vote Leave's Letter to David Cameron," *The Telegraph*, June 4, 2016, https://goo.gl/fuy9FM.
19 Johnson and Gove, "Getting the Facts."

20 Boris Johnson, "This Is a Turning Point: We Have to Fly the Flag for Britishness Again," *Telegraph*, July 14, 2005, https://goo.gl/u2HNdD.
21 Farage, *Flying Free*, 238, 240. Also see "UKIP's Nigel Farage Tells Van Rompuy: You Have the Charisma of a Damp Rag," *The Guardian*, 25 February 2010.
22 "Nederland Weer Van Ons!," "Partij voor de Vrijheid" Concept Party Program, accessed May 1, 2018, www.pvv.nl/images/Conceptverkiezingsprogrammma.pdf.
23 Geert Wilders, "Let My People Vote," *The New York Times*, January 15, 2018, Print edition, sec. Opinion, https://goo.gl/wVdtuF.
24 Peter Davies, *The National Front in France: Ideology, Discourse and Power* (London: Routledge, 2012), 101–102.
25 Marine Le Pen, "May 1 Speech," (Paris, May 1, 2016), www.frontnational.com/videos/1er-mai-2016-discours-de-marine-le-pen/.
26 Marine Le Pen, Interview with Marine Le Pen: "I Don't Want this European Soviet Union", interview by Mathieu von Rohr, in *Der Spiegel*, June 3, 2014, https://goo.gl/t1bWPR.
27 Marine Le Pen, "Marine Le Pen: After Brexit, the People's Spring Is Inevitable," *The New York Times*, January 20, 2018, Print edition, sec. Opinion, https://goo.gl/BgHR.
28 Victoria Friedman, "Marine Le Pen in Euro Parliament: 'UK Sent a Signal of Freedom Out to the Entire World,'" *Breitbart*, June 28, 2016, https://goo.gl/5geg38; July 18, 2016, www.politico.eu/.../marine-le-pen-bastille-day-nice-attacks-proof-of-islamic-fundame.
29 Horst Seehofer, Heimat-Minister Horst Seehofer (CSU) in BILD-Interview: "Der Islam gehört nicht zu Deutschland!," in *BILD*, May 1, 2018, https://goo.gl/Usyg5p.
30 "AfD: What You Need to Know about Germany's Far-Right Party," *Deutsche Welle*, September 24, 2017, https://goo.gl/FKYJJ9.
31 "Just How Far to the Right Is AfD?," *BBC News*, October 13, 2017, sec. Europe, www.bbc.com/news/world-europe-37274201.
32 "Italian Vote Points to Impasse," *BBC News*, February 25, 2013, sec. Europe, www.bbc.com/news/world-europe-21574116.
33 "Just How Far to the Right Is AfD?," BBC News, October 13, 2017, sec. Europe, www.bbc.com/news/world-europe-37274201.
34 Niki Kitsantonis and Matthew Saltmarsh, "Greece, Out of Ideas, Requests Global Aid," *The New York Times*, April 23, 2010, sec. Global Business, www.nytimes.com/2010/04/24/business/global/24drachma.html.
35 Alexis Tsipras, "Europe at Crossroads," *Le Monde*, May 31, 2015.
   Yanis Varoufakis, "Germany Won't Spare Greek Pain – It Has an Interest in Breaking Us | Yanis Varoufakis," *The Guardian*, July 10, 2015, sec. Opinion, www.theguardian.com/commentisfree/2015/jul/10/germany-greek-pain-debt-relief-grexit.
36 Steven Erlanger, "Rise of Far-Right Party in Denmark Reflects Europe's Unease," *The New York Times*, June 19, 2015, sec. Europe, www.nytimes.com/2015/06/20/world/europe/rise-of-far-right-party-in-denmark-reflects-europes-unease.html.
37 Matt Golder, "Far Right Parties in Europe," *Annual Review of Political Science* 19, no. 1 (May 11, 2016): 477–497, doi:10.1146/annurev-polisci-042814-012441.
38 John Fund, "Right-Wing Victory in Austria Today," *National Review*, October 15, 2017, www.nationalreview.com/2017/10/right-wing-populist-victory-austria-election/.
39 Martin Eiermann, "The Austrian Election Showed Populists yet Another Path to Power," *New Statesman*, October 25, 2017, www.newstatesman.com/world/europe/2017/10/austrian-election-showed-populists-yet-another-path-power.
40 Yaron Steinbuch, "EU Worried about Other Countries Taking Brexit-like Leave," *New York Post*, June 24, 2016, https://nypost.com/2016/06/24/eu-worried-about-other-countries-taking-brexit-like-leave/.
41 Reiss Smith, "What Is the Five Star Movement? Meet 'Italy's Ukip'," *Express*, September 21, 2016, www.express.co.uk/pictures/pics/6717/Brexit-Nexit-Frexit-Who-s-next-to-leave-the-EU.

6

POPULISM FLOODED EASTERN EUROPE AND THE BALKANS— UNDERMINING THE EU

A real home for populism

Populism is a worldwide phenomenon: it exists from the US to the Philippines; from Britain to Western Europe to Central and Eastern Europe and the Balkans. The latter areas, however, became the real home of this movement. Right-wing populist, nationalist parties created governments in several of the region's countries. In one of them, Hungary, half of the electorate voted for two of those parties—*FIDESz* and *Jobbik*—in April 2018. The former had been in government for three terms, while the latter—an openly extreme-right-wing party—led the opposition from even farther to the right. Recently, however, they followed in the footsteps of Marine Le Pen, officially dropping anti-Semitism messaging to become more *comme il faut* to govern.

In Poland, the governing right-populist *Prawo i Sprawiedliwość* (Law and Justice Party) of Jarosław Kaczyński topped opinion polls in summer 2017, leading by eight percentage points ahead of the center-right Civic Platform Party. In mid-December of that year, the polls reflected 41 percent support 12 points ahead of the main centrist opposition party.[1] In Slovakia, populism had ruled most of the time after the collapse of communism. In the 1990s, Vladimir Mečiar's populist-nationalist Movement for Democratic Slovakia controlled the country. In the early twenty-first century, the leftist populist-nationalist *Smer* Party of Robert Fico (Direction – Social Democracy) dominated, but in 2016 it only gained 28.3 percent of the vote. Several ultra-right-populist parties, such as the Ordinary People Party (whose campaign slogan was "We Protect Slovakia") and the far-right People's Party Our Slovakia of Marian Kotleba, were also rather influential. In the Czech Republic, multibillionaire Andrej Babis won the last election. Babis, a former minister of finance, was removed because of major corruption charges but later established his own party, the *Akce nespokojených občanů* (Action of Dissatisfied Citizens), or ANO, in 2011. Babis gained votes by advocating for anti-corruption policy, stating, "It's the last chance to knock down this corrupt system" and, as a successful business-man, to elevate the country to the place it belongs: "We belong somewhere else and we're not there."[2] In early summer of 2018, Slovenia also elected a populist party to govern the country.

The nucleus of Central Europe, the four so-called Visegrád countries,[3] is under populist rule. "The Visegrád Group, formed immediately after the demise of the old order by presidents Havel, Wałęsa and Göncz," stated Jacques Rupnik,

> stood for democratization, overcoming the nationalist legacies of the past, and for the shared goal of European integration. Back then, Visegrád meant orientation towards the West. Today, particularly on the migrant issue, Visegrád asserts itself in opposition to Brussels and Berlin, with Orbán and Poland's Jarosław Kaczyński calling for a counter-revolution in Europe. So how did we get from there to here?[4]

To answer Jacques Rupnik's question, one has to go a bit backward in time and history. In the modern era, Central and Eastern Europe have mostly been ruled by right- or left-wing nationalist, authoritarian populism. Fascism and communism dominated the region's politics for most of the twentieth century. These revolts were rooted in the relative backwardness of the area. This histor-ical past, unfortunately, has strongly reemerged in the present. Historians call this phenomenon "path dependence." This experience of history is poetically expressed by Thomas Mann's Joseph tetralogy. Thomas Hollweck summed up this tetralogy's message in the following way:

> modernity reveals a far stronger concern with the past, be it as the founda-tion of modernity, be it as the reaction against the perceived or real speed of material and social change, or be it as the unquiet search for something that is experienced as having been lost and that should by all means be recovered. ... In short, the argument must be made that modernity, for all its dreams about new worlds and new ways of being, is deeply wedded to the past.[5]

The Nobel laureate economist Paul Krugman also felt the heavy hand of the past in the region when he wrote about its present populist turn. He argued:

> I would suggest, however, that there's a deeper story here. ...When the Berlin Wall fell, a political scientist I know joked, 'Now that Eastern Europe is free from the alien ideology of Communism, it can return to its true path: fascism.' We both knew he had a point.[6]

In the 2010s, the Visegrád Four (V4) was a populist-nationalist bloc against im-migration, liberal democracy, and further integration after Brexit. Following the

European Commission's release in March 2017 of a White Paper outlining five scenarios for the future of the European Union (EU) (discussed in Chapter 10), the V4 issued a declaration stating that it neither wants a strict single market nor federalization and that the concept of a multispeed EU is especially unacceptable for them. In V4's view, such a structure would degrade them by making them second-class countries in the Union.[7] In other words, the four Central European countries oppose any kind of further EU development.

In a joint declaration in January 2018, the four countries demanded national sovereignty within the EU: "EU institutions should treat all member states equally and act strictly within the remits of their respective ... competencies. The right of member states to carry out domestic reforms within their competences should be respected," the statement said. On migration, the four restated their focus on "effective, responsible and enforceable [EU] external border protection to avoid obligatory quotas [being] applied, which are ineffective and have already divided Europe." They also said they should not be punished for having different opinions within the bloc.

Joseph Leinen, a German member of the European Parliament who participated in the drafting of the European Constitution, characterized the Visegrád declaration in a strongly worded statement as

> an attack on European democracy. ... The Visegrád governments call for a Europe of the executives, where decisions are taken in small circles and without proper parliamentary control. They ignore the democratic structure of the European Union and the role of the European Parliament as equal co-legislator. ... There is a danger of a split not only on single issues, but regarding the democratic nature of the European Union ... Viktor Orbán and Jarosław Kaczyński propagates nationalism and apparently see the European Union only as a source of structural funds.[8]

Already in 2016, the Nations in Transit organization,[9] reviewing the entire former communist bloc, announced that the year

> was marked with populist successes. ... After a long period of stagnation and decline in democratic governance across the 29 countries of order in Central and Eastern Europe and the Balkans, years of populism and corruption have eroded once-promising democratic institutions. In Eurasia, personalist authoritarianism has gone from a burgeoning trend to an entrenched norm. This year, 18 of the 29 countries in the survey suffered declines in their overall Democracy Scores, the most since 2008, when the global financial crisis fueled instability and stalled political reforms. There have been more declines than improvements in each year of the survey since 2005, following the first big wave of EU expansion to the east. For the first time in the report's history, there are now more Consolidated Authoritarian regimes than Consolidated Democracies.[10]

In the last decade, populism connected with authoritarianism flooded the Balkans. Populist leaders are rising all over: Alexandar Vučić in Serbia; Nikola Gruevski in Macedonia (since 2006); Milorad Dodik in the Republika Srbska (in Bosnia and Herzegovina); Albin Kurti and Levizja Vetevendosje in Kosovo; Ivan Vilibor Sinčić and Ivan Pernar in Croatia, where the populist Human Shield Party established itself as a third party with more than 22 percent support; and Janez Janša in Slovenia, who won the June 2018 parliamentary elections.[11]

Ljubomir Danailov Frckoski analyzed *"authoritarian populism* in the countries in transition, especially in the Western Balkans" and concluded that it is "completely warping the young democratic institutions in the very beginning of their establishment. This populism appears as a lethal threat to them and to democracy too, especially a threat to the rule of law and human rights." As a common feature, they are all based on anti-immigration, nationalism and anti-Europeanism. In the

> Western Balkans, there are different degrees of developed authoritarian populism: from Macedonia, where the system has been completed (in the last 7 years), to Serbia where the elements of the system can be detected in ... Montenegro, Albania under Berisha's rule, Kosovo, and Bosnia too.[12]

The eastern part of Germany

That Central and Eastern Europe are the real homelands of populism is perhaps best illustrated by the case of the eastern part of the Federal Republic of Germany. The former communist German Democratic Republic has been part of the reunited Germany for almost three decades. This region of Germany, east from the River Elbe, is actually a historical part of Central and Eastern Europe that remained outside the Carolingian Empire. It has had very similar economic and social characteristics to Poland and Hungary since the early modern period. It remained mostly agricultural and was dominated by huge latifundia. Industrialization remained mostly limited to food processing in the nineteenth century. All the economic and sociopolitical characteristics of Eastern Europe were dominant there, including communist rule after World War II.

This past is still present in the relative triumph of the right-wing *Alternative für Deutschland* (AfD), or Alternative for Germany Party, during the 2017 German parliamentary elections. The relative success of this newly emerged party in rich and stable Germany was strongly based on the party's exceptional success in the former communist East Germany. On a sociohistorical basis, even after German reunification in 1991, the area exhibited rather similar sociopolitical phenomena as that occurring in Eastern Europe. Left wing was replaced by right wing. Already in 1992, extreme right-wing organizations became strong. They launched violent attacks against foreigners, including burning a high-rise apartment building with Roma and Vietnamese immigrants in it. In depopulated rural areas, advocates of extreme right-wing ideology sit on town councils and organize local sports and youth activities.[13]

Some of these people recently joined the right-wing populist Alternative for Germany Party in the mid-2010s, which became the second-most powerful party in the region and the strongest in Saxony. In regional elections in Saxony-Anhalt in March 2016, the party secured 24.3 percent of the vote, its best result in Germany up to that point. In the 2017 national elections, the party became the second-strongest party in the former communist East, where it captured nearly 22 percent of the vote (compared with less than 11 percent in the West). Strange but typically for it, Alternative for Germany displaced Die Linke—a far-left party with origins in the East German Communist Party—as the East's main alternative to the center-right bloc that had existed since the first post-reunification decades.

Today, a great part of the population in former East Germany shares the same feelings as the lower levels of society in rural areas and in industrial centers in various societies across Europe. These self-identified "left behind" or "forgotten people" are the usual base for populists worldwide. Although West Germany invested nearly €2 trillion in the East after reunification and generated a major catching up process, it stopped after the mid-1990s, and the region never surpassed two-thirds of the West German GDP and living standard. Certain areas were depopulated. Young and entrepreneurial people left for the West. As a typical example, half the inhabitants of Weisswasser, a small city, moved away. "Bus routes in the surrounding countryside were canceled. Stores and schools in local villages were closed." The media also discussed a supposed "collective psychological disorder spurred by the fact that the experience of two dictatorships was never properly dealt with."[14]

The region left behind

The feeling of "left behind" that characterizes certain layers of Western societies and the bulk of the population of the Central and Eastern European countries is the exact soil in which populism is most fertile. What factors caused this huge difference? One of them is the radically increasing income inequality. Although it is a common feature across the Continent, after the extreme equalizer state socialist regimes, it is more pronounced in Central and Eastern Europe than in the West. Several of the transforming countries introduced autocratic capitalism with a small oligarchy that was closely connected to political power and "crony capitalism"; together these factors sharply increased income inequality. Russia is one of the most extreme examples. In the midst of the Soviet era in 1980, the lower 50 percent of the population received 32–33 percent of the country's national income, while the top 1 percent's share was only 4 percent. In contrast, in 2016, the elite 1 percent's share jumped to more than 20 percent, while the share of the lower 50 percent of the population dropped to 17 percent.[15] Several of the former Soviet republics, such as Ukraine and Moldova, exhibited similar changes: overall inequality rose in the Balkans and in most of Central and Eastern Europe (as was discussed in Chapter 2).

The population's strong disappointment mobilized the masses against the ruling elite. Antiestablishment revolt is a central feature of populism. The masses considered the elite to be self-serving and corrupt. And indeed, Central and Eastern Europe are currently characterized by extreme, everyday corruption. Although corruption is almost universal, its scale and penetration of society are rather different in the two halves of the Continent. Among the ten least corrupt countries in the world, seven are European, all from Northwest Europe: Denmark, Luxembourg, the Netherlands, Sweden, Norway, Switzerland, and Finland, followed by Britain.[16] In 2015, corruption in Denmark, Finland, and Sweden was ranked between 89 and 91 on a scale measuring lack of corruption (where 100 means a total lack of corruption).

On the other hand, several of the Continent's peripheral countries have extreme levels of corruption, which becomes a "substitute" for good institutions and the rule of law.[17] Corruption oils the machine of the state apparatus and of business life. To arrange something, to get the required permission from a state office, to receive good health care, to get a job, to find important products that are not freely available, to receive a fair decision in court, to get accepted by a university (or just get a university diploma without studying), or to avoid punishment for violation rules, people (who pay less taxes than in more developed Western European countries) have to bribe and corrupt state officials, city employees, tax collectors, medical doctors, judges, shop clerks, university officials, and even parking meter inspectors.

Corruption penetrated everyday life and became a widespread disease in the region. It somewhat paralyzed normal life in Central Europe, but absolutely devastated it in the Balkans, Russia, Ukraine, and other backward (now independent) former Soviet republics. Bribing is so natural that it belongs to life, and therefore bribery prices are virtually fixed. For example, in Greece, receiving various state services—ranging from tax auditing to getting a driver's license— requires a bribe of €1,400. The International Corruption Perception Index ranked Greece in 80th place among 185 countries in the world. Greece was considered a "Western country" during the Cold War decades—the only one in the eastern half of the Continent, although it was ruled by a bloody anti-communist dictatorship. In reality, Greece is one of the typical Balkan countries. Corruption is also combined with tax evasion. According to certain calculations, in Greece, tax evasion costs the country about $20 billion per year. About one-third of the value-added tax (VAT) is never paid and consumes 7–8 percent of the country's GDP.[18] In 2016, Romania was regarded as the fifth most corrupt country in the EU, after Bulgaria and Greece, and at the same level as Hungary between 2007 and 2015 (as revealed by the annual Corruption Perceptions Index conducted by Transparency International).[19] Between 2016 and 2018, Hungary descended nine places in this ranking, dropping behind Greece and Romania to the same level as Malaysia and Montenegro. Typical for crony capitalism, almost one-third of the government's public orders and expenditures, a great part of the EU's aid, goes to friends and family of the governing new elite, the newly created "native business elite," without the competition technically required by state orders.[20] The European Anti-Fraud Office (OLAF) discovered irregularities in two-thirds of them using the EU aids. One case, connected to the company of the son-in-law of the prime minister, caused €43.7 million losses for the EU. Among the countries named by OLAF, Romania occupied the first place, and Hungary occupied the second, together with 21 serious irregularities from the 102 OLAF found within EU countries.[21]

The Corruption Perceptions Index—the most widely used indicator of corruption worldwide—ranks Ukraine among the worst: sometimes the country is ranked at 142nd in the world, alongside Uganda and even behind Nigeria. The people, who are the true sufferers of this chronic corruption, easily believe in strong populist leaders who promise its elimination. In Slovakia, young people established an anti-corruption movement to "get back" their country or leave it for the West.[22] Unfortunately, these populist promises, like several others, were not realized. Moreover, the populist regimes that created their own oligarchs and sometimes promoted the enrichment of the authoritarian populist leaders' friends and families became equally or even more corrupt.[23]

History also matters. Central and Eastern Europe is a traditional home for corruption, left- and right-wing populism, and authoritarianism. The century-long past is reemerging again. Populism offers to resolve central issues of relative backwardness, including lower living standards, corruption, and endangered independence by rich countries' exploitation and dominance. Rather, it exploits the dissatisfaction and despair of the layers of the population that were left behind. Populists accuse an "enemy" who is responsible for all of the misery of the people and promise efficient policies to change the situation in order to make the country "great" or "great again."

In Central and Eastern Europe, except a small rich layer at the top, members of societies have the feeling that they were "left behind." After the collapse of communism and especially after joining the EU, people in the region believed that in a few years, their country and themselves personally would be on a similar level with the populations of the Western countries. Naturally, it did not happen. Although the hope was a false delusion, the disappointment was bitter and overwhelming. As an average, the nine countries of Central Europe and the Baltic area reached only 32 percent of the West European average per capita GDP in 2016. The 18 countries of Eastern Europe and the Balkans—including the successor states of the Soviet Union and Turkey—had only slightly more than 11 percent of the income level of the West. In the most Western parts of that region (not including Asian or Caucasian republics), East Europe and the Balkans, the average income level is 13 percent of Western Europe's per capita GDP. They are even far behind neighboring Central Europe, reaching only 40 percent of their income level. The West Balkan countries and Ukraine had hoped to be accepted soon by the EU but had to realize that their hopes were misplaced. Together with former superpower Russia, they declined into poverty, became marginalized by the West, and felt deeply disappointed and angry.[24] In other words, the psychology of feeling "left behind" and neglected or even "exploited" by the rich West European EU member countries penetrated these societies and fueled disappointment and bitterness among the people. This feeling is almost unconnected from reality but is deeply rooted nonetheless.

A lower per capita GDP is, of course, equal with a lower standard of living. A lower GDP means people have less money for food, housing, education, vacation time, traveling, and leisure. Living in these areas of Europe and being cognizant that much higher standards of living exist in countries only a few hundred or even thousand kilometers away in the West is frustrating. People feel that they have been cheated and even exploited.

The reverse migration crisis of the region

One of the main socioeconomic problems in Central and Eastern Europe, the Baltics, and the Balkans that members and candidates of the EU struggled to address was the European immigration crisis, which occupied the central place in populist politics during the 2010s. Defending the "white" population and the Christian identity of the countries, "attacked"—as they complained—by robust immigration and the EU's tolerant immigration policy in 2015–16, was an essential weapon for Viktor Orbán, Jarosław Kacziński, the so-called V4 countries, and others in the region during the 2015–16 migrant "offensive." During that time, Europe indeed suffered a major shock from the chaotic inflow of millions of migrants.

The shares of foreign non-EU citizens in the population of the EU is, on average, slightly above 4 percent, while in Central Europe—Bulgaria, Croatia, Hungary, Lithuania, Poland, Romania, and Slovakia—it is less than 2 percent. The only exceptions are Estonia and Latvia, where this share is about 15 percent because of the large Russian population. Nevertheless, populist governments exploited the crisis atmosphere to maximum effect. Anti-immigration hysteria penetrated the population. It is highly characteristic that in the EU as a whole, only 31 percent of the people thought that immigrants received more than they contributed, and in Hungary and the Czech Republic, these shares were 43 and 45 percent, respectively. In the EU on average, only 28 percent of the people felt that immigrants took their jobs (in Germany 13 percent, and in Sweden 7), but in Hungary and the Czech Republic, these numbers reached 52 and 51 percent, respectively. And this polling was done in 2014, before the real crisis and exaggerated hysteria became dominant.[25]

In Hungary, the harsh, permanent, and virtually hysterical anti-immigrant propaganda worked and successfully revitalized the old, traditional sentiments of part of the population. On public transportation, trains, and trams, vulgar verbal attacks against African or Indian people of color and Hungarian girls who occasionally accompanied them were reported in the media from time to time.[26]

The migration crisis in this region, however, is rather different than in most countries on the Continent, as it actually experienced the reverse of the EU's crisis. The few thousand immigrants—7,000 for Poland and about 1,300 for Hungary—that the EU Commission wanted to distribute to these countries did not present a real danger at all. Central and Eastern Europe suffered from a new *emigration* crisis. This was especially dangerous because the region had already declined into a demographic crisis around the turn of the millennium. Birth rates had declined and remained at very low levels for decades in Europe as a whole since the 1960–70s. The fertility rate was much lower than the reproduction rate (2.1 children per family). The EU's average reproduction rate in 2015 was only 1.58. In Central and Eastern Europe, however, it was even lower. In Poland, it was 1.32; in Slovakia and Croatia, it was 1.40; and in Hungary, it was 1.45. Deaths outnumbered births: in Bulgaria by 6 percent; in Romania, Lithuania, Latvia, Croatia, and Hungary, by between 3.2 and 3.7 percent. Thus, populations were decreasing. According to the EU's report in 2009, if the trend had remained unchanged, the reduction in labor input would have been a dramatic 20 percent in 18 Member States between 2007 and 2060, among them virtually all of the Central European and Balkan member countries: Bulgaria, the Czech Republic, Estonia, Latvia, Lithuania, Hungary, Poland, Romania, Slovenia, and Slovakia.[27] The region was thus in a deep demographic crisis.

On top of that, since the 1990s, the region's emigration rate was higher than the immigration rate. A complex analysis of emigration from the region was prepared by a subsidiary of the International Monetary Fund (IMF). Let me sum up their findings.

> The past quarter century has seen a persistent and much larger wave of mostly economic migration from Central, Eastern, and Southeastern Europe (CESEE), mainly to Western Europe. Many of the CESEE emigrants were young and highly skilled, more so than in other emigration episodes. … This 'brain drain' coincided with rapid aging of the population in many Eastern European countries, with far-reaching effects on their output and productivity. … CESEE emigration appears to be more permanent than migration observed elsewhere. … During the past 25 years, nearly 20 million people (5½ percent of the CESEE population) are estimated to have left the region. By the end of 2012, Southeastern Europe (SEE) had experienced the largest outflows, amounting to about 16 percent of the early-1990s population. Emigration has also been persistent— annually, reaching as high as 0.5–1 percent of the 1990s population— and has tended to pick up following each new wave of EU expansion [in 2004, 2007 and 2013]. The non-EU SEE countries have seen easing access for their citizens for travel to Western Europe, and thus stay and work.

[After 1990, outward migration from SEE shaved off more than 8 percentage points from cumulative population growth.] "As a result, local populations in most countries in the region have been stagnant or shrinking. Every eight in ten CESEE migrants go to Western Europe, with Germany, Italy, and Spain receiving the bulk (nearly one-half)." [Additionally—and most damagingly— the emigrants']

> education levels tended to be higher than their home country averages. As of 2010, the share of emigrants from the Czech Republic, Hungary, Latvia, and Poland with tertiary education was well above the equivalent ratio in the general population and has been increasing over time. For Croatia and Romania, which have already low shares of people with tertiary education in the population, the brain drain from emigration may have had particularly important implications for productivity. Migration shaved off 0.6–0.9 percentage points of annual growth rates in some countries in SEE and the Baltics. Overall, emigration has lowered growth and slowed income convergence. Empirical analysis suggests that in 2012 cumulative real GDP growth would have been 7 percentage points higher on average in CESEE in the absence of emigration during 1995–2012, with skilled emigration playing a key contributing factor. In turn, this has slowed per capita income convergence, in particular in SEE countries (Albania, Bulgaria, Croatia, and Romania), which had a high share of young and skilled emigrants in their populations. Significant effects are also observed in the Baltics and in Slovenia. On average, CESEE countries would have reduced their per capita income gap with EU28 by an additional 5 percentage points by 2014 in the absence of skilled emigration during 1995–2012.[28]

Another EU document presents a dramatic picture of emigration from the Baltic countries and Croatia. While on average, Central and Eastern European net emigration was equal to 0.23 percent of the population in 2015, by far, the largest net outflows occurred in Lithuania (−0.64 percent of the population), Latvia (−0.58 percent), and Croatia (−0.52 percent). In Latvia and Lithuania, most of the population decline in 2008–12 was the result of the emigration of young cohorts. The resident population of younger people declined by about 20–25 percent, causing major losses to these countries. Large-scale emigration from Latvia and Lithuania continued through 2013–16.[29] In Hungary, during the 2010s, more than half a million people—5 percent of the population—went abroad; in Poland, the number was nearly 2 million. The emigration crisis in Central and Eastern Europe and the Balkans is thus a rather devastating factor but is hardly discussed by populists in the region. Ironically, while they concentrate on "saving their countries" from non-European immigrants, their economies need a new additional labor force.

The crisis of 2008 and austerity policy—authoritarian nationalism

On top of the migration crisis and inherited backwardness, the 2008 economic and financial crisis hit most of these countries hard and made several of them highly indebted. They were unable to repay their loans, and several of them had to be bailed out by the IMF and the EU. Consequently, they were forced to introduce austerity measures that made them even poorer and undermined the hope for a very rapid catch up. This situation generated a strong anti-EU feeling. The populations in all these countries were easily influenced by populist parties, especially because the bulk of the population, often two-thirds and even three-quarters of them, were traditionally strongly attracted to nationalist ideas and policy. All in all, the region's population—which had been almost extraordinarily optimistic after the collapse of communism—now became dominated by bitter feelings of "missed opportunities." As Norman Davis phrased it, they longed for the payoff "of the freedom they received in 1989."[30]

Populists offer strong leadership and often realize it in authoritarian rule. They all are antiestablishment and anti-elite, and cast these groups as responsible for the misery of the people and the decline of the country. They promise the rule of the people. Populists are often xenophobes; the enemy is a minority, immigrants, "others," some hostile neighbor, or a great power—nowadays, a commanding, and even "colonizing" and "exploitative," EU. The migration crisis and the severe mistakes the EU made in handling it during 2015 and 2016 were excellently exploited by the populist parties and leaders in countries where right-wing nationalism had a long history.

It is also a common phenomenon that left- and right-wing populism sometimes replace one another. They often follow similar policies and name similar enemies, such as neoliberalism, multinational companies, globalization, and the EU, while right-wing populists often play the nationalist card against the "other," the minorities or immigrants. Viktor Orbán's speech in February, before the April 2018 elections, is one of the characteristic examples in Europe of white supremacism: "We do not want to be a multi-colored country … [and as he said he] did not want Hungarians to interact with immigrants in such a way that our color is mixed with others' colors."[31]

Nowadays, populism prefers combining left- and right-wing slogans and promises, and sometimes even rejects the label of "right" or "left" as obsolete. The main difference that distinguishes countries under populist rule from others in Europe is separatism and the ideal of a closed "sovereign'" country, compared to open and integrating nations. Left or right, separationist populism purports to offer an immediate solution to serious problems and malaise, and often combines leftist views with nationalism. (That also happened in Latin America, another traditional home of populism. A few decades ago, about 60 percent of populist leaders and presidents of countries were right-wing populist; nowadays, 70 percent of them are left-wing populists.)

After World War I, Hungary was taken over by left-wing communist populists, but after their defeat, a right-wing nationalist regime ruled. One to two decades after the collapse of communism in Eastern Europe in 1989–91, right-wing populism is starting to dominate the region. Greece was under a right-wing military dictatorship for a long time during the post-World War II decades but is now ruled by left-wing populists. Early twenty-first century Central and Eastern European populism is mostly right-wing, nationalist, and authoritarian. The cases of Hungary and Poland, where populists are stably in power, clearly exhibit the main characteristics of populist regimes. In the first place, one has to mention the measures they proposed to gain popularity and mass support. Their governments promised and introduced tax cuts (in Hungary personal taxes went from 35 to 15 percent), lowered the retirement age (in Poland the age went from 65 to 60 years for men), decreased utility bills (in Hungary by 25 percent), and increased the minimum wage (in Hungary by 50 percent). As Viktor Orbán declared, his government elevated the people, unlike the EU, which was preoccupied with the migrants and "forgetting the white working class."

They often stated that a strong nation must first have a strong government. A whole series of measures introduced authoritarian rule in those countries. First, they subordinated the constitutional courts and the judiciary to the executive branch of government. If needed, they enacted new constitutions and changed laws in order to gain unchecked power. (Hungary not only introduced a new constitution but also made five amendments that enabled the government to get rid of democratic control.) They also subordinated the National Bank to the government either by law or (because the EU stepped in and did not allow it in Hungary) by personal appointments of friends and supporters to leading positions. The Orbán government eliminated the autonomy of the universities by appointing chancellors to aid the rectors that traditionally led these institutions, ensuring that every decision made at the universities involved governmental control.

Populist governments eliminated checks and balances and made drastic steps to destroy the opposition. Both Hungary and Poland changed the electoral laws to strengthen the positions of their parties and launched vicious attacks against nongovernmental organizations, George Soros (the American liberal philanthropic donor who runs his "Open Society" funds all over the region), and the Central European University in Hungary, supposedly to support democratic values (discussed in Chapter 7). Liberal institutions were characterized as foreign-financed anti-national centers. Jarosław Kaczyński went so far as to denounce party opposition as treasonous. "In Poland," he said, "there is the bad tradition of national treason. This takes place in the genes of some people who are the worst sort of Poles. And right now this worst sort is incredibly active."[32] On another occasion, he went even further: "In Poland, there was and … still is a genuine front for the defense of German interests. One must also say to oneself clearly that this front … consists of informants of the German secret services. … This is a very big group of people who live from German money and act as if they were independent scholars and journalists."[33]

In the focus of their populist rhetoric stands the national agenda, the "defense of the nation." "Our country is now run by politicians," Kaczyński declared, "accountable to Polish voters, not to German, British or French left-wing intellectuals."[34] Both Kaczyński and Orbán proudly acted as defenders of their country's' independence against the "colonizing" EU: "Europe, our common home, is not free!" stated Orbán.

> Today in Europe, it is forbidden to speak the truth. … It is forbidden to say that Brussels is now stealthily devouring more and more slices of our national sovereignty. … We should not allow Brussels to place itself above the law. … We must put steel in our spines, and we must answer clearly, with a voice loud enough to be heard far and wide, the foremost, the single most important question.…

Orbán quoted the popular mid-nineteenth-century Hungarian poet Sándor Petőfi, whose words on March 15, 1948, started the revolution against the Habsburg Empire: "Shall we be slaves or men set free — That is the question, answer me!"[35]

In one sense, extreme nationalism for Orbán means the "unification of the *entire* nation," the 15 million Hungarians (10 million in Hungary, 3 million in neighboring countries, and 2 million all over the world, including the descendants of early twentieth-century emigrants to the US). Post–World War I peace accords and the Trianon Treaty, which cut off two-thirds of the territory of Hungary, became a central propaganda question again. The situation recalls debates in the interwar Horthy regime, which pushed the country into Hitler's arms, leading to a Nazi alliance and war in order to recapture lost territories that had huge majority non-Hungarian populations, including the Romanian population in Transylvania and the Slovaks in the so-called North Hungarian area (today Slovakia).

At this point, it pays to quote Viktor Orbán at some length to illustrate the rhetorical strategies that this pioneer and informal leader of the Central European populist bloc employs. My quote comes from a public speech that he delivered three weeks before the parliamentary election in the country on March 15, 2018, on the occasion of the 170th anniversary of the day when the country's major 1848 revolution and fight for independence started. Incidentally, 2018 also marks the 100-year anniversary of the Trianon Treaty. His speech was a masterpiece of nationalist, xenophobic, and coded anti-Semitic demagoguery. Orbán painted Hungary as a country endangered by liberal cosmopolitan conspiracies and betrayed by the EU. He explicitly threatened retribution against those who serve "alien interests":

> They want to take away our country. … They want us to give it voluntarily to others in a few decades, to aliens who arrive from other parts of the world, do not speak our language, do not respect our culture, law and way of life. … Europe and we Hungarians arrived to a historical turning point.

Never before confronted the national and global forces so openly … Brussels does not defend Europe, does not want to stop immigrants but help and organize them … it wants to change the population of Europe. We have to struggle against a network organized as an empire. Against the media, paid by foreign corporations and domestic oligarchs, against paid-activists and organizers of demonstrations, against NGOs financed by international speculators, embodied by the name of George Soros. … We will fight against the Soros Empire and what it does and plans against Hungary. … Soros' candidates are running against our candidates at the elections. They, if gain power, want to realize the big plan to crash Hungary that blocks the road of immigrants. … They don't tell you who is paying them … they are not national but international, they do not believe in work, they are speculators without a fatherland and they believe that the whole world belongs to them. … After the elections we will take our revenge in moral, legal and political ways.[36]

As he proclaimed on September 5, 2010:

We are sailing under a Western flag, though an Eastern wind is blowing in the world economy. … We are doing our best [he promised], to find a way to part with West European dogmas, to free ourselves from them.[37]

He explicitly named the new "stars" of the world—Singapore, Russia, China, Turkey—as ideal instead of the "declining West." In his famous speech about establishing an "illiberal democracy" in Hungary, he added, "We have to abandon liberal methods and principles of organizing a society, as well as the liberal ways of understanding the world."[38]

After having won the national elections in May 2018, at his inauguration speech in Parliament, Orbán went much farther than ever before. He declared that he was going to fight to change the EU as well:

Now, we will be hunting for big game. … We must and we will enter the arena of European politics, in order to stop the Europe … climbing to the next step towards self-immolation. … The Union must function as an alliance of free nations and give up on its delusional nightmares of a United States of Europe. … The era of liberal democracy is over. … We are ready to be reformers in the changes that the EU can't avoid.[39]

In the leading Visegrád countries of Central and Eastern Europe, the populist "national saviors" of their countries are gradually limiting and eliminating democracy. The method of killing is a combined policy of legislation and appointments. Using their parliamentary majority, governments changed constitutions and legal systems according to their specific interests. They changed the electoral rules and redesigned the electoral districts. As a consequence, although opposition parties received more votes than FIDESz and Orbán's party, Orbán's party gained 48 percent of the votes in April 2018 in key districts, allowing it to attain a two-thirds majority in Parliament. In Hungary, the FIDESz government enacted 1,000 laws at an unparalleled speed. They changed the Supreme Court personnel, the national body of judges, the National Bank, and the rules of public broadcasting. In areas where legislation did not work, the government appointed its most loyal followers and friends. They also limited the freedom of the media by appointing their own candidates to lead the media regulatory offices and bought up opposition newspapers.[40]

Both Orbán and Kaczyński went so far as to refuse to accept the EU's decision that Hungary and Poland would receive and settle a few thousand immigrants because, they argued, Muslim immigrants would "destroy the Christian Hungarian values" in the country of 10 and nearly 40 million inhabitants, respectively. Meanwhile, even as they reject solidarity and the sharing of essential tasks with other EU member countries, their countries continue to pocket huge amounts of EU aid for backward regions and agriculture. In the Polish case, this aid totaled €27 billion annually, while Hungary received €40 billion during this budgetary period (until 2020). From the annual €156 billion EU budget, about 9 percent goes to Poland and another 2.5 percent to Hungary. These amounts cover the greatest part of infrastructure spending: 61 percent in Poland and 55 percent in Hungary. In the latter, without EU support, the annual 3 percent growth would drop to 1 percent. "Parting from the West" and the "colonizing" EU, but pocketing their money? The Hungarian government spokesman, Zoltán Kovács, stated that these amounts constitute payback for the profit that the West has made in the region: "Don't try to suggest that EU cohesion fund is a gift for central and eastern member states."[41]

Viktor Orbán was one of the very first to denounce immigration and build fences to hermetically close the borders to aliens. It is worth mentioning an interesting episode in connection with the anti-immigration policy: in 2018 at the South Korean Winter Olympics, the Hungarian media exaltingly reported on "The biggest Hungarian sporting sensation of the last 30 years." Indeed, for the first time ever, Hungary won a gold medal at the Winter Olympics (in short track speed skating, men's 5,000m relay). However, the most exciting fact in the news was that from the four-member Hungarian team, two men were non-Christian and Chinese. Liu Shaoang and Liu Shaolin Sándor were both Hungarian-born sons of a Chinese economic immigrant father, who had settled in the country 30 years before and married a Hungarian woman. Their coach, Zhang Lina, was also Chinese. Ignoring the multicultural nature of this victory, Orbán welcomed the great "Hungarian success": "Köszönjük, hogy ezt is megélhettük. Hajrá magyarok! [Grateful for living to see this day! Go Hungarians!]"

A public debate erupted. To quote one view,

> After three years of government propaganda against 'migrants,' the Chinese background of the two brothers on the team became part of a debate about

immigration. I don't know what went through Viktor Orbán's head. … But those who disapprove of Orbán's hate campaign against migrants felt a certain degree of satisfaction. Here it is. Orbán has to face the uncomfortable truth that sons of an 'economic migrant' made up half of the Hungarian speed skating team that turned out such an outstanding performance.[42]

The populist, nationalist, authoritarian wave had already undermined democracy in the region. Nationalist-populist right-wing regimes were created in Hungary and Poland, and gradually emerged around the four Visegrád countries. In those countries, "a political greenhouse for an odd kind of soft autocracy [emerged], combining crony capitalism and far-right rhetoric with a single-party political culture."[43] In Slovakia, one of the Visegrád countries, even the murdering of journalists, often and many times happened in Russia. Jan Kuciak, an investigating journalist who went after a government corruption case, was killed execution-style with his fiancée in their apartment.[44]

All this is happening under the watch of an EU that can make very little difference, partly because sufficient measures and procedures are missing from its legal arrangement. As Vivian Reding, the EU's justice commissioner, stated, "The main problem was that the founders of the European Union never considered the possibility that a member country would backslide, and did not create procedures to deal conclusively with such an event. … It was unthinkable."[45] The other part of the truth is that the EU did not even use the insufficient weapons it had. The spread of autocratic right-wing nationalism among member countries is weakening the integration process of the EU and is threatening to paralyze it.

This development was one of the central topics of French President Emmanuel Macron's speech at the European Parliament in April 2018.

> Europe is in a battle between the liberal democracy that shaped its postwar vision and a new populist authoritarianism that brushes aside dissidents and cares little about the rule of law. … Europe has to turn away from selfish nationalism. … We see authoritarians all around us, and the answer is not authoritarian democracy, but the authority of democracy,

he said. He has suggested deeper European integration, especially in the euro-zone.[46] Meanwhile, a group of intellectuals published an open letter to German Chancellor Angela Merkel, stating, we

> are convinced that the survival of Hungarian democracy is now acutely imperiled; some even believe that it has already been effectively dismantled. And yet, you as German chancellor have so far failed to condemn either Orbán's anti-Semitic rhetoric or his concerted attacks on democratic institutions. … Worse, the party you lead remains allied in the European Parliament with Orbán's political party … helped to legitimize Orbán, you have never called for them to change course. This silence makes you

complicit. … The European Union is founded on values including democracy, the rule of law and respect for human rights. By allowing the Hungarian government to destroy democratic institutions and to demonize minorities with impunity, the EU risks turning into little more than a regional trade bloc devoid of common values.[47]

This danger is especially strong because it is accompanied by outside support, Russian political alliances and energy cooperation, and Chinese alliances that include the building of infrastructure through huge investments (discussed in Chapter 9). These outside entanglements help the autocratic, anti-EU populist leaders in their "fight for independence against Brussels." A revitalized EU should punish and somewhat marginalize the revolting countries by closing the lines of the eurozone countries and leave those who do not want to go together in the outside-zone of the EU members.

Rising prosperity in the world economy and in Europe may have had a positive impact on the region from 2017 to 2018 onward. The countries of Central and Eastern Europe were closely built into the regionalized economy of the EU, which had a 2.4 percent growth rate in the early twenty-first century. The region's most important companies are subsidiaries of foreign giant corporations or parts of their supply network; thus, a great part of their industries is producing for major outside companies. In the new prosperity, the countries' industrial output increased in the early twenty-first century by 7.4 percent in Poland, between 6.9 (January) and 4.1 (February) percent in Hungary, and by 2.7 percent in the Czech Republic. An emerging labor shortage led to wage increases. The jobless rate, which, as an average, was 8.5 percent in February 2018 in the EU, dropped to 2.4 percent in the Czech Republic (one of the lowest in Europe), to 6.8 percent in Poland, and to 8.6 percent in Hungary. In the Czech Republic, monthly wages increased by 8 percent in 2017, rising from €1,400 to €1,600; this amount is already one-third of the average German wage level.[48] Automation and robotization, which provide substitutes for labor force shrinkage, are also improving, which elevates productivity. At the moment, populist governments are quick to portray the improvements as the consequences of their own politics; however, this development may have the positive outcome of enabling these countries to catch up with the West and increasing the living standard in the long run, which may take the steam out of populist politics as well.

Notes

1 "Poland's Illiberal Law and Justice Party Is Still on Top," *The Economist*, July 3, 2017, sec. Debeatified, www.economist.com/europe/2017/07/03/polands-illiberal-law-and-justice-party-is-still-on-top. "Poland's Prime Minister Gets the Chop," *The Economist*, December 14, 2017, sec. Debeatified, www.economist.com/europe/2017/12/14/polands-prime-minister-gets-the-chop.
2 Philip Heijmans, "The Populist Tide Has Spread to One of Central Europe's Last Liberal Democracies," *Public Radio International (PRI)*, October 20, 2017, Web edition, sec.

GlobalPost, www.pri.org/stories/2017-10-20/will-populist-tide-spread-another-eu-liberal-democracy.

3 The Four Visegrád countries, the Czech Republic, Slovakia, Hungary, and Poland, signed an agreement of collaboration after the collapse of communism in the small Hungarian township of Visegrád.

4 Jacques Rupnik, "Evolving or Revolving? Central Europe since 1989," *Eurozine*, December 15, 2017, www.eurozine.com/evolving-or-revolving-central-europe-since-1989/.

5 Thomas Hollweck, "Thomas Mann's 'Work on Myth': The Uses of the Past," accessed June 6, 2018, https://sites01.lsu.edu/faculty/voegelin/wp-content/uploads/sites/80/2015/09/Thomas-Hollweck1.pdf.

6 Paul Krugman, "What's the Matter with Europe?" *The New York Times*, May 21, 2018.

7 Eva S. Balogh, "A Multi-Speed Europe and the Visegrád Four," *Hungarian Spectrum* (blog), March 7, 2017, http://hungarianspectrum.org/2017/03/07/a-multi-speed-europe-and-the-visegrad-four/.

8 Georgi Gotev, "Jo Leinen – Visegrad Four 'Attack European Democracy,'" *Euractiv.com*, January 30, 2018, www.euractiv.com/section/future-eu/news/jo-leinen-visegrad-four-attack-european-democracy/.

9 Nations in Transit is Freedom House's research arm covering 29 formerly communist countries in Central and Eastern Europe and Central Asia. Freedom House is a US-based nongovernmental organization, established in 1941, that conducts research and advocacy on democracy, political freedom, and human rights.

10 "Nations in Transit 2017: The False Promise of Populism," *Balkan Civil Society Development Network* (blog), April 5, 2017, www.balkancsd.net/nations-in-transit-2017-the-false-promise-of-populism/.

11 Dario Brentin and Tamara Pavasović Trošt, "Introduction: Populism from Below in the Balkans," *Contemporary Southeastern Europe* 3, no. 2 (2016): 1–16.

12 Ljubomir Danailov Frčkoski, "Authoritarian Populism in Transitional Democracies of Western Balkans," *South-East European Journal of Political Science* 2, no. 1 (2014): 329–340.

13 David Crossland, "The World from Berlin: In Eastern Germany, the Neo-Nazis Are Winning," *Spiegel Online*, August 21, 2012, sec. International, www.spiegel.de/international/germany/press-review-on-the-german-far-right-20-years-after-the-rostock-riots-a-851193.html.

14 Maik Baumgärtner et al., "A Country, Still Divided: Why Is the Former East Germany Tilting Populist?" *Spiegel Online*, November 17, 2017, sec. International, www.spiegel.de/international/germany/eastern-germany-and-its-affinity-for-populists-a-1177790-2.html. For related coverage, also see "The German Election was a Fault Line of East-west Tensions, Key to the Rise of the Far Right" (*The Washington Post*, September 26, 2017).

15 Eduardo Porter and Karl Russell, "It's an Unequal World. It Doesn't Have to Be," *The New York Times*, December 14, 2017, sec. Business Day, www.nytimes.com/interactive/2017/12/14/business/world-inequality.html.

16 "Corruption Perceptions Index 2015" (*Transparency International*, 2015), www.transparency.org/cpi2015.

17 The following paragraphs on corruption are based on Ivan T. Berend's "Populist Demagogues in Modern European Politics, forthcoming from Central European University Press," 2018–19.

18 Niki Kitsantonis, "Greece Publishes List of 4,000 Tax Scofflaws," *The New York Times*, January 23, 2012, sec. Europe, www.nytimes.com/2012/01/24/world/europe/greece-publishes-list-of-4000-tax-scofflaws.html. For the Italian case, see Beppe Severgnini, "If Only...," *The Economist*, November 16, 2011, www.economist.com/node/21537029. For more on Greece, see Stergios Babanasis, *Apo tēn stē viosimē anaptyxē* (Athens: Papazisi, 2011).

19 The Corruption Perceptions Index measures corruption on a scale between 0 and 100: 100 means no corruption at all, while 0 signals the worst possible corruption.
20 Millennium Intézet, Budapest, Hungary, Newsletter, February 24, 2018.
21 https://hirtv.hu/ahirtvhirei/megint-szegyenpadba-ulhet-magyarorszag-2462398; http://168ora.hu/kulfold/akkora-kart-okozott-az-eu-nak-tiborcz-istvan-volt-cege-hogy-mas-a-nyomaba-sem-er-a-kategoriaban-151030.
22 Rick Lyman, "Young and Idealistic, but Resolute," *The New York Times*, April 30, 2017, Print edition, sec. World, www.nytimes.com/2017/04/30/world/europe/slovakia-teenagers-corruption-david-straka-karolina-farska.html.
23 See Balint Magyar, *Post-Communist Mafia State: The Case of Hungary* (Budapest: Central European University Press with Noran Libro, 2016).
24 The facts and figures are shockingly similar in Latin America, the other natural home of populism. The 32 countries of Latin America had, on average, virtually the same per capita GDP as that of Central Europe in 2016. For them, the natural comparison is their northern neighbor, the US, which is even somewhat richer than Western Europe. The Latin American average per capita GDP is only 27 percent of the US's income level.
25 Uuriintuya Batsaikhan, Zsolt Darvas, and Inês Goncalves Raposo, *People on the Move: Migration and Mobility in the European Union*, Blueprint Series 28 (Breugel, 2018), http://bruegel.org/2018/01/people-on-the-move-migration-and-mobility-in-the-european-union/.
26 Pion István, "'A kurva anyád, te büdös, rohadék geci! Takarodj az országunkból!' – üvöltötte egy magyar férfi a vonaton egy indiai fiúnak," *Zoom.hu*, April 26, 2018, https://zoom.hu/hir/2018/04/26/a-kurva-anyad-te-budos-rohadek-geci-takarodj-az-orszagunkbol-uvoltotte-egy-magyar-ferfi-a-vonaton-egy-indiai-fiunak/.
27 "2009 Ageing Report: Economic and Budgetary Projections for the EU-27 Member States (2008–60)," Ageing Report, European Economy (European Union), accessed June 6, 2018, http://ec.europa.eu/economy_finance/publications/pages/publication14992_en.pdf.
28 Ruben Atoyan et al., *Emigration and Its Economic Impact on Eastern Europe*, IMF Staff Discussion Note SDN/16/07 (International Monetary Fund, 2016), Washington D.C.
29 Batsaikhan, Darvas, and Raposo, *People on the Move*.
30 Steven Erlanger, "In Eastern Europe, Populism Lives, Widening a Split in the E.U.," *The New York Times*, December 1, 2017, Web edition, sec. World, www.nytimes.com/2017/11/28/world/europe/populism-eastern-europe.html.
31 Marc Santora, "Hungary Election Gives Orban Big Majority, and Control of Constitution," *The New York Times*, April 9, 2018, sec. World, www.nytimes.com/2018/04/08/world/europe/hungary-election-viktor-orban.html.
32 Derek Monroe, "No Law, No Justice and No Civic Values: Why Poland's Constitutional Crisis Can Only Get Worse," *RT International*, accessed June 6, 2018, www.rt.com/op-ed/327882-poland-political-crisis-eu/.
33 Klaus Bachmann, "Reason's Cunning," trans. Christopher Gilley, *Eurozine*, Osteuropa, August 10, 2007, www.eurozine.com/reasons-cunning/.
34 "Is Poland a Failing Democracy?" *Politico*, January 13, 2016, www.politico.eu/article/poland-democracy-failing-pis-law-and-justice-media-rule-of-law/.
35 Viktor Orbán, "Speech by Prime Minister Viktor Orbán on 15 March," Government, Hungarian Government Website, March 15, 2016, www.kormany.hu/en/the-prime-minister/the-prime-minister-s-speeches/speech-by-prime-minister-viktor-orban-on-15-march. The quotation in the last sentence is of the mid-nineteenth century Hungarian poet Sándor Petöfi's 1948 poem that started the Hungarian revolution of that year.
36 Viktor Orbán, "Orbán Viktor ünnepi Beszéde Az 1848/49. évi Forradalom és Szabadságharc 170. évfordulóján" (Budapest, March 15, 2018), www.kormany.hu/hu/a-miniszterelnok/beszedek-publikaciok-interjuk/orban-viktor-unnepi-beszede-az-1848-49-evi-forradalom-es-szabadsagharc-170-evfordulojan.

37 Sean Lambert, "Eastern Opening," *The Orange Files* (blog), February 9, 2014, https://theorangefiles.hu/eastern-opening/.
38 Csaba Tóth, "Full Text of Viktor Orbán's Speech at Băile Tuşnad (Tusnádfürdő) of 26 July 2014," *Budapest Beacon*, July 29, 2014, https://budapestbeacon.com/full-text-of-viktor-orbans-speech-at-baile-tusnad-tusnadfurdo-of-26-july-2014/.
39 "Viktor Orbán Elected as Prime Minister," Hungarian Government Website, accessed June 9, 2018, www.kormany.hu/en/the-prime-minister/news/viktor-orban-elected-as-prime-minister.
40 Patrick Kingsley, "Taking an Ax to Democracy as Europe Fidgets," *The New York Times*, February 10, 2018, Print edition, sec. World, www.nytimes.com/2018/02/10/world/europe/hungary-orban-democracy-far-right.html.
41 Steven Erlanger, "To Punish Rogue States EU Mulls Funding Cuts," *The New York Times*, May 1, 2018, Print edition, sec. World, www.nytimes.com/2018/05/01/world/europe/poland-hungary-european-union-money.html.
42 Eva S. Balogh, "Amid Anti-Immigrant Propaganda, the Sons of a Chinese Immigrant Win Gold for Hungary," *Hungarian Spectrum* (blog), accessed February 24, 2018, http://hungarianspectrum.org/tag/winter-olympics/.
43 Kingsley, "Taking an Ax to Democracy as Europe Fidgets."
44 Marc Santora and Miroslava Germanova, "Ex-Model, Mob Suspect and a Murder Could Bring Down Slovakia's Government," *The New York Times*, June 8, 2018, sec. World, www.nytimes.com/2018/03/09/world/europe/slovakia-journalist-killing-protests.html. Indeed, the endless mass demonstrations led to the resignation of the populist Prime Minister Fico.
45 Ibid.
46 Steven Erlanger, "Fight Over Values Risks a 'European Civil War,' Macron Says," *The New York Times*, April 19, 2018, sec. World, www.nytimes.com/2018/04/17/world/europe/macron-european-parliament-strasbourg.html.
47 Yascha Mounk et al., "Merkel's Shameful Silence," *Politico*, April 17, 2018, sec. Opinion, www.politico.eu/article/angela-merkel-viktor-orban-shameful-silence-viktor-orban-hungarian-election-fidesz/.
48 "Economic and Financial Indicators," *The Economist*, March 20, 2018, www.economist.com/economic-and-financial-indicators/2018/03/20/economic-and-financial-indicators.

   "Population and Population Change Statistics," Statistics Explained (Eurostat, July 2017), http://ec.europa.eu/eurostat/statistics-explained/index.php/Population_and_population_change_statistics.

   Liz Alderman, "Robots Ride to the Rescue Where Workers Can't Be Found," *The New York Times*, May 14, 2018, sec. Business Day, www.nytimes.com/2018/04/16/business/labor-robots-jobs-eastern-europe.html.

7

CHRISTIAN EUROPE? THE USE AND ABUSE OF CHRISTIAN VALUES AND THE POPULIST DEBATE

Populism and Christianity

The terms "Christian values" and "Christian Europe" are in constant use in populist rhetoric, especially in public speeches and arguments. This is somewhat new in highly secular Europe. One of the first postwar European populists to invoke Christian rhetoric for political ends was Jean-Marie Le Pen, who represented "French values" as consonant with those of Christianity and the Catholic Church. His daughter, Marine Le Pen, frightened her believers by continuously referring to the "occupation" of France by 14 million Muslims and the transformation of Christian, French, and Western cultures by "Islamic France." This supposed occupation, she predicted in 1990, will "eradicate all that links France to Western, humanist and Christian civilisation."[1] More recently, Geert Wilders of the Netherlands stressed that Islam posed a dire threat to Judeo-Christian society in his country.[2]

Let me quote at some length from *The Paris Statement*, a recent populist manifesto signed in Paris by 13 populist politicians from across Europe. The declaration is a clear rejection, under the banner of Christianity, of universalism (including universal human rights) and multiculturalism. The signatories allege that their repudiation of the European Union (EU) is a consequence of the "decline of Christian faith" in Europe:

> The true Europe has been marked by Christianity. The universal spiritual empire of the Church brought cultural unity to Europe, but did so without political empire. This has allowed for particular civic loyalties to flourish within a shared European culture. ... It is no accident that the decline of Christian faith in Europe has been accompanied by renewed efforts to establish political unity—an empire of money and regulations, covered

with sentiments of pseudo-religious universalism, that is being constructed by the European Union. ... The true Europe affirms the equal dignity of every individual, regardless of sex, rank or race. This also arises from our Christian roots. Our gentle virtues are of an unmistakably Christian heritage: fairness, compassion, mercy, forgiveness, peace-making, charity. Christianity revolutionized the relationship between men and women, valuing love and mutual fidelity in an unprecedented way. ... [T]he Christian legacy of humane and dignified life, a living engagement with our Classical inheritance—all this is slipping away. As the patrons of the false Europe construct their faux Christendom of universal human rights, we are losing our home. ... Europe's multicultural enterprise, which denies the Christian roots of Europe, trades on the Christian ideal of universal charity in an exaggerated and unsustainable form. It requires from the European peoples a saintly degree of self-abnegation. We are to affirm the very colonization of our homelands.[3]

According to the populist manifesto, Christian Europe is the "true Europe," while the EU is a "false Europe."

The populist movements, however, are ambivalent on the issue of "Christian identity." As a European University Institute analysis maintains, they all reject Islam as "non-European," but some of them fight for the re-Christianization of societies (like the Polish populists). Others defend a Christian identity without faith (the Lega [Nord] in Italy and the FPÖ in Austria), while still others endorse contemporary secular values (such as Geert Wilders in the Netherlands). In France, Marine Le Pen currently also defends "laïcité" (secularism) as the root of the French identity (while her niece and the rising star of the Front National, Marion Maréchal Le Pen, promotes an old view of France with churches, processions, and a ban on abortion).

Generally speaking, however, when populists promote Christianity, it is in the form of a folkloric popular religion that uses the cross as a political symbol but ignores the teachings of the Church. It often fights against clerical authorities who call for hospitality to migrants and refugees. In fact, this Christian identity may run contrary to Christianity as Pope Francis interprets it.

As a matter of fact, the "European values" referred to after World War II were not associated with Christianity but were instead based on three pillars: political liberalism; human rights; and, less explicitly, strong state welfare policies. As human rights are by definition secular—that is, independent of any religion—in a sense, they epitomize the postwar European identity. Proponents initially established European human rights in opposition to totalitarian ideologies rather than religious beliefs. Since the 1980s, however, pro-human rights leaders have also advocated for the taming of religious norms perceived as oppositional (such as women's unequal status in some religious sects or freedom of speech limitations).[4]

A special feature of East European nationalist interpretations of Christianity

Although all contemporary populists cultivate the idea of a "Christian nation," it is much more frequent in Central and Eastern Europe, where the concept of the "Christian nation" has a centuries-old tradition. It originated during the long wars with the Ottoman Empire but gained new virulence after World War I in anti-Semitic and anti-communist contexts (Christianity against faithless communism). Modern propagandistic invocations of Christianity have thus been integrated into nationalist self-identification since the interwar decades.

Although it disappeared for half a century after World War II, the "Christian Nation" slogan reemerged in early twenty-first century right-wing, proto-authoritarian regimes like Hungary and Poland. When Viktor Orbán, who was previously not religious at all, gained power in Hungary, he declared that "we may finally build … a national Christian era."[5] A few years later, he praised his regime, saying, "within three years the civic-Christian government [has] led the country out of this hopeless, ruinous situation."[6] During the migration crisis of the mid-2010s, Christianity became a leading slogan against immigration: "Masses arriving from other civilizations endanger our way of life, our culture, our custom and our Christian tradition."[7]

In November 2012, Prime Minister Orbán went even further with his "Christian" national ideology. In his address at the fourteenth Congress of Catholics and Public Life in Madrid, entitled "Hope and Christian Response to the Crisis," he hailed a return to the principles of Christendom as Europe's only chance for salvation. He even argued that the economic depression undermining the European economy

> has not come by chance but by carelessness, the neglect of their responsibilities by leaders who have called into question the Christian roots, that is, the driving force that made European unity, the family, work and credit possible. … These values transformed the old continent into an 'economic power,' thanks to the development of those days being made in accordance with those principles.[8]

Jarosław Kaczyński, a close follower of Orbán, was elected to power with the program of "combating the de-christianisation of Poland."[9] His government launched harsh anti-abortion laws and a cultural war against modernity. It pays to quote one of his anti-modernization tirades: "We only want to cure our country of a few illnesses," such as the

> new mixture of cultures and races, a world made up of cyclists and vegetarians, who only use renewable energy and who battle all signs of religion. … What moves most Poles [is] tradition, historical awareness, love of country, faith in God and normal family life between a woman and a man.[10]

Kaczyński's new handpicked Prime Minister, Mateusz Morawiecki, while he started working on destroying the independence of the judiciary, in his first TV interview called for the "rechristianisation" of Europe since "in many places carols are not sung, churches are empty and are being turned into museums."[11]

While Kaczyński is a deeply religious man, Orbán and Vladimir Putin, the former Soviet KGB officer, previously had nothing to do with religion. Both of them, however, pretend to be religious for political ends. Putin is often photographed crossing himself at Orthodox services or standing alongside Patriarch Kirill, the head of the Russian Orthodox Church. They mutually assist one another. Putin has helped to rebuild the Church, which was destroyed during the communist period. In 1988, the millennium anniversary of Russia's Christianization, the Orthodox Church was in ruins, with only 76 eparchies (their version of dioceses) remaining in the country. By 2016, that number had jumped to 293; relatedly, in 1988, there were 6,674 priests, whereas by 2016, that number had increased to 35,000. In exchange, the Orthodox Church supports Putin's policies, including the incorporation of Crimea.[12] More importantly, the non-centralized Orthodox Church, which has more than a dozen self-governing eparchies in Eastern Europe and the Balkans (each with its own patriarch), is still under the strong influence of the powerful Russian Orthodox Church in Moscow. The Moscow Church is in close contact with the eparchies of Ukraine; Moldovia; and other, now independent countries from former Soviet republics. Together these religious organizations are helping Putin in his efforts to recreate the former empire. The Orthodox Church is also an envoy of Putin in the Balkans and supports Putin's European policies as well.

Christianity and Christian values thus became a major pillar of populist rhetoric and policy everywhere in Eastern Europe. Right-wing leaders used Christianity as a political weapon in order to gain mass popular support.

What are Christian values, and how do they influence European life?

There is, naturally, no place in this chapter for a detailed philosophical or theological discussion. From a historical perspective, however, Christianity broadly defined is central to European history. From the eleventh century onwards, Europe was indeed rarely called Europe but "Christianitas" (Christendom). Nevertheless, in modern times—beginning a few centuries ago but increasingly in the postwar decades—there has been a trend toward a secular, less religious Europe.

When discussing this issue, one has to ask the evident question: what kind of Christian values? One might just as easily focus on the tolerance of the early Christians or today's Vatican, on the one hand, as on the well-known intolerance of the medieval Church and the Inquisition, on the other.

Furthermore, one has to ask what the so-called Christian values mean for daily European life: does it influence daily eating habits, like Judaism or Islam do? Does it regulate clothing customs (as do Orthodox Jews, Saudi Muslims, Indian Sikhs, and people in many other religious cultures)? Does it influence science, business, politics, or economics? The Church was strongly against science for centuries, rejecting several key scientific discoveries as sins against God. The Church forbade moneylending with interest (usury), a ban that stifled banking activities in general, on the premise that it was unchristian, which shifted these activities into non-Christian domains. The Catholic Church has basically preserved its medieval feudal structure, in sharp contrast to the democratic political structures of Europe. European values, in reality, formed and emerged as the Catholic Church started losing its firm grip upon European life. It is an oft-mentioned commonplace that modern European values trace their origins to a mixture of Greek philosophy, Judaism, Christianity, the Renaissance, and the Enlightenment. The dominating values of democracy and human rights for all people (including non-male and minority populations) regardless of religion actually stem much more from the Enlightenment than from Christianity. The prospective but ultimately down-voted constitution of the EU rightly based European values on the complex "cultural, religious and humanist inheritance of Europe."[13]

Today the Catholic Church is strongly opposed to many of the populist politics that run under the banner of Christianity, including on several debated issues including immigration.

Pope Francis's differing interpretation of Christian Europe

It is valuable to compare populist "Christianity" with the Vatican's interpretation of Christianity. The Argentinian Jesuit Pope Francis, in his message at the Day of Migration and Refugees on August 15, 2017, quoted Leviticus and Matthew: "You shall treat the stranger who sojourns with you as the native among you, and you shall love him as yourself, for you were strangers in the land of Egypt: I am the Lord your God" (*Leviticus* 19:34). "Every stranger who knocks at our door is an opportunity for an encounter with Jesus Christ, who identifies with the welcomed and rejected strangers of every age" (*Matthew* 25:35–43). The Pope added, "In this regard, I wish to reaffirm that our shared response may be articulated by four verbs: *to welcome, to protect, to promote* and *to integrate*."[14] Similarly, in an address to a gathering of European cardinals in 2017, Pope Frances discussed the value of community and peace, emphasized the value of the EU in these respects, and stressed the importance of inclusiveness and acceptance of "strangers." The Pope's Christianity is the exact opposite of populist "Christianity." Pope Francis said:

> The contribution that Christians can make to the future of Europe, then, is to help recover the sense of belonging to a community. It is not by chance

that the founders of the European project chose that very word to identify the new political subject coming into being. ... This leads us to reflect on the positive and constructive role that religion in general plays in the building up of society. I think, for example, of the contribution made by interreligious dialogue to greater mutual understanding between Christians and Muslims in Europe. ... Leaders together share responsibility for promoting a Europe that is an *inclusive* community, free of one fundamental misunderstanding: namely that inclusion does not mean downplaying differences. On the contrary, a community is truly inclusive when differences are valued and viewed as a shared source of enrichment. Seen in this way, migrants are more a resource than a burden. Christians are called to meditate seriously on Jesus' words: 'I was a stranger and you welcomed me' (*Mt* 25:35). ... A Europe that rediscovers itself as a community will surely be a *source of development* for herself and for the whole world. ... Finally, the commitment of Christians in Europe must represent a *promise of peace*. This was the central concern that inspired the signatories of the Treaties of Rome. After two World Wars and atrocious acts of violence perpetrated by peoples against peoples, the time had come to affirm the right to peace. For it is a right. Yet today we continue to see how fragile is that peace, and how particular and national agendas risk thwarting the courageous dreams of the founders of Europe."[15]

Populism uses Christianity as a political weapon. The populist leaders' Christianity is diametrically opposed to the Pope's interpretation of scripture. Unfortunately, a large number of churches in most Central and Eastern European countries are allied with, and often directly serve, autocratic leaders and governments.

Notes

1 Marine Le Pen, *Identité*, No.6 (April 1990).
2 "CONCEPT – VERKIEZINGSPROGRAMMA PVV 2017–2021" (Partij voor de Vrijheid), accessed June 20, 2018, www.pvv.nl/images/Conceptverkiezingsprogrammma.pdf.
3 Philippe Bénéton et al., "The Paris Statement," October 4, 2017, https://thetrueeurope.eu/a-europe-we-can-believe-in/.
4 Olivier Roy, "The (re)construction and Formatting of Religions in the West through Courts, Social Practices, Public Discourse and Transnational Institutions," *Research Project ReligioWest* (European University Institute, March 2016), www.iris-france.org/wp-content/uploads/2016/03/RW-rethinking-the-place-of-religion.pdf.
5 "Mass Migration Can Indeed Be Stopped," *Hungarian Prime Minister's Office*, March 1, 2016, www.kormany.hu/en/the-prime-minister/news/mass-migration-can-indeed-be-stopped.
6 Viktor Orbán, "Prime Minister Viktor Orbán's State of the Nation Address" (Budapest, February 28, 2016), www.kormany.hu/en/the-prime-minister/the-prime-minister-s-speeches/prime-minister-viktor-orban-s-state-of-the-nation-address.

7 Dzsihadfigyelo, trans., "The Full Text of Viktor Orbán's Speech," Translated Speech Transcript (Gates of Vienna, March 19, 2016), https://gatesofvienna.net/2016/03/the-full-text-of-viktor-orbans-speech/.

8 "Viktor Orban on Christian Europe," *Unam Sanctam Catholicam*, accessed June 20, 2018, www.unamsanctamcatholicam.com/social-teaching/moral-issues/93-social-teaching/moral-issues/354-viktor-orban-on-christian-europe.html.

9 Pawel Sobczak and Justyna Pawlak, "Divisive Kaczynski Shuns Limelight in Polish Election," *Reuters*, October 23, 2015, www.reuters.com/article/us-poland-election-kaczynski/divisive-kaczynski-shuns-limelight-in-polish-election-idUSKCN0SH20N20151023.

10 Jan Cienski, "Polish Conservative's PR Pushback," *Politico*, January 4, 2016, www.politico.eu/article/poland-nato-bases-germany-pis-waszczykowski-commission/.

11 "Poland's Prime Minister Gets the Chop."

12 Gregory Freeze, "The Russian Orthodox Church: Putin Ally or Independent Force?" *Religion & Politics*, October 10, 2017, http://religionandpolitics.org/2017/10/10/the-russian-orthodox-church-putin-ally-or-independent-force.

13 "Preamble to the Treaty of Lisbon" (European Union), accessed June 20, 2018, www.lisbon-treaty.org/wcm/the-lisbon-treaty/treaty-on-european-union-and-comments/preamble.html.

14 Pope Francis, "Message of His Holiness Pope Francis for the 104th World Day of Migrants and Refugees" (104th World Day of Migrants and Refugees, Vatican City, August 15, 2017), https://w2.vatican.va/content/francesco/en/messages/migration/documents/papa-francesco_20170815_world-migrants-day-2018.html.

15 Pope Francis, "Address of His Holiness Pope Francis to the Commission of the Bishops' Conferences of the European Community" ([Re]Thinking Europe – a Christian Contribution to the Future of the European Project, Vatican City, October 28, 2017), https://w2.vatican.va/content/francesco/en/speeches/2017/october/documents/papa-francesco_20171028_conferenza-comece.html.

8

THE DEMONIZATION OF GEORGE SOROS AND ITS REAL MEANING IN CENTRAL AND EASTERN EUROPE

Right-wing anti-Soros hysteria all over

George Soros is a Hungarian-born American multibillionaire hedge fund manager. He was born in a Jewish family in 1930, survived the Holocaust, and left Hungary for England after the communist takeover of Hungary in 1947. He became a student at the London School of Economics, where he was strongly influenced by the ideas of one of his professors, philosopher Karl Popper, who published his famous book *Open Society and its Enemies* in 1945.[1] This early impression not only influenced but virtually determined his entire life. In the US, where he moved in 1956 and established his hedge fund in 1970, he soon made a fortune. As a multibillionaire, he started his worldwide philanthropy in South Africa in 1979, where he assisted South African blacks during apartheid to enroll in universities in other countries. His actions gradually spread to over 100 countries (half of the countries in the world). In 1993, he devoted almost $20 billion, or nearly 80 percent of his wealth, to establishing the Open Society Fund, which supports liberal democratic programs all over the world. Altogether, in a quite unique way, he spent $32 billion on philanthropic causes. Soros belongs to the top 20 biggest donors, and his philanthropist activities are among the most successful in the world.

One of his first major actions targeted communist Eastern Europe by supporting dissidents; during the 1980s, he helped opposition movements in several communist countries from Hungary to China. In Budapest, Soros established the Central European University (CEU), the best school in the country, which offers free studies for young people from countries throughout the region. In 2012, President Bronislaw Komorowski of Poland bestowed one of the country's highest orders on George Soros for his contributions to building a democratic civil society after communism.

This philanthropic attitude—supporting certain programs, social and educational goals, and political trends—has been quite common among American millionaires for a century. Around the turn of the millennium, however, quite a number of them were financing conservative, sometimes extreme, right-wing programs and movements. Some of the most notorious examples include brothers Charles and David Koch, who have been major Republican donors for years, and the conservative hedge fund billionaire Robert Mercer, who donated to the pro-Trump Make America Number One political action committee (super PAC). Sheldon Adelson, the billionaire casino mogul, donated to Newt Gingrich's failed presidential campaign, gave $10 million to the super PAC supporting Mitt Romney's senate race, and partly financed the building of the new American Embassy in Jerusalem in 2018.

While most super-rich Americans are conservative, Soros supports liberal causes globally and domestically. For example, he recently donated to the "Black Lives Matter" movement in the US. Consequently, he often became a target for right-wing American politicians and media. In 2017, Fox News host Bill O'Reilly labeled him "off-the-charts dangerous" and "an extremist who wants open borders, a one-world foreign policy, legalized drugs and euthanasia."[2] Glenn Beck, another former Fox News host and ultra-right radio host, called him "a puppet master"[3] who holds the strings of the world in his hands. In 2016, the right-wing media platform Infowars launched a video attack against him entitled "George Soros is about to overthrow the US."[4] Roy Moore, a far-right Republican Senate candidate in 2017, attacked him as an immigrant who does not understand American values. The extreme-right news outlet Breitbart called Soros "an octopus," using a favorite Nazi metaphor from the 1930s and 1940s that refers to Jews' supposed tentacle control of the world.[5] In the sharp debates after the Brexit referendum, how to leave the European Union (EU) in 2018, English Brexiters acridly pointed out that Soros had supported the "Stay" campaign to keep Britain in the EU. In other words, George Soros has been a favorite target for anti-liberal, anti-EU forces for quite a while.

However, the most extreme anti-Soros hysteria during the 2010s emerged and was fueled by right-wing populists in Central and Eastern Europe. Although this regional trend shares similarities with Western anti-Soros finger-pointing, it has characteristics and meanings unique to that area. Unlike the sporadic, if virulent, Western anti-Soros demagoguery, governments in Central and Eastern Europe made anti-Soros rhetoric part of their official state policies, with serious consequences for civil society organizations.

Putin's Russia gave the signal

In building his autocratic regime, Vladimir Putin openly and consistently destroyed his opponents including politicians, journalists, and rich oligarchs who turned against him. They were shot at in the streets, imprisoned, or pushed out of the country. He also destroyed nongovernmental civil organizations (NGOs) that supported liberal values and defended human rights. Putin signed the first laws against them in 2012, and Russia closed all of its Soros-financed NGOs in 2015–16.

The official Russian statement explicitly mentioned the "anti-government activity" of George Soros. Tellingly, an important portion of this statement included a list of blacklisted NGOs and strongly recommended that other Central European countries follow Russia's measures: as a Russian news outlet summarized, "This list [of NGO organizations] will be interesting for the East European and Balkan countries as well; banning the faked civil organizations under Western control and the groups that collaborate them is highly recommended for the East European countries."[6]

As László Valki showed in his aforementioned study, Viktor Orbán's government in Hungary—the number one opponent against George Soros—followed in the footsteps of Orbán's political ally Putin after a short delay. Hungary began its most vicious anti-Soros campaign in 2015 and decided to close all Soros organizations in Hungary in 2017–18. During these events, Russian foreign language propaganda broadcasting strongly supported Orbán. The Russian media website Sputnik News published an article supporting the Orbán parliament's actions against the Soros-founded CEU in Budapest. Russia Today, Russia's official TV program abroad, voiced its support for Orbán early on: on November 4, 2015, collaborator Paul Craig Roberts stated that Soros is a "threat to the existence of European peoples because they become dissolved in a so-called diverse society of different people, different religions, different cultures, different values. ... The Hungarian prime minister is the only one that has any sense."[7]

"Let's not leave Soros the last laugh"

Viktor Orbán, Hungary's populist-authoritarian prime minister—who as a young opposition politician himself received a grant from the Soros Foundation to go to Oxford University after the collapse of communism—initiated a passionate attack against George Soros, accusing him of trying to undermine Hungary and blaming him for the immigration crisis in Europe. His government planned to close the Soros Foundation and even the Soros-founded CEU in Budapest. Huge billboards and posters flooded the country, featuring a photograph of a smiling Soros and the text "Let's not leave Soros the last laugh." These posters were also put on the stairs of Budapest trams, forcing people taking the tram to step on Soros's picture.

Orbán stated in his speech at the EU Parliament,

> Our position is clear: we do not want, and do not think it is in accordance with the founding treaties of the Union, to settle migrants in our country in a mandatory way. The decision on who we live with can only be made by the Hungarian citizens. It is important information that George Soros and his NOGs [sic.] want to transport one million migrants to the EU per year ... and [he] provides a financial loan for it.[8]

In another speech on March 15, 2015, Orbán launched a vicious attack against the EU:

> We know how [it works]. If we allow first that they tell us who to accept, they will then force us to serve foreigners in our own country, and at the end they will push us out [of] our own country.[9]

In a statement representing Hungary's anti-Soros campaign as an action protecting citizens, the foreign ministry stated that Hungary "takes steps against anyone who represents a risk to the national security of the country and its citizens."[10] One of the central refrains of Orbán's *Fiatal Demokraták Szövetsége* (FIDESz) Party's election campaign in 2017–18 was a continued hysterical attack on Soros that positioned him as an enemy of the Hungarian people who wants the Islamization of Europe. The prime minister sent signed letters to families explaining the "Stop Soros" imperative. Orbán posed as Hungary and Europe's savior from Islamization, using traditional nationalist slogans, especially those often used in interwar Hungary. He stated that "dark clouds are gathering" again and that his country was a "last bastion" in the fight against the "Islamization" of Europe.[11]

The Hungarian government not only used this propaganda campaign but also arranged a "national consultation," or a referendum-like vote that 2.3 million citizens participated in, on their anti-Soros measures.[12] They afterward declared that this referendum amounted to a "national authorization" for a new harsh law against NGOs. The government presented "Stop Soros" legislation to the Hungarian Parliament in early 2018, which recommended the old requirement that all NGOs register with the Ministry of the Interior be replaced by an authorization for activity.[13] The new law criminalizes civil organizations who "support" immigration and introduces a 25 percent fee for NGOs with foreign financing.[14] The government-controlled media welcomed the law as a defense of the Hungarian nation's future. The still-existent opposition media criticized the new law as an existential danger for civil organizations and for society more broadly.

On April 4, 2017, the Hungarian Parliament adopted amendments to the country's 2011 Act CCIV on National Higher Education, in an attempt to force the CEU—which was established in 1991 by George Soros—out of the country. The effects would be dire because, as one report summarizes,

> Today close to 450 professors from some 50 countries teach 1,800 students from 120 countries at CEU. It is considered to be one of the most prestigious universities in Central and Eastern Europe for 25 years now. It has a high academic reputation, ranking 39th among the best young universities (below 50 years of age) worldwide, and 16th among emerging economies' university rankings, according to Times Higher Education.[15]

In his April 2017 ministerial exposé of the Hungarian Parliament's introduction of the amendment to the 2011 law, Zoltán Balog explicitly copied Russia's anti-Soros argument, saying, "The faked civil organizations of George Soros in Hungary and the world are spy organizations and we are determined to stop their activity." The new law was accepted by the Hungarian Parliament.[16] Having won the election in April 2018, Orbán forcefully continues his anti-Soros campaign. The Open Society Foundation left Hungary and moved to Berlin in the summer of 2018. The CEU already rented a campus in Vienna, but the international resistance against the action, including from the US, led only to some postponement of kicking out the CEU from Hungary; in the end, it happened in 2018.

Global media outlets reported that the Hungarian Parliament passed the "Stop Soros" law on June 21, 2018 (ironically, June 21 is also World Refugee Day). As the title of a *New York Times* article stated, the law "mak[es] it a crime to give aid to migrants." As the report summarizes, "Under the terms of the new law, helping migrants legalize their status in Hungary by distributing information about the asylum process or providing them with financial assistance could result in 12-month jail term."[17]

What other kinds of aid or assistance for migrants were criminalized? The text of the law is surprising:

> Any kind of program, action and activities that directly or indirectly help immigration to the country, including media campaigns, media seminars and the participation in those programs, any kind of propaganda activities that presents immigration as a positive phenomenon, any kind of operations, network activities that helps immigrants. The authorities are responsible to decide what kinds of activities belong to these categories.[18]

In addition, the government is already preparing a new amendment to the constitution (which has already been amended several times). According to the prepared text of the amendment, the EU directive to

> settle foreign population[s] in Hungary [is] a rebuke attempt by the EU to encourage Hungary to admit small numbers of refugees who had been living in other European countries. ... No one can settle in Hungary and [be] eligible to get asylum who arrives through countries where immediate danger for persecution does not exist.

(Note the smart wording: there is no danger of persecution in any of Hungary's neighboring countries; thus, no migrants are eligible for asylum in Hungary.) "Unlike liberal politics," the government stated, "Christian politics [are] able to protect people, our nation, families, our culture rooted in Christianity ... our European way of life." According to these constitutional changes "the freedom of speech and gathering must not disturb others' home, private, and family life that is defended by the state." The proposed amendment means that the government has the right to limit or ban demonstrations that "disturb" peoples' homes.[19]

Anti-Soros mania in Eastern Europe

Besides the right-wing Hungarian government, several other countries in the region also followed Russia's initiative. A vicious demonization campaign has swept across Central Europe. Liviu Dragnea, the chairman of the Romanian Social Democratic Party, has said that Soros "fed evil in Romania."[20] Krystyna Pawlowicz, a Polish parliamentarian who is close to Kaczyński, stated that Soros is "the most dangerous man in the world" and characterized him as a "supra-national lefty troublemaker" who is "openly and brazenly financing the anti-democratic and anti-Polish element with a view to fight Polish sovereignty and indigenous Christian culture." She talked about the covert, revolutionary activities of the global speculator, whose foundations "finance anti-Christian and anti-national activities." According to her, George Soros is promoting the "unconstitutional and immoral derailment of the society" and is responsible for the "financing of any initiatives directed against the current democratically elected Polish authorities."[21]

Even in the remote small Balkan country of Macedonia, right-wing politicians accused Soros of being behind an illegal wiretapping operation of top leaders that caused the fall of the government and a political crisis. They established the "Stop Operation Soros," or SOS.[22] In Bulgaria, some newspapers described George Soros as a "liberal terrorist."[23] In Serbia, local right-wing and pro-Russian publications have linked Soros to the Rothschilds, thus highlighting his Jewishness.[24]

Sometimes these campaigns were connected to American extremist rhetoric about supposed attacks against America, which propagated false, nonsensical accusations such as:

> George Soros is using his billions of dollars to prop up leftist groups across the globe. The real mystery is why American taxpayers are being forced to fund his schemes. ... The Obama administration helped use American tax dollars to support Soros's cronies. Millions of dollars were funneled through Soros's Open Society Foundation to help support left-wing organizations from 2012 to 2016.[25]

Soros's view on immigration in Europe

These propagandistic comments and accusations speak for themselves. But is there any truth to the accusation that Soros wants to "Islamize Europe" by settling one million immigrants in Europe every year, as Viktor Orbán said? In various essays and speeches, including one in the EU Parliament, George Soros indeed discussed the migration crisis and supported the acceptance of migrants in an organized way. As is well known, because Europe's population is shrinking and aging, he argued that Europe needs immigrants to keep its economy running. However, he also opposed compulsory quotas for member countries to settle immigrants and urged a system of voluntary cooperation where participating countries are well compensated.

Let me quote some parts of Soros's argumentation by way of answering these accusations against him: "First, the EU and the rest of the world must take in a substantial number of refugees directly from front-line countries in a secure and orderly manner, which would be far more acceptable to the public than the current disorder.... The EU [should] make a commitment to admit even just 300,000 refugees each year, and that commitment [should be] matched by countries elsewhere in the world.... The EU must regain control of its borders. There is little that alienates and scares publics more than scenes of chaos. ... At least 30 billion euros a year will be needed for the EU to carry out a comprehensive asylum plan. ... Once refugees have been recognized, there needs to be a mechanism for relocating them within Europe in an agreed way. It will be crucial for the EU to fundamentally rethink the implementation of its stillborn resettlement and relocation programs.... The union cannot coerce either member states or refugees to participate in these programs. They must be voluntary. ... The European Union, together with the international community, must support foreign refugee-hosting countries far more generously than it currently does. ... A sudden influx of more than a million asylum-seekers overwhelmed the capacity of the authorities, turning public opinion against migrants. Now the EU urgently needs to limit the overall inflow of newcomers, and it can do so only by discriminating against economic migrants."[26]

No doubt, the wild and vicious accusations that Soros is responsible for the migration crisis and is conspiring to undermine Hungary, other countries, or Europe as a whole is an enormous set of falsehoods. Soros does not "want" to settle one million immigrants per year in Europe; indeed, he opposes instituting a compulsory quota to distribute them among member countries. His view and suggestions about the need for immigrants in Europe are at least partly debatable. Because Europe's population is shrinking and aging, the Continent definitely needs an additional young labor force. From the late 1950s onwards, several West European countries have attracted immigrants to work. They already represent 15 percent (in Switzerland, 25 percent) of the labor force in several countries.

The solution, however, might not be mass immigration. Limited, selected immigration and an institutionalized guest worker program offer a better solution. The latter is already working in Switzerland and in the Arab world. Debates, of course, are not only possible but necessary. But rigorous debate is definitely not the motivating reason behind the vicious attacks against Soros.

The "Secret Message" of anti-Soros hysteria

Why did Viktor Orbán and several other populist politicians and movements from Central European and the Balkans viciously turn against Soros? What was behind these passionate attacks? First of all, the situation offered an excellent excuse for stopping the activities of NGOs, which advocate for liberal human rights issues and are thus in opposition to authoritarian, anti-democratic politics. It offered the opportunity to denounce them as foreign agents working against these nations. What was equally, or in some cases even more important, these attacks occurred because (as mentioned earlier) George Soros was born a Hungarian Jew who moved to the US, became a bold speculator genius, and elevated to join a group of super-rich multibillionaires. His biography fits the traditional ant-Semitic and nativist anti-American stereotypes propagated by right-wing European regimes.

As a top philanthropist who helped build open democratic societies, Soros became a target for the right, but especially for right-wing nationalist xenophobes in Central and Eastern Europe. During the years of the Great Recession in the 2010s, right-wing populist governments from Hungary to Poland launched an offensive against NGOs, which promote liberal values and thus had helped the liberal opposition to authoritarian governments. They wanted to create a scapegoat responsible for the problems that the countries were facing, and George Soros offered an excellent, well-known target for them. "You couldn't come up with a better enemy figure today," said Jan Orlovsky, director of the Slovak branch of the Open Society Foundation. "George Soros brings up all of the stereotypes we have lived with all our lives — about Jews, bankers and, in Slovakia, also about Hungarians." Rafal Pankowski, the head of an anti-racism organization in Warsaw, says the "current tendency to see Soros as a central figure in an alleged global Jewish conspiracy" is growing along with a rise in xenophobia. "Because he promotes liberal values, has a Jewish background and is a billionaire, he is the perfect figure for explaining to hard-core voters why the world is the way it is."[27]

The anti-Soros hysteria in Central and Eastern Europe is a well-considered political propaganda campaign that mobilizes the traditionally significant xenophobic and anti-Semitic layers of the population, the real base of the nationalist-populist right-wing parties in the region. This type of campaign has been especially profitable before parliamentary elections, helping right-wing politicians to gain or remain in power. Indeed, some Soros billboards in Hungary have been defaced with graffiti that reads "stinking Jew."[28] In the summer of 2017, an Israeli newspaper reported that "Israel envoy urges Hungary to halt anti-Soros campaign."[29] The Hungarian Jewish Federation (*Mazsihisz*) has also urged Orbán to halt the campaign. "This campaign, while not openly anti-Semitic, clearly has the potential to ignite uncontrolled emotions, including anti-Semitism," they said. In a reply to Mazsihisz, Orbán said that it was "his duty to protect Hungarians—including the country's 100,000-strong Jewish community—from illegal migration." Oddly, before Israeli Prime Minister Benjamin Netanyahu's official visit to Hungary (as Reuters reported), "Israel's foreign ministry … issued a statement denouncing US billionaire George Soros, a move that appeared designed to align Israel more closely with Hungary" and, of course, against Soros, who has often criticized Netanyahu's actions against the Palestinians.[30]

The calculated anti-Soros hysteria in Central and Eastern Europe—with its coded anti-Semitic, anti-American, anti-capitalist secret messages—serve right-wing nationalist-populist interests in that region excellently.

Notes

1 Karl Popper, *Open Society and its Enemies*, Vol I and II (London: Routledge, 1945).
2 Veronika Bondarenko, "George Soros Is a Favorite Target of the Right — Here's How That Happened," *Business Insider*, May 20, 2017, www.businessinsider.com/how-did-george-soros-become-the-favorite-boogeyman-of-the-right-2017-5.
3 "Glenn Beck Explains George Soros Conspiracy Theory On 'O'Reilly Factor'," *Huffington Post*, November 13, 2010, sec. Media, www.huffingtonpost.com/2010/11/13/glenn-beck-george-soros-bill-oreilly-_n_783174.html.
4 George Soros Is about to Overthrow the U.S. (Infowars, 2016), www.infowars.com/george-soros-is-about-to-overthrow-the-u-s/.
5 Bondarenko, "George Soros Is a Favorite Target of the Right — Here's How That Happened."
6 "Nemkívánatossá nyilvánítják Soros György alkalmazottait," *Hídfő*, May 24, 2015, www.hidfo.ru/2015/05/nemkivanatossa-nyilvanitjak-soros-gyorgy-alkalmazottait/.
   László Valki, "Lex CEU – a felsőoktatási törvény módosítása," in *Jogtörténeti Parerga II. Ünnepi tanulmányok Mezey Barna 65. születésnapja tiszteletére*, eds. Gosztonyi Gergely and Révész T. Mihály (Budapest: Eötvös Kiadó, 2018), 271–282.
7 "Soros's 'European Values' Mean Losing Your National Identity – Paul Craig Roberts," *RT International*, November 4, 2015, www.rt.com/op-ed/320747-soros-european-values-orban/.
8 Viktor Orbán, "Prime Minister Viktor Orbán's Speech in the European Parliament" (Political Speech, April 26, 2017), www.miniszterelnok.hu/prime-minister-viktor-orbans-speech-in-the-european-parliament/.
9 Viktor Orbán, "A Szabadság és a Függetlenség Történelmünk Vezércsillaga" (Political Speech, March 15, 2015), www.kormany.hu/hu/a-miniszterelnok/beszedek-publikaciok-interjuk/a-szabadsag-es-a-fuggetlenseg-tortenelmunk-vezercsillaga.
10 AFP, "Israel Envoy Urges Hungary to Halt Anti-Soros Campaign," *The Times of Israel*, July 8, 2017, www.timesofisrael.com/israel-envoy-urges-hungary-to-halt-anti-soros-campaign/.
11 Daniel Boffey, "Orbán Claims Hungary Is Last Bastion against 'Islamisation' of Europe," *The Guardian*, February 18, 2018, sec. World news, www.theguardian.com/world/2018/feb/18/orban-claims-hungary-is-last-bastion-against-islamisation-of-europe.
12 Gábor Baranyai, "Már a Parlament Előtt a Szigorított Stop Soros," *Magyar Idők*, February 14, 2018, https://magyaridok.hu/belfold/mar-parlament-elott-szigoritott-stop-soros-2796696/.
13 MH/MTI, "Megvitatták a Stop Soros-Törvénycsomagot," *Magyar Hírlap*, February 20, 2018, http://magyarhirlap.hu/cikk/111302/Megvitattak_a_Stop_Sorostorveny csomagot.
14 "Amnesty: 'A Stop Soros-Csomag a Létezésünket Fenyegeti,'" *Magyar Narancs*, February 14, 2018, http://magyarnarancs.hu/belpol/amnesty-a-stop-soros-csomag-a-letezesunket-fenyegeti-109329.
15 Petra Bárd, "The Open Society and Its Enemies: An Attack against CEU, Academic Freedom and the Rule of Law," *CEPS Policy Insights*, no. 14 (April 2017), www.ceps.eu/publications/open-society-and-its-enemies-attack-against-ceu-academic-freedom-and-rule-law.
16 Valki, "Lex CEU – a felsőoktatási törvény módosítása."
17 Patrick Kingsley, "Hungary Passes 'Stop Soros' Law, Making It a Crime to Give Aid to Migrants," *The New York Times*, June 20, 2018, Print edition, sec. World, www.nytimes.com/2018/06/20/world/europe/hungary-stop-soros-law.html.

18 András Jambor, "Lényegében Véleményadót Vet Ki a Fidesz a Másként Gondolkodókra," *Mérce*, June 20, 2018, https://merce.hu/2018/06/20/lenyegeben-velemenyadot-vet-ki-a-fidesz-a-maskent-gondolkodokra/.

19 D. Ildikó Kovács, "Megszavazták Az Alaptörvény Hetedik Módosítását," *24.hu*, June 20, 2018, https://24.hu/kozelet/2018/06/20/alaptorveny-hetedik-modositas/.

20 Vanessa Gera, "Demonization of Soros Recalls Old Anti-Semitic Conspiracies," *The Times of Israel*, May 16, 2017, www.timesofisrael.com/demonization-of-soros-recalls-old-anti-semitic-conspiracies/.

21 Przemek Skwirczynski, "Polish MP Demands 'Pest' Soros Is Stripped of Country's Highest Honour," *Breitbart*, September 21, 2016, www.breitbart.com/london/2016/09/21/polish-mp-demands-pest-soros-is-stripped-of-countrys-highest-honour/.

22 Jamie White, "'Stop Soros' Movement Sweeps Europe," *Infowars* (blog), January 26, 2017, www.infowars.com/stop-soros-movement-sweeps-europe/.

23 Rick Lyman, "After Trump Win, Anti-Soros Forces Are Emboldened in Eastern Europe," *The New York Times*, December 22, 2017, sec. World, www.nytimes.com/2017/03/01/world/europe/after-trump-win-anti-soros-forces-are-emboldened-in-eastern-europe.html.

24 Lianne Kolirin, "Anti-Soros Campaign across Europe Is Drenched in Antisemitism," *The Jewish Chronicle*, accessed July 8, 2018, www.thejc.com/news/world/anti-soros-campaign-across-europe-is-drenched-in-antisemitism-1.438614.

25 "Help Expose George Soros!" *Judicial Watch*, accessed July 8, 2018, www.judicialwatch.org/blog/poll/expose-soros/.

26 George Soros, "This Is Europe's Last Chance to Fix Its Refugee Policy," *Foreign Policy*, sec. Argument, accessed July 16, 2018, https://foreignpolicy.com/2016/07/19/this-is-europes-last-chance-to-fix-its-refugee-policy-george-soros/.

27 Lyman, "After Trump Win, Anti-Soros Forces Are Emboldened in Eastern Europe."

28 Krisztina Than, "Hungary's Anti-Soros Posters Recall 'Europe's Darkest Hours'…," *Reuters*, July 11, 2017, www.reuters.com/article/us-hungary-soros/hungarys-anti-soros-posters-recall-europes-darkest-hours-soros-spokesman-idUSKBN19W0XU.

29 AFP, "Israel Envoy Urges Hungary to Halt Anti-Soros Campaign."

30 Than, "Hungary's Anti-Soros Posters Recall 'Europe's Darkest Hours'."

9

IS THE EUROPEAN UNION A NEOLIBERAL CONSTRUCTION THAT DESERVES TO BE DESTROYED? A DEBATE WITH LEFT-WING ATTACKS

Does attacking the EU equate to anti-neoliberalism?

Another element of the European Union's (EU's) profound and complex crisis is that, in addition to being the enemy and target of right-wing populism, it is also attacked from the left. In the March 2017 issue of *Le Monde diplomatique*, the preeminent historian and essayist Perry Anderson joined the fray. His point of departure is that the antiestablishment revolts in Europe and the US target neoliberalism, which has been adopted by both center-right and center-left political parties since the 1980s.

This alignment with neoliberalism, Anderson maintains, is at the center of the revolt against the EU. When the EU was established in the 1950s and 1960s, it did not harm the nation-states, as French politician Phillipe Herzog put it. From the 1980s onward, however, the EU veered sharply toward supranationalization and neoliberalism. As Anderson concludes,

> The EU is now so path-dependent as a neoliberal construction that reform of it is no longer seriously conceivable. It would have to be undone before anything better could be built, either by breaking out of the current EU, or by reconstructing Europe on another foundation, committing Maastricht to the flames.[1]

The idea that the EU is a "neoliberal construction" is wrong. The term "United States of Europe" as an ideal future outcome for the continent first appeared in a letter written by the first president of the US, George Washington; it was subsequently repeated by the famous French writer Victor Hugo in the late nineteenth century and was advocated for by Winston Churchill in the 1940s. The founding treaty of the European Economic Community, the 1957 Treaty of Rome, clearly stated that the goal was an "ever-closer union"[2]—that is, a federal Europe. This happened long before the neoliberal turn and was certainly not a neoliberal idea. Rather, it was a response to historical development trends, most of all the lessons of the war (including the fragility of national sovereignty), and the emerging Cold War confrontation that threatened an even more devastating war.

True, the EU's founding fathers recognized that the process must be a gradual one, beginning with economic integration. The process turned out to be longer than anticipated because of two decades of near stagnation beginning in the mid-1960s. President Charles de Gaulle of France halted progress by opposing any additional steps toward supranationalization and insisting on maintaining veto rights for each member country, in defense of the nation-state. As the French Fouchet Plan (1960) detailed, de Gaulle wanted a "Europe of the nations" (*une Europe des États*): full national independence and intergovernmental cooperation on economic and foreign policy issues.

It is also true that large European corporations pushed for a stronger Union beginning in the mid-1980s, and that the leading "troika"—Jacques Delors (President of the Commission), President François Mitterrand of France, and Chancellor Helmut Kohl of Germany—supported them. The EU was able to create the Single Market and soon followed that accomplishment by establishing a common currency. These steps were indeed connected to expanding globalization and the predominance of American and Japanese multinational (especially high tech and semi-high tech) companies in the world market, including a huge part of the European market. In addition to cutthroat American competition, the "Four Asian Tigers" (Hong Kong, Singapore, South Korea, and Taiwan) also flooded the market with cheap consumer goods. This dangerous globalization rivalry was dramatically described by the French writer and journalist Jean-Jacques Servan-Schreiber in his *Le Défi Américain* (The American Challenge) in 1967. He described how competitors occupied a huge slice of the European market and threatened to undermine Europe's international status. This was a kind of wake-up call.

Globalization or regionalization?

Europe, indeed, began to defend itself, regaining its competitiveness and international stature. It did so through regionalization, creating a strong modern economy and a thoroughly integrated, centralized European market with a streamlined legal and regulatory system overseeing intra-European banks and corporations holding "European" passports. All of this purposely assured a free flow of goods, capital, and labor throughout a borderless EU. It was not a neoliberal attempt at globalization *à la* Friedrich von Hayek (as Perry Anderson has suggested), but rather the creation of a protected European region. Regionalization is in some ways a part of, or at least a contemporary of, globalization, but it is also a *safeguard* against it.

Thanks to the creation of the Single Market, European multinational corporations have largely pulled their business out of the global market. The Dutch-British Unilever, one of the very first multinational companies in the world, sold more than 70 of its factories and subsidiaries outside of Europe and turned toward the European market. After Brexit, the company is planning to close its London headquarters and move entirely to Rotterdam. Germany has drastically decreased its investments outside of Europe (from 40 to 17 percent) and redirected them to other European countries.

One must not confuse globalization and regionalization. Let me quote a few authors on the differences. "One motive for the formation of regional economic blocs," one interpretation explains,

> is that these help states to resist pressure from intensified global competition. These blocs therefore function as customs unions, 'fortresses' against the pressures from the wider global economy. In an increasingly interdependent global economy, states seek prosperity through the establishment of free trade areas that give them access to larger markets and facilitate economic specialization.[3]

According to Björn Hettne, "Regionalism is thus one way of coping with global transformation, since most states lack the capacity and the means to manage such a task on the 'national' level." He also adds:

> This process is similar to state formation and nation building, and the ultimate outcome could be a 'region-state', which in terms of scope can be compared to the classical empires, but in terms of political order constitutes a voluntary evolution of a group of formerly sovereign national, political units into a supranational security community, where sovereignty is pooled for the best of all.[4]

Bennett Collins maintains that

> New regionalism ... has taken shape out of the multi-polar world order and is a more spontaneous process from within the regions, where constituent states now experience the need for cooperation in order to tackle new global challenges. New regionalism is a more comprehensive and multidimensional process which not only includes trade and economic development but also environmental, social, and security issues.[5]

As the title of his study suggests, Grahame Thompson also confronts the question of "globalization versus regionalism." He explains that

> Regionalisation signifies a process that draws states and groups together on the basis of their proximity, perhaps because of economic advantages such as transport and information cost economies, or perhaps because

security or environmental issues can have a region-wide impact. In addition there is a possibly more pronounced *institutional* integration process that often accompanies such regionalisation which attempts to manage and regulate these local integrative processes, which can be termed regionalism.[6]

End of globalization? The increasing importance of regionalization

The argument against the EU on the basis of neoliberal globalization began to lose its strength in the early twenty-first century. Today globalization continues to decrease while regionalization has rapidly gained importance. The notion of the "end of globalization" has generated increased interest and is still gaining prominence. Globalization is "ending" partly because the political will and international alliances behind it have weakened significantly. America, formerly the main globalizer, is retreating; now, in 2018, an unpredictable tariff war is starting between the three major economic giants: the US and China, and the US and the EU.

Most importantly, globalization is losing its importance because of the ongoing technological revolution's effects. The impressive development of automation; robotization; software-driven technologies; applications of artificial intelligence; and the so-called additive manufacturing, or 3-D printing, that is able to produce multiple designs by the same machine radically changed the advantage of global value chains, which relied on cheap labor in less-developed countries and produced hundreds of products in hundreds of countries. (The Boeing 787 is produced in nine countries; a Honda Accord in two dozen countries. China, one major home of labor-intensive assembly engineering, is producing end products, such as smartphones, out of parts imported from Japan, the US, and several other countries.)

This technological revolution made cheap labor and labor-intensive assembly engineering in cheap-labor countries less important for advanced countries. Much less labor-intensive procedures are needed because they are being replaced by robots and automation. Consequently, the value chains are significantly shortening. This new development meaningfully increases the importance of regionalization, as a few countries allied together with a well-developed division of labor, such as the original North American Free Trade Agreement (NAFTA) or the EU, have the potential to become virtually self-sufficient.[7]

To sum up, the EU is not the product of neoliberal globalization but a defense against it in the form of regionalization from the 1980s. Regionalization became even more important in the early twenty-first century when globalization began losing ground. Regionalization is the best defense for small groups of cooperating neighboring countries in this new era of strengthening international competition and confrontation.

Austerity policy as exploitation of peripheral countries?

From Perry Anderson's perspective, the EU's "neoliberal construction" and bureaucratic machinery assure that "draconian austerity could be imposed on a helpless electorate, under the joint direction of the Commission and a reunited Germany." In an integrated neoliberal Europe, austerity; oligarchy; and the free movement of goods, capital, and labor "form an interconnected system" that precludes "popular sovereignty." Moreover, the EU's "bureaucratic authority" shields the EU from the people's will.[8] This is a theory of a neoliberal conspiracy. From this viewpoint, the EU has served oligarchs' interests by imposing policies that hurt poor peripheral countries and the proletariat of Europe's deindustrialized regions.

Why is this criticism unfounded? For one, there is a somewhat baffling disregard for the problems created by the ongoing technology revolution. Perry Anderson refers to populist antiestablishment and anti-EU critiques in his essay, but he fails to even mention the new technological revolution that is the main cause of deindustrialization, rather than neoliberalism. The technology revolution has led to the eradication of old-style mining and industrial jobs, while it has increased industrial and energy output. New partly reproducible energy sources and the robotization of several branches of industry have indeed destroyed millions of jobs. Various applications of artificial intelligence continue this process, further destroying jobs. They cannot be brought back with economic nationalism, tariffs, and restrictions of the free flow of goods and capital. This structural unemployment must be counterbalanced not with tariffs but with education and retraining (lifelong learning) to empower people to assume new, more intellectually demanding jobs. A revolt against technological revolutions has already happened in history. During the first British Industrial Revolution, the old handworkers, or Luddites, destroyed new machinery to get their jobs back. The Luddites at least understood that their "enemy" was new technology. Their revolt was no less hopeless than the populist one going on today.

Equally problematic is Anderson's criticism of the so-called EU "machinery" under the sway of the Commission and Germany, which supposedly imposes this neoliberal policy. There is a whole literature of criticism against the purported "democratic deficit" of the EU. But, as is well known, the Commission is not the decision-making body of the EU. Decisions are made by the Council of Europe, an intergovernmental body composed of government representatives from member countries. Their decisions are often subject to the approval of the European Council, where the heads of state and governments of member countries deliberate. For quite a while, the freely elected European Parliament has also served as a co-decision-making body. This is by far not a perfect institutional system and is certainly not the most representative, but it is not one that damages national sovereignty or shields the EU from popular sentiment.

Third, it is simply not true that the EU, when its "machinery was in place," imposed heartless austerity measures on poor peripheral countries such as Greece. The incident in question happened after the 2008 economic crisis, which unveiled the reckless spending and endemic tax evasion in some peripheral EU countries. Greece offers an extreme example. Alone in Europe, the country had three insolvencies between 2009 and 2015. It became the very first "advanced" country that joined Zimbabwe, Tunisia, and Somalia in being unable to repay an International Monetary Fund (IMF) loan. This was not very new. Greece was financially bankrupt around the time of the country's independence in 1830 and repeated this crisis four times during the nineteenth century.

Before the crisis, Greece lowered the retirement age to 58 for public employees and 45 for certain occupations; pensions amounted to 80 percent of the previous wages (compared to 46 percent in Germany). The country organized the 2004 Olympic Games with an original budget of €2.5 billion, but in the end spent nearly four times more (€10 billion), partly because they started the work much later than originally planned and had to work day and night. The money came partly from loans and was invested in areas that did not pay back. In terms of corruption, Greece ranks 80th among 185 countries; this level of corruption aligns the country with non-European nations that suffer from endemic corruption. As the deputy-head of Greece's tax collecting office acknowledged, "If tax collection worked, there would be no debt problem." Both households and (in some countries) governments of formerly poor, now *nouveau-riche* peripheral countries, flooded with cheap EU credit, have spent far beyond their means. Greeks have attained a much higher level of home ownership (80 percent) than affluent Switzerland, Germany (at hardly more than 50 percent), or the US (67 percent). Based on its (GDP), Greece has spent four times more for armaments (6–7 percent) than Germany has (less than 2 percent). The country joined the eurozone without fulfilling the strict prerequisite of having its financial household in order. Their banks and state institutions fell into bankruptcy.

Austerity measures that insisted on reduced spending fostered the creation of solid financial households in countries that used the common currency. Those measures were necessary for avoiding the collapse of the euro. Besides, there was also a kind of educational motivation to get eurozone member countries to adopt more reasonable fiscal policies. In fact, this policy, though arduous, was badly needed in these countries and worked in Ireland, Spain, and Portugal. Today, however, a decade on, these measures have become overly controversial and counterproductive, and definitely should be replaced or at least combined with stimulus measures. But presenting the austerity policy as ruthless neoliberal exploitation is more than one-sided. It is simply not borne out by the facts.

Serving the oligarchs?

The same can be said about the claim that the EU serves oligarchs' interests. The free flow of goods, capital, and labor within the EU has in fact benefited the largest part of the population by creating high prosperity, rapid growth, and higher living standards prior to the 2008 crisis. Welfare institutions are working; health care and education are free or inexpensive. Consumption has dramatically increased because spending on basics has dropped from 60 to 15 percent for the first time in half a century, with car and home ownership becoming ubiquitous even in the previously poor Mediterranean region. Income equality, although deteriorated, is still the most uniform and relatively balanced in the world. Inequality is much lower than in nonmember European countries outside the EU, for example, in Russia, or the US, let alone in Latin America and the Third World. The EU is not a typical neoliberal regime.

Furthermore, the EU has quite uniquely provided massive assistance to people in need. During the worst part of the economic crisis between 2007 and 2013, the EU reached over 50 million people via its Social Fund. In 2011 alone, it directly impacted the lives of 4.5 million unemployed and 5 million inactive people. It did so by providing €75 billion to help people fulfill their potential by giving them better skills and better job prospects.[9] EU assistance also supported the most backward regions of its member countries. A number of admitted Mediterranean and particularly Central and East European countries, which have been categorized as backward regions (below 75 percent of the average per capita GDP of the EU), have received huge amounts of aid. The former communist member countries of Central and Eastern Europe have been earmarked for one-and-a-half times more aid from the EU up through 2020 than what the 16 European countries got from the Marshall Plan over a four-year period. This definitely contributed to a spectacular catching-up process in Ireland and Spain, countries whose GDPs at the time of their entering the Union were only 55–60 percent of the GDPs of West European core countries. Today, Ireland is one of the richest countries in Europe, surpassing Britain, France, and Germany. Spain is now virtually on par with the average EU levels. Even the East European EU members have seen their per capita GDPs rise—all thanks to their Union membership; generous EU aid packages; and the free flow of goods, capital, and labor. Evaluating the EU must consider all aspects of Union membership. Strangely enough, Perry Anderson completely ignores Central and Eastern Europe in his analysis. Their case could prove the opposite of what Anderson maintains. Five of the countries in that region—Lithuania, Estonia, Romania, Latvia, and Slovakia—registered the best performance, gaining between 30 and 40 percent in one-and-a-half decades, compared to their relative position vis-à-vis the EU average in 2000. While overall income convergence has taken place over the last 15 years at both regional and country levels (in terms of higher growth in the poorest countries, as well as reduced differences in GDP per capita), detailed data suggest that the Central and Eastern European countries lead the convergence process.[10] Besides, the EU is responsible for giving the largest share of worldwide development and humanitarian aid, 56 percent; the aid given by the US and Japan together only amounts to 31 percent of the total.

The straitjacket of euro and national sovereignty

Perry Anderson's less important but more surprising criticism of the EU is that although it did not originally jeopardize national sovereignty, it most certainly did after its "neoliberal turn" and its introduction of the "straitjacket of the euro."[11] Anderson, in this area, shares Charles de Gaulle and Margaret Thatcher's national ideas. Smaller countries, of course, have long realized that their national sovereignty was more fiction than reality, especially during the 400 years that pre-EU Europe was almost permanently at war. Perry's brother Benedict Anderson convincingly demonstrated that the nation is only an "imagined community."[12] The Austrian philosopher Rudolf Bauer in some ways went even further when he spoke of the "Imagi-Nation" and the "Indoctri-Nation." In other words, national sovereignty cannot be considered an eternal or sacrosanct institution. Supranational institutions such as the standardized common market have created tremendous capital flow from rich to poorer countries, enabling their continuing modernization and providing critical assistance to Member States' most backward regions. This process has aided EU Member States much more than any imagined sovereignty (which would lack the free flow of production factors), could possibly have accomplished.

Real causes of revolt: social shock caused by complex societal changes

Was the populist revolt caused by EU neoliberalism? Neoliberalism definitely played a role by increasing inequality, largely causing the Great Recession, and aiding deregulation. Inequality among EU Member States, however, had nothing to do with neoliberal policy. Actually, in the globalized world economy, inequality among countries became somewhat more moderated during the rise of neoliberalism. As Thomas Piketty has proved through rich statistical facts, China, India, and other Asian countries have elevated millions of people from poverty; compared to the advanced Western world, income differences have decreased somewhat.

Income differences within EU member countries were not the result of "EU neoliberalism." They were caused by previous economic development on the periphery of the continent. The original founding member countries had a rather homogenous income level, and inequality in the Union emerged as a result of enlargements toward the southern and eastern peripheries in the 1980s and the 2000s. After lower-income periphery countries were included in the EU, several of them—such as Ireland, Spain, the Baltic countries, and some other Central European member countries of the EU—started increasing their income level faster than the traditional rich core countries of Europe. As a result, the inequality scissors began to close.

Nevertheless, neoliberalism definitely still contributed to the population's growing dissatisfaction. Neoliberalism was, however, more of an American and British invention under President Ronald Reagan and Prime Minister Margaret

Thatcher than a central idea behind the founding of the EU (as discussed). One of the most successful populist revolts within the EU, and the only one that succeeded in the rich Northwest, was Brexit. Was it a revolt against EU neoliberalism? If the Brits are revolting against neoliberalism, they will have to leave Britain itself to be free from it, not just the EU.

Populist revolts were more the result of a number of dramatic, disruptive, complex societal transformations. These include startling structural changes in advanced economies caused primarily by the technological revolution, which has halved industrial employment from 30–40 to 15–20 percent, and has increased service employment from 50 to 75 percent.

At the same time, Europe has become more integrated, its borders have been eliminated, and millions have flocked from poorer regions to affluent core countries that needed an outside labor force. Poverty and climate change, the collapse of colonial empires, and no fewer than 30 civil wars around the world uprooted tens of millions of people from the Middle East, Africa, and Asia. A huge migration of impoverished refugees began to pour into Europe. Suddenly, Europe, a continent of emigration up until World War II, became a continent of immigration. The proportion of non-Europeans increased in several European countries to more than 10 percent and comprised 13–15 percent of the labor force. In several of these instances, the majority of immigrants were Muslim and African peoples with different ethnicities, religions, and cultures. This unprecedented migration hit its climax in 2014–16 when a tumultuous flood of uncontrolled economic migrants and refugees invaded Europe.

Social change and transformation penetrated every sphere of life in Europe. The southern parts of the continent had moved from dictatorship to democracy after the 1970–80s. The eastern half of Europe underwent promising but invariably painful radical changes, transitioning from communist-planned economies and one-party rule to market democracies beginning in the 1990s. As Karl Polanyi has brilliantly demonstrated, major historical changes cause huge social shocks even if they are positive and lead to higher levels of development. All the old institutions, social environments, work arrangements, educational traditions, and behavioral patterns were undermined. Social shocks accompanied Britain's Industrial Revolution and the collapse of the colonial system as well.

The result of this vast array of changes, which invariably led to winners and losers, was populist revolt. That was the driving force of radically transformed political representation, the disappearance of traditional mass parties, and the rise of the new populist movements. Most of the power-hungry populists we see today are keenly exploiting this very situation and are presenting themselves as the "voice of the forgotten people." Brexit was not a revolt against "neoliberal EU" but against immigration, and for "regaining national sovereignty," by a part of the population mesmerized by delusions and the memory of British global power. Britain was and remains more neoliberal than most continental European countries.

Geert Wilders in the Netherlands and Marine Le Pen in France are running xenophobic anti-immigration, anti-Muslim, and anti-EU campaigns under the banner of defending "Christian European civilization." Viktor Orbán and Jarosław Kaczyński, in Hungary and Poland, are radical nationalists. The EU hinders their plans to build authoritarian "illiberal" regimes. Those populists are not revolting against neoliberalism but against the *liberal* democratic EU.

Perry Anderson seemingly does not accept the term "populism" and instead refers to the "stigmatization" of the people's revolt by the established order, "whether from the right or left, as a menace of populism." He criticizes the left for not being consistent enough in attacking the neoliberal EU. In his view, the left "cannot afford to be less radical in attacking the system [than the right], and must be more coherent in their opposition to it." This is not good advice. It has to be added that the distinction between the left and the right is not such a major divide any longer, and is strongly mixed in European populism. Right-wing white supremacists also have social slogans and demands. Populist parties attracted a great part of former supporters, including a lot of blue-collar workers from the left. Although this is a widespread phenomenon, the Italian Five Star Movement is probably one of the most characteristic examples of it. Who would want the remnants of the European left to compete with right-wing populism on an equally vicious anti-EU program?

Nevertheless, Perry Anderson is, one hopes, right when he says that the "populist danger" cannot destroy the EU and, as the title of his essay suggests, that "the system will still win." If that happens, it would offer further improvements for the European population, including the further catching up of relatively less-developed countries. On the other hand, all early signs signal and calculations show that Britain and its population outside the EU will pay a dear price for leaving it. That may be a good warning to other countries and should help them to understand the value and advantage of close integration in Europe.

Notes

1 Perry Anderson, "Why the System Will Still Win," *Le Monde Diplomatique*, no. March 2017 (March 1, 2017), https://mondediplo.com/2017/03/02brexit.
2 "Treaty of Rome," 1957, https://fullfact.org/europe/explaining-eu-deal-ever-closer-union/, February 22, 2016.
3 "Explain the Relationship between Regionalism and Globalisation," May 19, 2014, https://arqshah.wordpress.com/2014/05/19/explain-the-relationship-between-regionalism-and-globalisation/.
4 Björn Hettne, "Globalism and Regionalism," in' *96 Shonan Session* (Hayama: United Nations University Global Seminar, 1996), http://archive.unu.edu/unupress/globalism.html#Globalization, 2–6 September 1996.
5 Bennett Collins, "Does Regionalism Challenge Globalization or Build Upon It?" *E-International Relations* (blog), July 29, 2010, www.e-ir.info/2010/07/29/does-regionalism-challenge-globalization-or-build-upon-it/.
6 Grahame Thompson, "Globalisation versus Regionalism?" *The Journal of North African Studies* 3, no. 2 (June 1, 1998): 59–74, doi:10.1080/13629389808718320.

7 See, among others, Laurence Neville, "Is This the End of Globalization?" (*Global Finance Magazine*, December 8, 2016, www.gfmag.com/magazine/december-2016/ end-globalization) and Alan Tonelson, "Trump's Goal for NAFTA Should Be to Make North America Self-Sufficient" (*MarketWatch*, October 26, 2017, www.marketwatch. com/story/trump-should-return-nafta-back-to-basics-continental-self-sufficiency-2017-10-24).

8 Anderson, "Why the System Will Still Win."

9 EU Commission staff, "Social Investment through the European Social Fund. Social Investment Package," EU Commission - SEC Document (European Commission, February 20, 2013), http://aei.pitt.edu/45919/.

10 Cinzia Alcidi et al., "Income Convergence in the EU: A Tale of Two Speeds," Policy Paper, CEPS Commentary (Brussels: Centre for European Policy Studies, January 9, 2018), http://aei.pitt.edu/93160/.

11 Perry Anderson, "Passing the Baton," *New Left Review*, no. 103 (January-February 2017): 41–64.

12 Benedict Anderson, *Imagined Communities: Reflections on the Origin and Spread of Nationalism* (London: Verso, 2006).

10

OUTSIDE DISCONTENTS

The weakening alliance with the US, a hostile Russia, and Turkey and China at the borders

Discontent with the European Union (EU) within and among the member countries was unfortunately accompanied by the discontent of and attacks by rivals from outside the EU. A strong and integrated EU that attracted more and more countries to join became a superpower, which was disadvantageous for several ambitious rivals nearby, such as Russia, and even for faraway countries such as the US and China.

A loosening alliance with the US

For several decades the EU's strong alliance with the US, which was of the closest kind imaginable, and its membership in the US-led military alliance NATO, formed the adamantine base of the EU's foreign relations. This relationship was established before European integration started. The postwar Marshall Plan (1948–52) made cooperation among the recipient countries mandatory. From the 1950s onward, the US initiated and pushed West European integration, including the foundation of a joint European army against its Cold War enemy, the Soviet Union. The first three postwar American presidents—Truman, Eisenhower, and Kennedy—were strongly pro-European integration. They actively worked for it and tried pushing Britain to lead or, later, at least to join the European Economic Community.[1]

Consecutive American administrations did not stop advocating for further enlargement of the Community by accepting all NATO members, even including anti-communist dictatorships such as Francisco Franco's Spain and António Salazar's Portugal, and countries under military dictatorships such as Greece and Turkey. This relationship of patronage and assistance started changing in the mid-1960s, when President Lyndon B. Johnson stopped making further efforts to strengthen the European Economic Community because he was totally preoccupied with domestic reforms and the Vietnam War.

The real change, however, happened only in the 1970s during the Nixon-Kissinger era, when the American administration revised its European policy. They turned to the enemies, China and the Soviet Union, and made breakthrough agreements with them. The European allies lost their central importance for America. Moreover, Nixon and Kissinger looked to integrating Europe as a rival; instead of dealing with the EU Commission as a whole, they preferred forging bilateral relations with individual member countries. Nevertheless, the alliance and NATO remained intact and important during the entire century.

The new further distancing happened after the end of the Cold War during the 1980s and especially after 1991, the collapse of the Soviet Union. First of all, the stable (though sometimes dangerous) bipolar world system was gradually replaced by a multipolar world with about five major powers. That made the world system much less governable. As Robert Gilpin explains, this shift was especially significant from a European perspective: "the end of the Cold War ... and the decreased need for close cooperation [between] the United States [and] Western Europe ... have significantly weakened the political bonds"[2] between these entities. Furthermore, "during the Cold War, the United States and its allies generally subordinated potential economic conflicts within the alliance to the interests of political and security cooperation."[3] After the Cold War, "national priorities changed and the Western allies assigned a higher priority to their own national (and frequently parochial) economic interests. A shift in American policy had already become evident during the Reagan and Bush Administrations."[4] A greater emphasis on nationalism continued under the Clinton administration as economic security displaced military security.

Priorities also changed for Europe, which became less "willing to follow American leadership, much less tolerant of America's disregard of their economic and political interests, and more likely to emphasize their own national priorities."[5] According to Gilpin, protectionism slowly and gradually started to gain ground in America, as exemplified by the Multifiber Agreement of 1973 that restricted textile and apparel imports from developing countries, violating General Agreement on Tariffs and Trade (GATT) rules. Informal trade barriers emerged, and, in the US Trade Act of 1974, punitive actions were introduced against "unfair trade."[6] Nevertheless, the free trade system was not seriously endangered.

This gradual development eventually amounted to a dramatic shift, as exemplified by the new state of affairs that had already emerged during the first years of the Trump administration in 2017–18. During the presidential campaign, Donald J. Trump expressed his views several times about NATO. When two Bloomberg Politics journalists asked him about it on March 23, 2016, he answered in the following way:

> I think NATO may be obsolete. NATO was set up a long time ago ... when things were different. ... We were a rich nation then ... far more than we have today, in a true sense. And I think NATO ... doesn't really help us, it's helping other countries.[7]

In a foreign policy speech on April 27, 2016, he said:

> We have spent trillions of dollars over time on planes, missiles, ships, equipment, building up our military to provide a strong defense for Europe and Asia. The countries we are defending must pay for the cost of this defense, and if not, the U.S. must be prepared to let these countries defend themselves.[8]

The new president, elected at the end of 2016, signaled the changes with his "America First!" nationalist policy and his oft-repeated views that NATO was obsolete and the US carried an unequal burden for others. Together with his strong admiration of dictators (especially Vladimir Putin of Russia), Trump's views have cooled down US–EU relations to their chilliest level since World War II. Trump's first visit in Europe and the NATO summit made it crystal clear that the EU cannot count on him: in one particular episode, he refused to repeat the covenant that an attack of one of the member countries is an attack against all member countries.

Some of his lieutenants, namely, former Secretary of State Rex Tillerson and Secretary of Defense James Mattis, tried balancing US policy toward Europe, but they could not change the situation. Due to President Trump's mercurial tendencies, the US could not be counted upon as a solid and trusted ally any longer.

Several of Trump's other speeches and statements about European affairs were offensive for the EU. He declared that it was a good idea that Britain decided to leave the Union. A day after the Brexit referendum, just before his trip to his Scotland golf club during his campaign, a Washington Post journalist asked him, "How would the Trump administration approach the Brexit, should you be elected president? And Scotland voted 62-38 to remain. Should Scotland leave the UK, as many people are talking about?" Trump's answer was an enthusiastic, populist, anti-EU statement:

> People want to take their country back. They want to have independence, in a sense, and you see it with Europe, all over Europe. You're going to have more than just … what happened last night, you're going to have, I think many other cases where they want to take their borders back. They want to take their monetary back … They want to be able to have a country again. So, I think you're going have this happen more and more … I think it will turn out to be a good thing. Maybe not short term, not, but ultimately I think it will be a good thing … It's not staying together. It's a really positive force taking place.[9]

In his first interview in Britain with one of the leading Brexiters, Michael Gove, for *The Times* in January 2017, Trump said he thought the UK was "so smart in getting out." Speaking just before his inauguration, he also promised a quick trade deal between the US and the UK after taking office—without knowing that trade negotiations could not even start until Britain left the EU two years later.[10]

His first visit at NATO and the EU made a shocking impact. As the British *Guardian* reported,

> He denied saying things he had said, then said things that showed he did not understand. … It may, mercifully, have passed off without apocalyptic mishap, but Donald Trump's first transatlantic trip as US president still left European leaders shaken.[11]

Trump also praised the anti-EU French populist Marine Le Pen as the "strongest candidate"[12] during the French presidential campaign. His attitude toward the EU was clearly hostile. The EU thus lost the nation that had been its best and most powerful ally for more than half a century. Trump's anti-EU attitude became even more apparent during the 2018 G7 meeting in Canada when he refused to sign a joint agreement. Furthermore, at his second NATO meeting, he attacked Germany; during his 2018 visit to England, he undermined Theresa May, criticized her plan to remain in the European common market, and suggested that hard-liner, hard-landing advocate Boris Johnson would make a good prime minister.

On top of these open conflicts, the next day Trump met with President Putin in Helsinki. Trump treated him as a new friend and ally, rejecting the conclusions of the US's own intelligence agencies and the Department of Justice, which had indicted 12 high-ranking Russian intelligence officers for the 2016 cyberattack on the American elections days before his visit with Putin.

In addition to security issues, Trump and his administration expressed similar hostility toward economic connections. Trump's America turned sharply against the global free trade regime. The US pulled out of the so-called Trans-Pacific Partnership Agreement and started renegotiating the North Atlantic Treaty Organization (NAFTA) agreement with Mexico and Canada. In the framework of his new "America First" policy, he said that he has "a lot of problems"[13] with the EU's trade policy. Moreover, he entered into an open trade war against the EU, declaring it not only a rival but a foe. As one EU commentary phrased it, "The utterances of President Trump about the 'terrible Europeans,' or Germans, 'giving a bad deal' to the US for decades also emerge from an irrational belief that bilateral or even sectoral trade surpluses are somehow caused by 'bad deals.'" It is elementary economic knowledge that

> fundamental drivers of trade surpluses or deficits in the case of the US [have] essentially macroeconomic determinants (e.g. spending more abroad), complemented by sectoral competitiveness in terms of price, quality, reputation or design. They are therefore first of all US-driven—US deficits begin and end at home—and the sectoral issues are largely a matter of competition on their own merits and not at all of a 'deal.'[14]

Europe responded immediately to America's warning: "The European Union stands ready to react swiftly and appropriately in case our exports are affected by any restrictive trade measures from the United States."[15] The European Commission's spokesperson warned that "restrictive trade measures from the United States" would face a robust response from Europe. "If European exporters have to pay tariffs that will become a two-way street. Then U.S. exporters will have to pay tariffs here,"[16] announced the EU's budget commissioner Guenther Oettinger. Although this exchange was just a war of words, it was followed by a real trade war.

In the spring and summer of 2018, President Trump, indeed, announced the introduction of 25 and 10 percent tariffs for steel and aluminum imports to the US, respectively. The president's own party mildly disagreed, and his chief economic adviser resigned. The countries that were punished, China and the EU, immediately responded. The EU announced the introduction of tariffs against major US export items to Europe, with about $3.5 billion in EU duties. As the *New York Times* reported in early March 2018, "Trade partners respond in kind to tariff plans."[17] Trump immediately reacted by announcing that in the event those tariffs went into effect, he would introduce tariffs for European car exports to the US, a major item responsible for about €38 billion in business in 2016. A tariff war was in the making. Meanwhile, the White House trade adviser, Peter Navarro, rushed to declare that "the administration would take a tough line toward Europe."[18]

Economic alliances and cooperation were undermined. The Trump administration announced a fierce trade war that certainly marked the end of the free trade era that America initiated after the war. The US decided to go it alone, against Europe and its other former allies. Furthermore, the American president could not find one single word to support America's European allies when Russian double agents poisoned former Russian double agents in London using military nerve gas. This was a brutal attack against Britain and against Europe.

Meanwhile, President Trump dismissed most of the people from his administration who tried to somewhat counterbalance his trade war, his hostility against allies, and his extreme unpredictability in international conflicts.[19] The "America First" policy was quickly transforming into an "America alone" strategy.

Trump's America is closing the chapter of close friendship and cooperation with the EU as well as the era of American leadership in the postwar world system. But Trump probably cannot change the system itself. In a symbolic way, on the same day Trump signed the new tariffs, 11 countries with 500 million combined inhabitants signed the new Comprehensive and Progressive Agreement for Trans-Pacific Partnership in Santiago de Chile—without the US. Japan, Canada, and several other allies of the US are among the members. It is open for China to join. The tariff war against China, however, may have major consequences for the entire postwar world economic system. The World Trade Organization is also endangered, and Europe, losing its closest ally, remains more and more alone.

This new situation became more pronounced as differences and conflicts also emerged in various other areas of US–EU connections. The two allies have worked together on other initiatives such as crafting agreements about bank regulation, the Basel I and Basel II agreements, to create a fair and equal system throughout the West. Since the new administration occupied the White House, however, American and EU regulatory policies are diverging. The US started deregulating to provide more opportunities for high-risk speculation and to stimulate businesses regardless of consequences, while the EU kept regulation to guarantee solid business activity and avoid a new collapse. Similar distancing and diverse policies separated the two former allies in the arena of environmental policy as well. America introduced deregulations in environmental issues and, as President Trump declared in the summer of 2017, left the globally accepted (by 175 countries) Paris Climate Agreement of April 2016; the EU remains one of the most strident advocates and supporters of responsible environmental policy.

Differences also surfaced in foreign policy. The most outstanding conflicts emerged as a result of Donald Trump's statements about his eagerness to build a cooperative relationship with President Vladimir Putin. Trump's desires, formerly thinly veiled, took their most explicit and true form at their meeting in Helsinki in July 2018. It could be argued that Putin's Russia is a threat to the EU because its policies may undermine and endanger the EU borders through provocations and information warfare.

When Trump announced his decision to recognize Jerusalem as the capital of Israel and resettle the US Embassy there from Tel Aviv, the EU rejected his policy.

> European leaders' harshly worded rebukes of the Trump declaration … suggested that they view it as his latest contribution to a growing list of disagreements on foreign policy. Some EU states see the U.S. government's declaration as an incentive to double down on the union's official neutral position on the Holy City pending the result of peace talks between the Israelis and Palestinians.[20]

After hardly more than a year and a half in office, the Trump administration one-sidedly canceled the agreement with Iran, which had served as a deterrent to the existence of Iranian atomic bombs and had introduced strict international controls that worked well. The European allies, together with China and Russia, were also part of that agreement and decided not to go together with Trump's America. This may lead to the introduction of strict American sanctions against countries and corporations that continue trade connections with Iran. John Bolton, Trump's new hawkish security adviser, telephoned London, Paris, and Berlin in early May, warning that "there would be no sanctions exemptions for European companies."[21] The new American ambassador to Germany, Richard Grenell, "ordered" that German companies doing business with Iran "should wind down operation immediately."[22] All these, together with possible sanctions against European

Airbus exports due to EU subsidies, generated a furious European reaction. The German magazine *Der Spiegel* expressed this common sentiment in "its depiction of Mr. Trump as a middle finger proclaiming, 'Goodbye Europe'.... The West as we once knew it no longer exists ... [Trump] ignores 70 years of trust." Emmanuel Macron, who tried convincing Trump to stay with the Iran agreement and had behaved in the friendliest way possible during his visit to Washington a week before, stated that if Europeans allowed other powers to make security decisions for them, "we are not more sovereign and we cannot be credible to public opinion."[23]

The decline in American-European relations is rather multifaceted. On the one hand, it endangered European security and economic interests, but on the other hand, it became a wake-up call for the EU. One of the leading American media organizations concluded:

> Trump's bullying could turn out to be exactly what a fractured European Union (EU) needed in order to band closer together. His attacks on the European Union's shared policies—like climate change, free trade and defense—have forced EU countries to jointly defend their goals and strengthen ties with other global allies.[24]

The failure to keep Turkey in the EU's orbit

Another factor in the EU's worsening foreign relations was the failed effort to pacify and stabilize the neighborhood regions in the south, southeast, and eastern strip around the EU; incorporate new neighboring countries into the Union as members; and build friendly cooperation with others. Two main sets of policy attempts were geared toward serving this goal.

The first was the further enlargement of the EU by accomplishing the integration of Europe. The number one targets of EU membership expansion were Turkey and the Western Balkans. Previous American governments had already pressured the EU to accept Turkey because of its NATO member status, which eventually led (in a painfully slow manner) to Turkey obtaining official candidacy. However, Turkey is largely an Asiatic country: geographically, it only has a single edge on the Balkan Peninsula, and just 5 percent of the country's population lives on the European continent. Responding to American pressure, the European Economic Community signed the Ankara Treaty in 1963, which granted Turkey associated status in the European Economic Community. Turkey applied for full membership in 1987, joined the EU's Customs Union in 1996, and became an official EU candidate in 1999. In 2005, the accession negotiations started and the full membership seemed to be within reach.

Meanwhile, economic ties significantly strengthened. Turkey's attainment of membership in the EU's Customs Union in 1996 led to a sevenfold increase in Turkish-EU trade, amounting to €140 billion annually (41 percent of Turkey's global trade). The EU ranks first in Turkish foreign trade. In addition, two-thirds of the foreign direct investment in Turkey currently originates from the EU.[25]

As a 2008 report by the Commission clearly reflected, the EU concluded that Turkey's strategic importance to the EU had continued to increase in key areas such as energy security, conflict prevention, and regional security in the Southern Caucasus and the Middle East. The country's entrance into the EU, they considered, would make it a stronger force for stability in the region. In 2008, the Commission also declared that Turkey qualified for the first time as a functioning market economy based on the Copenhagen economic criteria.[26]

Nevertheless, the entire accession process hit a dead end in 2005, during the phase that had seemed like it would be the final turning point. The first major roadblock was Cyprus's acceptance of EU membership in 2004. Because Turkey attacked and had militarily occupied the eastern half of the island since 1974, serious discussion about Turkish membership could not happen without Turkey's withdrawal from the country.

Equally important was that to be accepted by the EU, the candidate country had to realize the requirements of membership, summed up in 35 chapters of the so-called *Acquis Communautaire*. The occupation of parts of Cyprus itself violated six of those accession chapters. Besides, in more than a decade since the negotiations had begun, only one chapter's requirements had been fully accomplished, and only half the chapters' prerequisites had been started. Turkey was unable to fulfill the full requirements of membership by realizing those few requirements. Unsolvable questions blocked the road toward membership: in addition to the Cyprus question, Turkey's harsh violations of women's rights and human rights in general made the possibility of full membership unattainable. (In contrast to this painful progress, accession negotiations with Croatia started at the same time as Turkey, and the country became a full member in 2013.)

Meanwhile, the EU's attitude toward further enlargement also changed. It became evident that the acceptance of ten Central European and Balkan countries in 2004 and 2007 was rather controversial and had led to dangerous over-enlargement. Those countries could not adjust well to the EU's values and even started forming a hostile "illiberal" anti-EU bloc. The Western European member countries' populations started opposing further enlargements.

Another motivation for the Northwestern member countries was the occurrence of several Islamist terrorist attacks that hit Western Europe in the 2010s. Strong anti-immigration and anti-Muslim attitudes spread in France, the Netherlands, Italy, and other member countries. French President Nicolas Sarkozy opposed Turkish membership, and Germany also looked for an alternative form as "privileged partnership" instead of full membership. More and more EU member countries became skeptical about Turkish membership. In 2016, the Austrian government called for ending talks with Turkey.[27]

The final blow came in 2016, when, after a failed military coup against Recep Tayyip Erdoğan in July, Erdoğan eliminated all of his oppositions and the free press: 170,000 "suspects" were investigated or arrested, and 50,000 people remained in prison, including journalists and teachers. Although Turkey's official candidacy has not yet been nullified by the EU, it has no real meaning any longer. As *Deutsche Welle* reported in October 2017,

> speaking to parliament … President Tayyip Erdogan had some strong words for the European Union and Turkey's 12-year accession talks, which have ground to a halt. 'We will not be the side which gives up. To tell the truth, we don't need EU membership any more. … Today, Europe has become a place where terrorists can move around freely and carry out all kinds of activity against Turkey's legitimate administration.'[28]

The relationship became even more hostile when Turkey arrested a number of German citizens in Turkey and after Erdoğan called upon the naturalized constituents of the three-million-member Turkish expat community in Germany to vote against Merkel in the 2017 elections. Erdoğan also went ahead with the re-Islamization of the country and turned to the archenemy of the EU: Putin's Russia.

The two isolated countries, Russia and Turkey, started to look to each other for alliances. Putin visited Ankara and Erdoğan received an ornate reception in the Kremlin. Putin rushed to exploit the cracks in the NATO alliance when both the EU and the US denounced Turkey's harsh dictatorial steps after the coup attempt. Putin immediately expressed his full support for Erdoğan. "We have received unconditional support from Russia, unlike other countries," Mevlut Cavusoglu, Turkey's foreign minister, said in a TV interview. The two countries also started cooperating in Syria. As the government's spokesman said to the Russian news agency TASS, "We would like to look at the future with more hope. In cooperation with Russia, we would like to facilitate a political transition in Syria as soon as possible."[29] Both sides also want to build robust trade relations: trade between the two amounted to about $30 billion annually in the mid-2010s, but the two presidents pledged to increase this to $100 billion by 2020.

One of the most spectacularly hostile steps was the Turkish purchase of a Russian S-400 air defense missile system instead of the interoperable weapon system of the allies, an unusual step by a NATO country. James Mattis, the US Secretary of Defense, immediately stated, "Clearly, it will not be interoperable with NATO, so they're going to have to consider that if they go forward."[30]

Instead of a friendly military ally and an EU candidate country, Turkey became a hostile neighbor allied with Putin's Russia. Turkey's crucially important strategic location and military strength in the areas of the Middle East closest to the EU dangerously weakened the EU's security.

The failure of the Balkans' policy toward the EU

Two Balkan countries, Romania and Bulgaria, were accepted as full members in 2007, and Croatia, formerly part of Yugoslavia, was accepted in 2013. These admissions were definitely too early since the countries were not prepared. The EU, nevertheless, wanted to pacify those newly independent countries from former Yugoslavia, which had fought a devastating war against one another in the first half of the 1990s.

The agreement on enlargement toward the southeast was made at the December 2006 European Council meeting. In order to create peace and cooperation on the troubled peninsula, the EU promised membership to all the West Balkan countries and initiated its Stabilization and Association Process, followed by the Stabilization and Accession Agreement.[31] The Western Balkans, meaning Serbia, Montenegro, Macedonia, Bosnia-Herzegovina, Albania, and Kosovo—or as they were called in EU jargon, the West Balkan Six (WB6)—became either official or potential candidates. This region has about 20 million inhabitants and a roughly €27 billion total GDP, meaning that its per capita GDP is only about €2,000, a non-European Third World level.

The European Council maintained "that the future of the Western Balkans lies in the European Union." The Commission therefore recommended that "negotiations for accession to the European Union should be opened with Serbia as soon as it achieves further significant progress," especially in the normalization of "its relations with Kosovo."[32]

The EU policy toward the region was accompanied by aid and rapidly increasing economic connections.[33] The EU provided €7 billion until 2006, €9 billion between 2007 and 2017, and €1.07 billion in 2018.[34] Meanwhile, the EU became the most important trade partner of the region, accounting for more than 76 percent of the region's total trade.[35] In 2003, the European Council made an important statement at its Thessaloniki meeting: "Welcoming the progress made by the countries of the region ... the EU remains committed and engaged at all levels to support them in conducting EU-oriented reforms and projects."[36]

The EU was convinced, as its Commission report of October 2009 reflected, that "Enlargement is one of the most effective foreign policy instruments of the EU." It is surprising to read the optimistic text of the "Enlargement Strategy." On the one hand, the EU clearly recognized that:

> the Western Balkans and Turkey continue to face major challenges related to the rule of law, in particular the fight against corruption and organised crime. These issues are key for a functioning democracy and economy and largely condition the EU accession process. Corruption is prevalent in many areas and affects the every-day life of citizens and the business environment. ... Additional efforts are needed to fight against organised crime which remains a problem throughout the region. ... In most enlargement countries, freedom of expression remains an issue of concern. ... It is in the EU's interest to keep up the momentum of the enlargement process, on the basis of the principles and conditions agreed and the renewed consensus on enlargement.[37]

On the other hand, how could the EU Commission and other institutions believe that all those inherited, deeply rooted, and traditional weaknesses could be cured within a few years?

In November 2010, the EU Commission was still optimistic and tried convincing the populations of member countries that enlargement was the solution to various problems the EU was facing:

> The Commission has redoubled efforts to support enlargement countries to prevent and tackle organised crime and corruption and to strengthen their law enforcement capabilities. ... This year's package of reports, and accompanying conclusions and recommendations, show that the enlargement process is part of the solution to many of our citizens' concerns, whether in the prevention and tackling of organised crime and corruption or in the creation of growth and jobs. The EU institutions and its Member States need to work hand in hand to strengthen understanding and support for the enlargement process and to explain how it can help us achieve our common objectives. By making a success of further enlargement, the EU will be able better to address the many other challenges which it faces.[38]

Both of the aforementioned documents exhibit an optimistic attitude and an effort to convince themselves about the possibility of radical change in a few years.

After the 2008 crisis and various unpleasant developments, however, several EU member countries changed their minds about the Balkans. Accepting new member countries from the Balkans became very unpopular in the EU member countries, as the Balkans experience was not very promising. After more than a decade of the acceptance of Romania and Bulgaria, their incorporation was not really digested. Corruption remained devastating; Bulgaria, after its acceptance, even stopped fighting against it. Kosovo's independence was still not recognized by five member countries; the 2015–16 migration crisis and several Islamist terrorist attacks in France, Britain, and Germany generated broad anti-Muslim public anger. This led to a reconsideration of three of the six potential West Balkan countries that had significant Muslim populations. The region remained in rather bad economic shape. Unemployment in Bosnia and Montenegro remained at 40 and 23 percent, respectively. Mafia killings were everyday phenomena.

However, the Union's consolidation solved the crisis by shelving the potential acceptance of those candidate countries. The new president of the European Commission, Jean-Claude Juncker, announced in 2014 that new members would not be accepted for five years. In March 2017, the European Council meeting made clear that further enlargement is not on the agenda in the foreseeable future at all, and the new deadline became 2025.

The WB6 countries are disappointed. The prime minister of Macedonia expressed the group's feelings, stating, "we are locked in the waiting room."[39] Some of the countries of the region are looking toward Russia as a possible ally, while others are considering some of the Arabic countries. As a member of the European Council on Foreign Relations stated, Russia "looks to the Balkans as a battle field in its political war" against the EU.[40] Some analysts maintain the Balkans became a "new Cold War battlefield." Nevertheless, Russia's economic strength is not comparable to the EU's. However, Russia's strategy is to concentrate heavily on Serbia, Montenegro, and Bosnia. In small Montenegro, one-third of the companies are in Russian hands, and one-quarter of tourists arrive from the Russian Federation. Since 2000, Serbia has received $20 billion in investments from Lukoil and Gapzprom Neft, which acquired 51 percent of Naftena Industrija Srbije in 2008, which is linked to the prospect of the South Stream gas pipeline. In Bosnia, the Russian Zarubezhneft built refineries at Bosanski Brod and Modrić in 2007. Yet the Moscow-Belgrade Free Trade Agreement (FTA) signed in 2000 has not yet been fulfilled. Trade with Russia is unimportant, mostly less than 10 percent (in Serbia 8.5 and in Bosnia 6.3 percent), while trade with the EU is 60–80 percent (in Albania 60.4, in Serbia 62.4, and in Bosnia 84.1 percent). Exports to Russia total less than 1 percent (in Serbia, 2.5 percent), while exports to the EU are around 20 percent (in Serbia 21.9 percent, and in Bosnia 21.7).[41]

Russian political influence is somewhat bigger than its economic impact, and therefore in the debate on the Balkans, some European politicians urge the acceptance of the West Balkan countries into the EU. As Carl Bildt, former Swedish foreign minister, said, "the EU took its eye off the ball for several years with detrimental effects." Johannes Hahn, EU Commissioner for Enlargement, declared a new deadline: "We have set 2025 as an indicative date for Serbia and Montenegro, which is realistic but also very ambitious."[42]

Accepting the unprepared West Balkan countries, where, according to a realistic report, "the countries show clear elements of state capture, including links with organized crime and corruption at all levels of government and administration," would be the wrong way to compete with Russia. As Norbert Rottgen, the chairman of the German Bundestag, rightly stated,

> The argument is that only by taking in the Balkan states are we assured to strengthen stability. But is that true? If we import fragile states into the EU, we import fragility. If we compromise on conditions, we let in fragile countries open to foreign influences, so we have to be tough on the entry requirements.[43]

He is right. Most of the West Balkan countries are not prepared for membership, and in a realistic evaluation, they will not be in the foreseeable future. It pays to quote at length from the EU's annual progress report on Bosnia and Herzegovina's preparedness in 2013:

> Complex connections between political actors, business and the media are putting democratic institutions and procedures at risk and making the detection of corrupt practices more difficult. The implementation of the State-level anti-corruption strategy and action plan 2009–2014 has been significantly delayed. ... The overall level of effective investigation, prosecution and conviction of corruption cases remains low. Joint

investigation teams and mechanisms to detect corruption have still to be developed. There is 48% increase of corruption reports filed with the prosecutors' offices throughout Bosnia and Herzegovina, 3,174 reports were filed in 2012 compared to 2,142 from the previous year. ... Bosnia and Herzegovina is at an early stage in the fight against corruption. ... Bosnia and Herzegovina has made limited progress in the fight against organised crime and terrorism. ... Bosnia and Herzegovina remains a source of arms and ammunitions for criminal groups operating in the EU and the Western Balkans region. Organised crime activities are mainly linked to illicit drugs trafficking, arms trafficking, economic crime, trafficking in human beings and money laundering.[44]

The situation is not better in other countries in the region. An EU evaluation of Albania's preparedness in 2010 also clearly reflected essential weakness, including high corruption and a lack of independence between legal institutions and the executive branch.[45] The Commission's 130-page-long report on Montenegro reflected a similar picture.[46] In the southern and southeastern neighborhoods (the areas covered by Turkey and the West Balkans), the EU's further enlargement policy aimed at stabilizing the neighboring zone failed but was then reconsidered, although it definitely remained more than controversial.

The failure of the EU's southern and eastern neighborhood policies

In an even more ambitious way, the EU initiated a neighborhood policy toward countries around its borders (and future borders). The goal of this policy was not the enlargement and later acceptance of those countries, but rather, as an EU analysis stated, the creation of a ring of peaceful, stable, and prosperous friends at Europe's borders. The Euro-Mediterranean Partnership started in 1995, in one of the most promising times for the EU after the collapse of communism. Several rich, neutral countries such as Sweden, Finland, and Austria joined the EU, opening a new chapter in the history of European integration. The Single Market project, launched in the mid-1980s, was finally realized. German re-unification led to the common currency initiative. A new and strong federalist wave united the European Economic Community, which was renamed the EU, more than ever. It is also clear that the initiator of this new development was in large part the European corporate business world, which was seeking protection against the overwhelming competition presented by the US and Japan in the globalizing world during the 1970s–80s. The regionalization of Europe, which created a huge integrated market, a legal system, and the standardization of the 500-million-person market across Europe, with a common currency and unlimited business activity, offered a strong defense.[47] The collapse of communism had already made an economic backyard with cheap labor and 100 million hungry consumers accessible. With its neighborhood policy, both European security and the enlargement of a backyard with an even larger market and a cheaper labor force could be secured.

In this optimistic atmosphere, the EU initiated a rather broad partnership program. At a 2011 meeting with African leaders, the EU declared that

> The Partnership between Africa and the European Union is one of the most enduring global relationships and is of strategic significance to both sides. We will continue the work launched at the Cairo Summit in 2000 and Lisbon Summit in 2007, where we decided to put our relations on a new, equal and strategic level.[48]

Leaders accepted a new Action Plan for 2011–13 with new commitments.

In the mid-1990s, the EU organized the Barcelona Euro-Mediterranean Conference, or the so-called Barcelona Process, to strengthen the relationship with its southern neighbors in the Mashriq and Maghreb regions and with nine countries—Algeria, Egypt, Israel, Jordan, Lebanon, Morocco, the Palestinian Authority, Syria, Tunisia, and Libya (which has held observer status since 1999).[49] Agreements were signed between 1995 and 2006 "to establish a common area of peace, stability, and shared prosperity in the Euro-Mediterranean region."[50]

> The neighbors were to be drawn closer to the EU's values through its 'power of attraction.' A review of the first decade of implementation shows that this conception was based on misguided, often Eurocentric assumptions and that the ENP [European Neighbourhood Policy] failed to attain its core objectives. A growing number of crises and conflicts stretching from Ukraine to North Africa have destabilised the EU's neighbourhood. ... During the first decade, the ENP's resources and tools expanded. In 2000–2003, the total funding for the Eastern and Southern neighbourhood ... amounted to €3.72 billion.

In 2007, under the European Neighbourhood Instrument,

> the EU allocated €11.81 billion to the ENP partners for 2007–2013 and €15.4 billion for 2014–2020. ... The ENP has served as a platform for closer political and economic integration with a number of neighbours. The EU has concluded Association Agreements including Deep and Comprehensive Free Trade Agreements with Georgia, Moldova and Ukraine. Negotiations on [similar agreements] with Morocco and Tunisia are ongoing, and so are preparatory talks with Egypt and Jordan. The EU has also developed its cooperation in the field of migration and has concluded Mobility Partnerships with Armenia, Azerbaijan, Georgia, Jordan, Moldova, Morocco and Tunisia. Since April 2014, Moldova has benefitted from visa-free travel to the EU. Meanwhile, Georgia and Ukraine are advancing in the implementation of their Visa Liberalisation Action Plans.

After one decade of implementation, analyses concluded, the neighborhood policy had failed, and the EU was surrounded by a "ring of fire."[51]

The failure of the neighborhood policy was spectacular. The main reason for its demise was, as another EU analysis stated, that the revolts in Tunisia, Egypt, and Libya in 2011 or

> the so-called Arab Spring has degenerated into a winter carrying heavy socio-political consequences for the Mediterranean region. The ascent of the Islamic State (IS), the 'unravelling of the state' in former autocracies and forced displacements have emerged as adverse outcomes of the uprisings that had originally left the world spellbound.[52]

The Carnegie Europe Institution, the third most influential think tank in the world, looked back and evaluated the EU's most comprehensive and forward-looking foreign policy initiatives, concluding:

> Two decades later, virtually none of the EMP's ambitions have been fulfilled. ... Despite many well-meaning policies ... conditions in the southern Mediterranean have worsened since 1995. ... War rages in four Arab states: Libya, Syria, Iraq and Yemen. Sunni radicalization, especially in the form of Islamic State (IS) jihadis, is challenging national borders. ... Egypt is rocked by instability and polarisation. The Arab-Israeli peace process is for now moribund, if not definitively dead. ... The region is suffering its worst-ever humanitarian crisis.[53]

The failure of the Southern Neighborhood Policy strongly contributed to the 2015–16 tragic migration crisis, where millions of Middle Eastern and African refugees flooded the EU in an uncontrolled and chaotic way. Even more tragic was the failure of the Eastern Neighborhood Policy initiative. The EU had ambitious plans for that region. The European Commission presented a plan, "The Black Sea Initiative," to the European Council and Parliament in April 2007. It maintained that "the Black Sea region is a distinct geographical area rich in natural resources and strategically located at the junction of Europe, Central Asia and the Middle East." The EU's presence in that region, as the document stated, would "[open] a window of fresh perspectives and opportunities."[54] This initiative also served both the security and the business interests of corporate Europe.

The Eastern Neighborhood Policy was officially launched at the EU's Prague Summit in May 2009 and targeted six countries: Armenia, Azerbaijan, Belarus, Georgia, Moldova, and Ukraine. Unlike the Mediterranean Partnership Program, which did not target future EU membership, the Eastern Partnership was ambiguous and open to future enlargement. The main focus of the Eastern Partnership project was Ukraine, a country of more than 50 million inhabitants and a close neighbor of the EU countries. As the EU announced, "the key goal is to bring Ukraine closer to the EU."[55] The European Commission, in its "Action

Plan for Ukraine," had already stated in 1996 that it wished to add Ukraine to "the European architecture drawn up by the Copenhagen European Council, to develop partnership relations with Ukraine."[56] A few days later, the EU Council of Ministers quite openly added that it wanted "a privileged partnership with Ukraine" that would be beneficial economically[57] and also prevent "any possible return to the former ways [and] will loosen the grip of dependence upon their powerful neighbor [Russia]."[58]

Actually, the EU had already offered a partnership agreement to Ukraine that had been signed as early as June 1996. The EU's summit meeting in Vilnius in November 2013 ratified the thousand-page Association Agreement, seeking "further Europeanization" of Armenia, Georgia, Moldova, and Ukraine. These countries also wanted to establish closer connections with the EU in the 1990s and early 2000s. Nicolae Timofti, then president of Moldova, stated when he signed the FTA that the EU was "the only chance that Moldova has in order to develop itself as a European country and in the European spirit."[59] Demonstrators in Kiev on February 20 shouted, "We want to live in Europe."

In 2010, the EU Commission prepared a 70-page-long report, "A 2020 Vision for the Black Sea Region," which stated,

> The Black Sea region has gradually evolved into one of geopolitical significance. It has emerged as one of the key areas in an intensified competition between the major global powers; Russia, the United States and to a certain extent, the EU. All three have developed their own regional policies ….

In

> negotiations over a new generation of agreements with Russia and other regional players, the EU can be expected to play a more assertive role. … Euro-Atlantic policy … in the early post-Cold War period [was] trying to prevent the then newly independent states from falling under the Russian sphere of influence and assuring a steady and secure supply of Caspian oil and gas. … The European Security Strategy of 2003 … emphasised the need for stability, security and prosperity in its wider neighbourhood. … The Black Sea has become a new strategic arena for Europe… [and in] consequence the Union has elaborated a number of policies towards the region. The first was the European Neighbourhood Policy of 2004 which offered a privileged relationship but without the promise of accession. Then came the Black Sea Synergy with its promotion of regional cooperation and a region-wide, projects-based approach. … Finally, hot on the heels of the August 2008 war, came the Eastern Partnership with its emphasis on deeper integration with the EU through bilateral action. … The EU has also become, for those states of the region which are not members, their most important economic partner.

In 2010, however, the Commission already clearly recognized the impending conflict with Russia regarding the Black Sea region. The report described the

> increase [in] Russia's perception of insecurity. Its fear of encirclement was clearly discernible in its government's statements made prior to and during the August 2008 war. In this context, the Russian position has gravitated towards bolstering its influence around its borders … [and] preventing the emergence of anti-Russian coalitions, curbing NATO expansion.[60]

Nevertheless, the EU did not give up its influence-building policy toward the Black Sea region, especially Ukraine.

In the coming paragraphs, let me quote various facts about the EU's ambitious activities regarding Ukraine. On March 2014, the European Commission announced a large support package for Ukraine to help stabilize its economic and financial situation. It offers €11 billion in assistance over the next seven years from the EU budget, including up to €1.4 billion in grants from EU Member States.

The European Commission established its Support Group for Ukraine in 2014, and in 2015, Ukraine became fully associated with the Commission's Horizon 2020 program. That meant that Ukrainian researchers, businesses, and innovators could participate in EU programs under the same conditions as EU Member States. As part of the EU's €11 billion package supporting Ukraine in April 2015, the European Commission established a Neighborhood Investment Facility and adopted a €70 million Special Measure for Private Sector Development and Approximation. This measure was responsible for supporting recovery and economic developments in Ukraine, especially for small- and medium-sized companies. The EU planned to complement the program with a €40 million loan guarantee facility.

After his appointment, EU Commissioner Johannes Hahn visited Ukraine five times in a short period of time and participated in the International Conference on Support for Ukraine in April 2015, as well as the 12th Annual Meeting of the Yalta European Strategy in Kiev in September 2015. In July 2015, the first meeting of the EU-Ukraine Association Committee reviewed Ukraine's reform progress and the challenges ahead.

As a statement announced, the Eastern Partnership aimed to explore the possibility of upgrading the legal basis of the relationship between the EU and the Eastern neighbors. It sought to do so by replacing the existing Partnership and Cooperation Agreements through the Association Agreements, which established the Deep and Comprehensive Free Trade Areas (DCFTA) and visa liberalization between the EU and partner states.[61]

It was not a secret that the EU had even more ambitious plans: namely, integrating the former Soviet republics into the Union. In the 2010s, Štefan Füle, the European Commissioner for Enlargement and European Neighborhood Policy, called in several public speeches for full EU membership for Ukraine, Moldova, and Georgia. In a May 2014 speech in Kiev, he stated, "If we want to be serious about transforming the countries of Eastern Europe, then we must seriously use the most powerful instrument we have for transformation: enlargement." In an interview for the German newspaper *Die Welt*, Füle also announced that "the Association Agreement with Ukraine is not the ultimate goal of our mutual cooperation"; rather, the EU's long-term aim is the "continuation of the enlargement policy beyond the current ambitions, together with deeper integration."[62]

The EU's Eastern Partnership Program, together with a similarly overambitious NATO enlargement plan toward that region (especially Ukraine) pursued by the George W. Bush administration, was a miscalculation. Incorporating the western former Soviet republics into the EU and NATO orbits was more than just humiliating for Russia: it endangered the country's traditional historical sphere of interests. Henry Kissinger and Zbigniew Brezinski, both veteran American foreign policy experts, criticized the NATO and the EU policies toward Russia and Ukraine. Kissinger spoke of the mistaken goal of "breaking Russia" instead of trying to "integrate it." He added that the EU "did not understand the implications of some of their own conditions" regarding Ukraine.[63] Brezinski spoke about the need for "finlandization," or the neutralization of Ukraine in order to avoid violating Russia's "sphere of interests."[64]

President Putin did not hesitate to launch counterattacks. As Ukraine and Moldova became closer to the EU, Russia blackmailed those countries by blocking imports from them and canceling oil deliveries. They pushed President Viktor Yanukovych of Ukraine not to sign the proposed European Association Agreement but instead to turn to Russia. That step generated a revolution in Ukraine that ousted the president. At that crucial moment, Putin went much further, mobilizing and assisting the Russian minority in the Donets Basin in eastern Ukraine, generating a Ukrainian civil war and militarily occupying Crimea.

As a special subcommittee of the British House of Lords that investigated the failure of the EU policy in Ukraine stated:

> Britain and the European Union made a 'catastrophic misreading' of Russia ... and 'sleepwalked' into the Ukraine crisis, treating it as a trade issue rather than as a delicate foreign-policy challenge ... Member nations [were] insensitive to the degree of Russian hostility toward European Union efforts to negotiate a closer political and economic relationship, known as an 'association agreement,' with Ukraine.[65]

The failure of the planned further enlargement toward the Western Balkans and Turkey, as well as the collapse of the ambitious neighborhood policy in the South and East, strongly endangered the EU's foreign relations, security, and business interests. Moreover, it generated vicious Russian hostility and overreactions. A strong and aggressively antagonistic Russia created immense dangers for the EU.

In the previous subchapters, I often used the term "failure": failure of further enlargement and failure of the neighborhood policy. By "failure," I only intended to signify that the planned and prepared enlargement was removed from the agenda. I do not mean to suggest that further enlargement would have been a positive and vital development for the EU.

Regarding the neighborhood policy, "failure" also meant that the effort to create a peaceful and friendly neighborhood around the Union did not succeed. It did not mean that the Eastern Neighborhood Policy that targeted and prepared further enlargement toward former Soviet republics was a good policy. If it had succeeded, it would have caused terrible consequences for the EU.

Russia against the EU: its counterattacks and provocations

"Russia"—as an EU analysis clearly stated in 2016—

> has repeatedly tried to portray European integration as a malign force. Whereas the European Commission prefers to operate as a Union of 28 states, Russia by contrast, prefers to employ a tactic of 'divide and rule' whereby it either aims at weakening the centre (Brussels) by playing off one Member State against the other, or undermine EU cohesion and coherence as a whole.[66]

Russia's attitude toward the West was the result of an early mistake by the West after the collapse of the Soviet Union, in which it antagonized instead of integrated Russia. The West installed NATO missiles next to the Russian borders and tried to incorporate areas that historically belonged to the core of the Russian sphere of interests, especially Ukraine, where the Russian state was born in the ninth century (Kievan Rus). All these generated a hostile Russian overreaction.

In several speeches, President Putin declared that Russia was ready to defend Russian and Russian-speaking peoples' interests if they were endangered and asked for help, even militarily.[67] He weaponized the 25 million "Russian speaking" minorities in the former Soviet republics. In Ukraine, it was easy to generate a deadly civil war since Ukraine is a severely divided country comprised of Western-oriented, Catholic, Ukrainian-speaking, West Ukraine and Russian Orthodox, ethnically Russian, and Russian-speaking East Ukraine.

In order to counter European attempts to incorporate the western republics of the former Soviet Union, which had become independent states, into the European integration process, Putin launched a rival integration plan, the Eurasian Economic Union. In an article in *Izvestia*, he spoke about a "new integration project for Eurasia, the future in the making."[68] Copying the EU, in January 2010, he started the formation of a Customs Union that included as many former Soviet republics as possible. At first, Russia, Belarus, and Kazakhstan joined. Somewhat later, Armenia's leadership changed its policy, gave up its EU orientation, and also joined together with Kyrgyzstan. Together these five countries have 183 million inhabitants, but Russia has an overwhelming dominance: it produces 86 percent of the GDP of this Union. According to the organization's ambitious future plans, a common currency will also be introduced, and ideally, economic integration will lead to political integration. Russia and Belarus have already signed an agreement about the proposed political union, which is a future aim of Putin's to include more countries and to restore as much of the former Soviet Union as possible. President Putin also initiated a military alliance with several former Soviet republics: in 2002, he signed the Collective Security Treaty Organization with eight other former Soviet republics.

The Russian reaction to the EU's enlargement plans went even further than that. In the tradition of old Soviet policies, Russia, an economically weak country, tried to increase its international status by military strength. One should not forget that even after the collapse of the Soviet Union and the dramatic economic decline that followed, Russia remained a strong military power. In the middle of the transformation crisis in 1998, Russia had almost twice as many combat tanks as America (more than 16,000 compared to more than 8,000), more than twice as many artillery (16,500 compared to 7,200), and more than twice as many strategic ballistic missiles (almost 1,600 versus 750), and more submarines. Russia remained behind the US only in combat aircraft (less than 3,000 compared to 4,500).[69] With its nuclear arsenal and military strength, the country became especially dangerous due to its autocratic political structure, its suppression of democracy, and its introduction of a modernized form of dictatorship (the "Muscovite model").[70]

President Putin, however, went much further in modernizing and developing the Russian military. The country did not recover from the economic crisis of 2009 (when the GDP dropped by nearly 8 percent); in 2015, it dropped by another 4 percent. The ruble lost half of its value compared with the US dollar. While inflation was at 13 percent, food prices increased by 20 percent and wages were cut by nearly 10 percent (and in several cases were paid only after long delays). According to official statistics, more than three million people, or 13 percent of the population, lived under the subsistence level, while 40 percent became unable to buy enough food or any clothing. The economic and social crisis was reminiscent of, though it did not become equal to, the situation in the late 1990s.[71]

In connection with these economic hardships, emigration reached a new peak: between 2010 and 2013, nearly 400,000 people left the country. In 2016, according to a poll, almost 20 percent of the population wanted to leave. In those years, a devastating capital flight occurred, reaching $50–60 billion annually; $150 billion in 2014 also signaled trouble.[72]

Nevertheless, the new Russian National Security Strategy stated in December 2015 that its goal is "strengthening Russia's status as a leading world power." Besides the inherited nuclear arsenal, Putin started investing nearly one-third of Russia's budget, a huge part of the revenue obtained from the country's significantly increased oil income, into new armaments, modernizing and increasing the nuclear arsenal, and strengthening the country's military power. While in 2006, the country dedicated $27 billion, or 2.4 percent of its GDP, to these goals, in 2016, it spent $69 billion, or 5.3 percent of its increased GDP. As a consequence, Russia elevated to become the second most commanding military power in the world.[73] In a two-hour televised speech to a joint session of both houses of parliament in early 2018, Putin announced the successful development of a new type of missile. He said the weapons were a response to the US's development of its missile defense system. One system Vladimir Putin described included a "low-flying, difficult-to-spot cruise missile … with a practically unlimited range and an unpredictable flight path, which can bypass lines of interception and is invincible in the face of all existing and future systems of both missile defense and air defense."[74]

In 2015, Russia started its first expeditionary military operation in Syria in order to demonstrate its strength and build up its influence in the Middle East, complementing its earlier installment of an air base in Egypt. Increasingly flexing its military muscles (especially since its Ukrainian intervention and the Western reaction to it), Russia regularly launches military provocations in the air and seas against NATO and the EU, especially in its neighboring Baltic and Nordic countries. Between March and October 2014 alone, it committed 40 provocations, including flying long-range "Bear" bombers over the Caribbean and near America and Canada. In 1999, 2009, and again in 2017, Russia performed its usual "Zapad" (West) military exercises next to the EU's borders. In December 2017, the Royal Navy monitored Russian warships in the North Sea and escorted one of them that skirted British waters. Several similar provocations happened in that area. In January and April of that year, provocations happened in the English Channel. Russia also often attacks the undersea cables that carry most of the global communications and monetary transactions. The head of the British Armed Forces, Air Chief Marshal Stuart Peach, warned of a catastrophic threat."[75]

Another form of provocation was the regular use of classic KGB methods, including the killing of Russian dissidents and enemies of Putin on European soil by Russian agents. From time to time in Britain, the mysterious death of emigrant Russian oligarchs occurred, and former spies or double agents were killed. In March 2018, former double agent Sergei Skripal and his daughter Yulia were poisoned by military nerve gas. Soon after, another Russian businessman, Nikolai Glushkov, died under suspicious circumstances. The British journal *The Independent* reported after these killings that "Ten deaths on British soil have been linked to Russia." Among the victims in 2006 were the 41-year-old Russian diplomat Igor Ponomarev and former KGB officer Alexander Litvinenko, who was killed with radioactive polonium. Other victims include Yuri Golubev, cofounder of the Russian oil giant Yuko, in 2007; 32-year-old codebreaker Gareth Williams in 2010; businessman Alexander Perepilidruy (whose autopsy revealed the remains of a poisonous plant in his stomach) in 2012; and Boris Berezhovsky, the former oligarch and member of the inner circle of the Russian leader, who was hanged in his home in 2013.[76]

Various Russian provocations became commonplace phenomena in Europe. In the spring and summer of 2016, the fear of conflict with Russia was rather high, and several leading newspapers discussed the issue. The British newspaper *The Guardian*, arguing against Brexit, added:

> What makes everything even more dangerous is Russia preying on the EU. Putin's Russia has a vital interest in its break-up. The risk is that Brexit could trigger a Breakit through a succession of other exits forced by the angry factions and thereby add too many crises for the EU to cope with. What happens then to Europe's nations big and small, one dares not imagine.[77]

A few weeks later in July 2016, just before the two-day NATO summit in Warsaw met to discuss the Russian danger, the *Financial Times* reported from Berlin that Chancellor Angela Merkel "said Moscow had undermined European security in 'words and deeds' by infringing Ukraine's borders and 'profoundly disturbed' Nato's [*sic.*] eastern members who therefore require the unambiguous back-up of the alliance."[78]

Military threats and provocations, however, are not the most important elements of the Russian political strategy. The Kremlin's goal is to weaken and, if possible, dismantle the Western alliance. In 2013, an article published in a Russian military journal explained the so-called "Gerasimov Doctrine," as it has become known. It discussed "hybrid" warfare, preferring the use of nonmilitary over military measures.

Exploiting the conflicts and weaknesses of the West, the Russians are working to build alliances with some of the member or candidate countries of the EU and NATO, including Italy, Hungary, and Turkey, and to establish security cooperation, arms sales, and joint military exercises with Western Balkan countries such as Bosnia, Serbia, Kosovo, and Macedonia. President Putin supported Serbia, opposed Western interventions and the decision regarding Kosovo's independence, and sought to build political cooperation. In 2015, the London School of Economics and South East European Studies at Oxford held a conference on Russia's presence and policies in the Balkans.[79]

In addition to diplomacy, a primary component of Moscow's strategy is launching a war of disinformation in order to influence elections and referenda. That was an old Soviet KGB method called "active measures." Using a forged letter supposedly by Lee Harvey Oswald, they spread conspiracy theories, including the news that the CIA was behind the Kennedy assassination. This psychological warfare nowadays uses broad modern communication technology, such as Facebook and Twitter, to spread narratives through social media about the corruption of the political elite, migration problems, the negative social consequences of globalization, and the negative role of the European Commission's bureaucrats. These beliefs have all found fertile soil in both left-wing anti-globalization circles and among right-wing cultural traditionalists in Europe, and contributed to the undermining of public trust. Russia also continues to try to influence important elections and referenda. Out of ten million Twitter messages about Brexit surveyed, Russian bots spread impressions that totaled one-third of those generated by the "Vote Leave" campaign.[80] Similar intervention penetrated the 2016 American presidential election, where the Russians supported Donald Trump in part in order to damage US–EU connections. As the American Department of Homeland Security reported, Russian state-supported hackers tried to breach election systems in 21 states in the US.[81] The facts of the Russian information warfare against American democracy were corroborated by Special Counsel Robert Mueller's investigation.

Russian organizations also made an agreement with populist parties in Western Europe, such as the Italian Northern League, the Austrian Freedom Party, and the Alternative for Germany Party. After the March killing of a former Russian double agent in England, the West and the EU demonstrated solidarity with Britain and expelled hundreds of Russian diplomats. Putin's alliance building in Europe was clearly demonstrated by the fact that a few EU member countries—Greece, Bulgaria, Austria, Slovakia, Slovenia, Cyprus, and Malta—did not join the solidarity demonstration. As *Politico Europe* summed up in an article titled "Russia's plot against the West,"

> Moscow sees liberal democracy as a threat and therefore must defeat it, either by force of arms in Ukraine and an attempted coup in Montenegro, or through non-violent means in the West, bringing us down to the Kremlin's own, depraved level through corruption, disinformation and support for nationalist political movements. ... Europe's political stability, social cohesion, economic prosperity and security are more threatened today than at any point since the Cold War, Russia is destabilizing the Continent on every front.[82]

Europe's dangerous oil dependence on Russia and the EU's plans to eliminate it

An important weapon of Russian policy and alliance building is the Kremlin's oil diplomacy. Because of Putin's complex warfare, Europe's strong dependence on Russian energy delivery poses an important security threat. In various cases, especially against Ukraine or Moldova, President Putin used this weapon. On January 1, 2006, Gazprom suspended all gas supplies to Ukraine, following Ukraine's refusal to sign a renewed supply contract which would have envisaged a significant price increase. This weapon was used again in 2009, as well as during the Ukraine crisis and annexation of Crimea in 2014. The shutdown of pipelines and refusal to deliver oil became a "tool for intimidation and blackmail."[83] By the EU, this "dependence on Russia is increasingly viewed as [a] vulnerability." It takes account of the political leverage that Russia possesses as a result of supplying more than one-third of total EU gas imports via its state-controlled export monopoly Gazprom (37.5 per cent in 2015).[84] In several countries such as Estonia, Lithuania, Finland, Slovakia, and Bulgaria, dependence on Russian gas imports reached 100, or nearly 100, percent. Starting from the late 1990s, Russian energy firms such as Lukoil and Gazprom have made inroads into Romania, Serbia, and Bosnia as well. The Balkan countries use between 87 and 100 percent Russian natural gas. The dependence of Greece, the Czech Republic, Hungary, Slovenia, and Poland is also between 50 and 75 percent.

Russia is also Europe's main supplier of crude oil. About 35 percent of the EU's crude import needs are supplied by Russia (33 percent comes from Organization of the Petroleum Exporting Countries (OPEC)). Germany, the Netherlands, and Poland are among the main receivers. Besides crude oil, Russia is also an important producer of refined products: products from Russia account for 84 percent of the refined products exported into Europe. Including coal (where 28 percent of Europe's imports originate from Russia as well), 53 percent of Europe's energy is imported from Russia.[85] Even in 2016–17, Gazprom, Russia's state-run export monopoly, shipped a record amount of gas to the EU; the company is still responsible for about 34 percent of the EU's fuel imports from Russia. Royal Dutch Shell and British Petroleum both forecasted that achieving European energy independence may not happen soon. This calculation was based upon the realization that these plans need time, and the recognition that several member countries have long-term legal contracts with Russia that reach even beyond 2025–30.[86]

This strong dependence has had major security implications: it led to a European effort to reorient its energy trade and replace imports with other, mainly reproducible, energy sources as much as possible. In October 2014, the European Council accepted a plan to establish energy security by 2030. According to this idea, an Energy Union among the countries would work closely together to decrease demand and diversify suppliers, making common purchasing agreements. The EU adopted the 20-20-20 Energy Program (decreasing consumption, reducing emission each by one-fifth compared to 1990, and covering 20 percent of the energy consumption by renewable energy). This plan was modified in 2014 to include a call to cut greenhouse emissions by 40 percent compared to 1990 levels, reduce consumption by 30 percent, and use 27 percent renewable energy by 2030.[87]

The EU countries developed an Integrated National Energy and Climate Plan covering the period from 2021 to 2030. The cooperating countries have to report on the progress they make in implementing the Integrated Plans on a biennial basis. The Commission monitors the progress of the EU as a whole and reports it in the annual State of the Energy Union report.

To reach the goals of the energy plans, the EU wants to halve the use of conventionally fueled cars in urban transport by 2030 and eliminate them entirely in cities by 2050, as well as set a 40 percent requirement for the use of sustainable low-carbon fuels in aviation. According to the long-term plans, the amount of freight transported by road will be shifted to other transport modes (30 percent by 2030 and 50 percent by 2050 for distances over 300 km).[88]

Special focus will also be given to heating and cooling buildings and industrial activities, which account for 40 and 25 percent of total energy consumption in the EU, respectively. The EU is also increasing energy production and diversifying supplier countries and routes, thus entailing effective negotiations with Norway, Saudi Arabia, and new partners like countries in the Caspian Basin region.

The plan also calls for close cooperation among the member countries in order to complete the internal energy market and build missing infrastructure links. These developments will enable the EU to respond quickly to supply disruptions and to redirect energy across the EU to where it is needed, strengthening emergency and solidarity mechanisms and protecting critical infrastructure. This increased coordination between EU countries will help optimize existing storage facilities, develop reverse flows, conduct risk assessments, and put in place supply plan security at regional and EU levels.[89]

These are long-term plans, but as the European Commission has reported, a radical transformation is already underway in the areas of energy production and use. Important progress happened in the employment restructuring that is at the heart of this energy transition. By 2015, the EU had 1.6 million people working on renewables and energy efficiency. This represents a growth of 13 percent since 2010—more than seven times faster compared to the 1.7 percent employment increase for the whole EU economy. The EU-wide share of renewable energy use increased from 9.7 percent in 2007 to 16.4 percent in 2015. By 2040, projections indicate that renewable energy sources will represent 60 percent of the European electricity mix, up from 24 percent in 2015, with solar representing half of the additional installed capacity and wind receiving half of all power capacity investment.[90]

China is entering the ring: the Balkan Silk Road

Besides the problem of Turkish and Russian hostility, China, the new rising world power, also expressed economic and political interests in the traditional spheres of the EU, the Balkans, and Eastern Europe. This ambitious new superpower strengthened its domestic front by eliminating freshly introduced democratic rules and reintroducing autocratic power structures. President Xi Jinping's power became lifelong and absolute. He is trying to gain international influence by weakening rival great powers. The US gave up this ambition under President Trump, and the Atlantic alliance was weakened. The EU, however, remained a strong rival. China is playing the economic card as a political weapon to weaken it.

China was actually welcomed by anti-EU populist forces in Central Europe. The Hungarian government of Viktor Orbán declared its Global Opening Policy in 2011. This was followed in 2012 by a new foreign economic policy—the Eastern Opening strategy. "The main objective of this policy," an EU analysis stated, "has been to reduce the dependency of Hungary's economy on trade with Europe through increased economic relations with the East." Poland also

> strives to diversify its exports, which it sees as overly dependent on the EU (77% in 2014), provide support for Polish companies entering developing markets, and attract new investments. ... Poland has the most developed

relations with China, with which it signed a strategic partnership in December 2011 … Hungary has a specific strategy towards China … and was the first to work towards a closer partnership. Poland is the only country among the V4 that is a founding member of the China-led Asian Infrastructure Investment Bank (AIIB) and a strategic partner. … Domestic media echoed the importance of the country's role as a gateway to China while international media reported about a new Chinese-Hungarian 'special relationship,' which caused mixed feelings … [at] the EU institutions.

In 2010, Hungary alone took in 89 percent of the Chinese capital flow to the Central-East European region. Between 2005 and 2014, the amount of Chinese investment had increased from $0.65 million to $556 million, which is by far the highest in the region. In the coming years, China wants to transform two countryside airports in Szombathely and Debrecen into major European cargo bases.[91]

In May 2017, President Xi Jinping organized a conference, the "Belt and Road Forum," in Beijing. Presidents and prime ministers from Russia, Turkey, Greece, Hungary, Poland, Serbia, and the Czech Republic participated. The Chinese government signed economic and trade agreements with 30 governments, including several former Soviet republics such as Belarus, Georgia, and Armenia, and with a series of Balkan countries, among them Albania, Bosnia, Montenegro, and Serbia. The Chinese Export-Import Bank also signed a loan agreement with the Serbian government regarding the modernization of the Hungarian-Serbian Railway Line. President Xi Jinping launched the Belt and Road Initiative in 2013 and started building a transport route and logistic corridor in the Balkans called "The Balkan Silk Road." In 2014, China also signed the "Gate towards Europe" agreement with Greece. Chinese investment in this country started in 2009 when the Ocean Shipping Company, the biggest in China, leased half of the Greek state-owned Piraeus Port Authority's container port for 35 years for €678 million and then bought a 51 percent majority of the port for another €280.5 million in 2016. In the same year, China's State Grid Corporation purchased a 24 percent stake in Greece's power grid operator ADMIE.

The Chinese investments in Greece are only a part of the "16+1 Initiative" established in Warsaw in 2012, which targeted trade and economic relations with 16 Central and East European countries. Summits of this group were held every year in one of the capital cities organized by the Beijing-based "Cooperation between China and Central and Eastern European Countries." In 2013, the Chinese-CEE Investment Cooperation Fund was opened with a $500 million amount paid by two Chinese banks. In 2016, a second China-CEE Investment Fund was launched with $11 billion. In 2017, the Bank of China opened a subsidiary in Hungary and a branch in Belgrade. Chinese companies are building a Danube bridge in Belgrade with a $260 million Chinese loan. The Chinese Export-Import Bank will finance 85 percent of the Belgrade-Budapest high-speed railroad as well. The $2.89 billion project triggered an EU investigation because the Hungarian government did not keep the EU law about proper public tender.

In connection with major Chinese investment projects in the region, trade contacts also increased. Between 2009 and 2014, the total trade between China and the region doubled to more than $60 billion. This was highly concentrated on five countries of the region—Poland, the Czech Republic, Hungary, Slovakia, and Romania—which constitute 80 percent of the trade exchange. The possible political consequences and dangers for the EU are evident.

Trade connections were partly realized on the EU-China rail transports, which have increased by hundredfold from 2011, when the first regular connections were introduced. Nearly 7,000 freight trains were launched in both directions and transport about 4 percent of overall EU-China trade. There are also plans to build industrial parks along the railway routes to attract Chinese investors. China was also interested in developing the so-called China-Europe Land-Sea Express Line connecting Chinese ports with the port of Piraeus in Greece. "China's involvement in expanding transport corridors via the Balkans has sparked major controversy within the EU."[92]

"The 16+1 framework for cooperation is China's most advanced sub-regional diplomatic initiative in Europe," *The Diplomat* summed in November 2017. The agreement involves

> 11 Central and Eastern European EU member states and five Balkan states, each in the process of negotiating their accession to the EU. In the aftermath of the financial crisis, Beijing initiated this format with the promise to foster investment, economic and trade cooperation, and to bring connectivity projects to the region … with the aim to facilitate Chinese access to the European market, to export China's excess capital and labor, and to build its global power.

The European Parliament recognized the danger and, in 2015, "called on EU member states to 'speak with one voice to the Chinese government, particularly in view of Beijing's present diplomatic dynamism. … The 16+1 group should not divide the EU or weaken its position vis-à-vis China.'"[93]

The Chinese Balkan Silk Road project is a long-term economic connection building plan that has already made China a major complement to the EU's partner investors. "The Balkan Silk Road project," as the author of the major study on this topic concluded, "cannot ignore the risks of creating investment and lending dependencies for countries in the region. … [I]ndividual countries subject to the Balkan Silk Road project are at risk of excessive dependence on Chinese state-led investment."[94] This dependence may significantly strengthen the Central European populist-authoritarian governments by weakening the EU's economic supremacy in this region. In countries where populism is emerging and where it is already in power (such as Greece, Hungary, Poland, and some others), Chinese economic connections, major investments, and trade relations may significantly strengthen the governments' anti-EU policies and independence from Brussels.

This is especially true because the ambitious European project is only part of China's worldwide expansion project. Investments in Europe sharply increased during the 2010s from about $10 billion to $40 billion by 2016. Chinese investors took over a huge part of the Portuguese electric system and bought up high tech companies in several West European countries, which generated some EU measures to control and decrease it. China is on the economic offensive all over the world. Its major pillar is a three-year plan of infrastructural investments in Africa and other parts of the world. This $174-billion plan includes building the "digital Silk Road" with about 30 satellites, which will start in 2018 with a $25 billion investment. By 2020, China will have its own Global Positioning System (GPS)—which will compete with the American one—shared with 30 countries with already signed agreements. All these are parts of the planned $1 trillion belt and road investment in Asia, Russia, Eastern Europe, and the Middle East.[95] With this plan, China entered the ring against the EU.

With their endangered and partly hostile neighborhood, without a rock-solid and unquestionable Western alliance system, and without Britain as a member country, further integration and deeper cooperation of continental Europe became more important than ever.

Notes

1 Ivan T. Berend, *The History of European Integration: A New Perspective* (London: Routledge, 2016).
2 Robert Gilpin, *The Challenge of Global Capitalism: The World Economy in the 21st Century* (Princeton, NJ: Princeton University Press, 2000), 9.
3 Ibid., 16.
4 Ibid., 17.
5 Ibid.
6 Ibid., 93.
7 Kendall Breitman and Kevin Cirilli, "'Unpredictability' on Nukes among Trump Keys to Muslim Respect," *Bloomberg.com*, March 23, 2016, www.bloomberg.com/news/articles/2016-03-23/trump-lays-out-vision-for-gaining-respect-from-muslim-world.
8 Chris Cillizza, "Here's What Was Missing from Donald Trump's Foreign Policy Speech," *Washington Post*, April 27, 2016, www.washingtonpost.com/news/the-fix/wp/2016/04/27/the-gauzy-generalities-of-donald-trumps-foreign-policy-vision/.
9 Cillizza, "Here's What Was Missing from Donald Trump's Foreign Policy Speech."
10 Michael Gove, "Donald Trump: 'Brexit Will Be a Great Thing … You Were so Smart,'" *The Times*, January 16, 2017, sec. *News*, www.thetimes.co.uk/article/brexit-will-be-a-great-thing-you-were-so-smart-to-get-out-09gp9z357.
11 Jon Henley, "Donald Trump's Europe Tour Leaves Leaders Strangely Shaken," *The Guardian*, May 27, 2017, sec. *US news*, www.theguardian.com/us-news/2017/may/27/donald-trumps-europe-tour-leaves-leaders-shaken.
12 Ben Jacobs, "Donald Trump: Marine Le Pen Is 'Strongest Candidate' in French Election," *The Guardian*, April 21, 2017, sec. *US news*, www.theguardian.com/us-news/2017/apr/21/donald-trump-marine-le-pen-french-presidential-election.
13 "Trump Hints at Retaliation at 'Very Unfair' EU Trade Policies," *Reuters*, January 28, 2018, https://ca.reuters.com/article/topNews/idCAKBN1FH0WI-OCATP.

14 Jacques Pelkmans, "Trade Policy-Making under Irrationality," *Centre for European Policy Studies*, March 12, 2018, www.ceps.eu/publications/trade-policy-making-under-irrationality.

15 Jon Stone, "The EU Just Threatened Donald Trump," *The Independent*, January 29, 2018, www.independent.co.uk/news/world/europe/eu-donald-trump-trade-war-us-tariffs-european-union-protectionism-policy-a8183156.html.

16 "EU Official Warn US on Trade: EU Will Hit Back If Needed," *AP News*, accessed August 13, 2018, www.apnews.com/61bd98695fbc4b3793f4d02d58aafd46/EU-official-warn-US-on-trade:-EU-will-hit-back-if-needed.

17 Ana Swanson, "Trade Partners Respond in Kind to Tariff Plans," *The New York Times*, March 2, 2018, Print edition, sec. U.S., www.nytimes.com/2018/03/02/us/politics/trump-tariffs-steel-aluminum.html.

18 Jack Ewing, "Why Europe Isn't Grateful for Reprieve from Tariffs," *The New York Times*, May 1, 2018, Print edition, sec. *Business Day*, www.nytimes.com/2018/05/01/business/trade-tariffs-trump-europe.html.

19 Secretary of State Tillerson was replaced by Mike Pompeo, and Security Adviser H. R. McMaster by John Bolton, in March 2018.

20 Cnaan Liphshiz, "Following Trump's Declaration, European Union Doubles Down on Its Jerusalem Policy," *Jewish Telegraphic Agency*, December 6, 2017, www.jta.org/2017/12/06/news-opinion/world/following-trumps-declaration-european-union-doubles-down-on-its-jerusalem-policy.

21 Karen DeYoung, "Allies Fume over Trump's Withdrawal from Iran Deal but Have Few Options to Respond," *Washington Post*, May 14, 2018, www.washingtonpost.com/world/national-security/allies-fume-over-trumps-withdrawal-from-iran-deal-but-have-few-options-to-respond/2018/05/14/c7232052-57a7-11e8-b656-a5f8c2a9295d_story.html.

22 Rick Noack, "Hours into His New Job, Trump's Ambassador to Germany Offends His Hosts," *Washington Post*, May 9, 2018, sec. *World*, www.washingtonpost.com/news/world/wp/2018/05/09/hours-into-his-new-job-trumps-ambassador-to-germany-offends-his-hosts/.

23 The Editorial Board, "An Indecent Disrespect," *The New York Times*, May 16, 2018, sec. *Opinion*, www.nytimes.com/2018/05/15/opinion/europe-allies-iran-deal-trump.html.

24 Elizabeth Schulze, "How Trump's Criticism of the EU Makes the Region Stronger," *CNBC*, August 14, 2017, www.cnbc.com/2017/08/14/how-trumps-criticism-of-the-eu-makes-the-region-stronger.html.

25 "Turkey-EU Relations," Government, Republic of Turkey Ministry of Foreign Affairs, accessed August 13, 2018, www.mfa.gov.tr/relations-between-turkey-and-the-european-union.en.mfa.

26 "2007 Annual Report on Phare, Turkey Pre-Accession, Cards and Transition Facility," EU Commission - COM Document (Commission to the EU Council, the European Parliament and the Economic and Social Committee, December 22, 2008), http://aei.pitt.edu/45571/.

27 Kathleen Schuster, "Turkey-EU Relations: Which Countries Are for or against Turkish Accession? | DW | 06.09.2017," *Deutsche Welle*, September 9, 2017, www.dw.com/en/turkey-eu-relations-which-countries-are-for-or-against-turkish-accession/a-40381533.

28 "Erdogan: Turkey No Longer Needs EU Membership but Will Not Abandon Talks," *Deutsche Welle*, October 2, 2017, www.dw.com/en/erdogan-turkey-no-longer-needs-eu-membership-but-will-not-abandon-talks/a-40771731.

29 Neil MacFarquhar and Tim Arango, "Putin and Erdogan, Both Isolated, Reach Out to Each Other," *The New York Times*, December 21, 2017, sec. *World*, www.nytimes.com/2016/08/09/world/europe/russia-putin-turkey-erdogan-syria.html.

30 Jim Mattis, "Hallway Press Gaggle by Secretary Mattis," *Transcript*, accessed August 13, 2018, www.defense.gov/News/Transcripts/Transcript-View/Article/1371000/hallway-press-gaggle-by-secretary-mattis/.

31 "2007 Annual Report on Phare, Turkey Pre-Accession, Cards and Transition Facility."

32 "Commission Opinion on Serbia's Application for Membership of the European Union. Communication from the Commission to the European Parliament and the Council," EU Commission - COM Document (European Commission, October 12, 2011), http://aei.pitt.edu/44516/.

33 Regarding the planned but shelved membership of the West Balkan countries, see Michael Schmunk, "The Western Balkans' EU-Perspective in an Era of New Challenges and New Uncertainties," *Südosteuropa* 57, no. 4–5 (2017): 26–39.

34 "Strategy for the Western Balkans," Weekly Meeting Notes (Strasbourg: European Commission, February 6, 2018), https://ec.europa.eu/commission/news/strategy-western-balkans-2018-feb-06_en.

35 "Western Balkans," Government, European Commission, accessed August 13, 2018, http://ec.europa.eu/trade/policy/countries-and-regions/regions/western-balkans/.

36 "Communication from the Commission to the European Parliament, the Council, the European Economic and Social Committee and the Committee of the Regions," European Commission Communication (Strasbourg: European Commission, June 2, 2018), https://ec.europa.eu/commission/sites/beta-political/files/communication-credible-enlargement-perspective-western-balkans_en.pdf.; "Conclusions by the President of the European Council in March 2017," https://ec.europa.eu/commission/sites/beta-political/files/communication-credible-enlargement-perspective-western-balkans_en.pdf.

37 "Enlargement Strategy and Main Challenges 2009–2010. Communication from the Commission to the European Parliament and the Council," EU Commission - COM Document (European Commission, October 14, 2009), http://aei.pitt.edu/44749/.

38 "Enlargement Strategy and Main Challenges 2010–2011. Communication from the Commission to the European Parliament and the Council," EU Commission - COM Document (European Commission, November 9, 2010), http://aei.pitt.edu/44755/.

39 Marc Santora, "What's in a Name? For Macedonia, the Key to Peace and Security," *The New York Times*, April 10, 2018, sec. *World*, www.nytimes.com/2018/03/20/world/europe/macedonia-greece-name.html.

40 Steven Erlanger, "In a New Cold War with Russia, Balkans Become a Testing Ground," *The New York Times*, April 11, 2018, sec. *World*, www.nytimes.com/2018/04/10/world/europe/european-union-balkans.html.

41 Dimitar Bechev, "Russia in the Balkans," *Conference Report* (London: The London School of Economics, March 13, 2015), www.lse.ac.uk/LSEE-Research-on-South-Eastern-Europe/Assets/Documents/Events/Conferences-Symposia-Programmes-and-Agendas/2015-Report-Russia-in-the-Balkans-merged-document.pdf.

42 Erlanger, "In a New Cold War with Russia, Balkans Become a Testing Ground."

43 Ibid.

44 "Bosnia and Herzegovina 2013 Progress Report, Accompanying the Document 'Communication from the Commission to the European Parliament and the Council: Enlargement Strategy and Main Challenges 2013–2014,'" EU Commission - SEC Document, October 16, 2013, http://aei.pitt.edu/58244/.

45 "Commission Opinion on Albania's Application for Membership of the European Union. Analytical Report Accompanying the Communication. Commission Staff Working Document," EU Commission - SEC Document (European Commission, November 9, 2010), http://aei.pitt.edu/44522/.

46 "Commission Opinion on Montenegro's Application for Membership of the European Union. Communication from the Commission to the European Parliament and the Council," EU Commission - COM Document (European Commission, November 9, 2010), http://aei.pitt.edu/44518/.

47 See Berend, *The History of European Integration*.

48 "Tripoli Declaration after the 3rd Africa EU Summit" (The Africa-EU Partnership, December 1, 2010), www.africa-eu-partnership.org/en/stay-informed/news/tripoli-declaration-after-3rd-africa-eu-summit.

49 "The Barcelona Process or Euro-Mediterranean Partnership," *Barcelona*, accessed August 13, 2018, www.barcelona.com/barcelona_news/the_barcelona_process_or_ euro_mediterranean_partnership.

50 "Euro-Mediterranean Partnership," Government, European Commission, accessed August 13, 2018, http://ec.europa.eu/trade/policy/countries-and-regions/regions/ euro-mediterranean-partnership/.

51 Nicole Koenig, "Taking the ENP Beyond the Conception-Performance Gap," Jacques Delors Institut – Berlin, no. 160 (March 22, 2016), www.delorsinstitut.de/2015/ wp-content/uploads/2016/03/ENPStrategicOrientation-Koenig-JDIB-Mar16.pdf.

52 Tamirace Fakhoury, "Tangled Connections between Migration and Security in the Wake of the Arab Uprisings: A European Perspective," Istituto Affari Internazionali Working Papers, New-Med Research Network, 16, no. 6 (March 2016), www.iai.it/ sites/default/files/iaiwp1606.pdf.

53 Richard Youngs, "Introduction to 20 Years of the Euro-Mediterranean Partnership," *Mediterranean Politics*, May 2015, https://carnegieeurope.eu/2015/05/18/20-years-of- euro-mediterranean-partnership-pub-60337.

54 "Black Sea Synergy - A New Regional Cooperation Initiative. Communication from the Commission to the Council and the European Parliament," EU Commission - COM Document (European Commission, April 11, 2007), http://aei.pitt.edu/38857/.

55 European Commission, "Ukraine - European Neighbourhood Policy and Enlarge- ment Negotiations," *European Commission*, accessed August 13, 2018, /neighbourhood- enlargement/neighbourhood/countries/ukraine_de.

56 "Action Plan for Ukraine. Communication from the Commission to the Council," EU Commission - COM Document (European Commission, November 20, 1996), http://aei.pitt.edu/6288/.

57 "European Commission Press Release - 1977th Council Meeting," Press Release (Brussels: European Commission, December 6, 1996), http://europa.eu/rapid/ press-release_PRES-96-366_en.htm?locale=en.

58 "Action Plan for Ukraine. Communication from the Commission to the Council."

59 David M. Herszenhorn, "Russia Putting a Strong Arm on Neighbors," *The New York Times*, October 22, 2013, sec. Europe, www.nytimes.com/2013/10/23/world/ europe/russia-putting-a-strong-arm-on-neighbors.html.

60 Mustafa Aydin and Dimitrios Triantaphyllou, "A 2020 Vision for the Black Sea Re- gion: A Report by the Commission on the Black Sea," Other (The Commission on the Black Sea, 2010), http://aei.pitt.edu/7413.

61 For more information about the relationship between Ukraine and the EU, see "Euro- pean Neighbourhood Policy (ENP)," Government, European Commission, Decem- ber 21, 2016, https://eeas.europa.eu/headquarters/headquarters-homepage_en/330/ European Neighbourhood Policy (ENP) and "Ukraine-EU Relations - Mission of Ukraine to the European Union," Government, Mission of Ukraine to the European Union, 2012, https://ukraine-eu.mfa.gov.ua/en/ukraine-eu/relations.

62 Chris Schiltz, "Osterweiterung: Ukraine, Moldau und Georgien sollen in die EU (Ukraine, Moldova and Georgia are to join the EU)," *Die Welt*, May 30, 2014, www. welt.de/politik/ausland/article128540032/Ukraine-Moldau-und-Georgien-sollen- in-die-EU.html.

63 Henry Kissinger, "The Interview: Henry Kissinger," interview by Jacob Heilbrunn, *Transcript*, August 19, 2015, https://nationalinterest.org/feature/the-interview-henry- kissinger-13615.

64 Terry Atlas, "Brzezinski Sees Finlandization of Ukraine as Deal Maker," *Bloomberg. com*, April 12, 2014, www.bloomberg.com/news/articles/2014-04-11/brzezinski-sees- finlandization-of-ukraine-as-deal-maker.

65 Steven Erlanger, "Britain and Europe 'Sleepwalked' Into the Ukraine Crisis, Report Says," *The New York Times*, December 21, 2017, sec. World, www.nytimes.com/2015/02/21/ world/europe/britain-europe-ukraine-house-of-lords-report.html. The article is based on the report of the European Union External Affairs Subcommittee of the British House of Lords.

66 Sijbren de Jong, "Confuse, Divide and Rule - How Russia Drives Europe Apart," Institute for European Studies, Policy Brief, no. 2 (March 2016), www.ies.be/files/Policy%20Brief%202016:2.pdf.

67 See Vladimir Putin, "Russia: The National Question," *Nezavisimaya Gazeta*, January 23, 2012, www.ng.ru/politics/2012-01-23/1_national.html; and Patrick Nopens, "Beyond Russia's 'Versailles Syndrome,'" *Security Policy Brief* (Brussels: Royal Institute for International Affairs, November 2014), www.egmontinstitute.be/publication_article/beyond-russias-versailles-syndrome/.

68 Vladimir Putin, "A New Integration Project for Eurasia: The Future in the Making," *Izvestia*, October 3, 2011, https://iz.ru/news/502761.

69 International Institute for Strategic Studies, The Military Balance: 1998/99 (Oxford: Oxford University Press, 1998), 20–27, 108–112.

70 Steven Rosefielde describes the Muscovite Model in the following way: postcommunist Russia is sustained by

> modernized forms of autocracy, sovereign authority over private property (patrimonialism), de facto tenure grants to servitors (pomestie), rent seeking (kormlenie), network mutual support (krugovaya poruka), plunder (duvan), protectionism (Slavophilism), subjugation, and extreme inequality ... Putin grants revocable charters or sinecures to lesser favorites, who are also required to serve the state.

They are "dismissible without cause. ... their properties and privileges aren't protected by the rule of law. They must play the Muscovite game or fall from grace." Steven Rosefielde, *Russia in the 21st Century: The Prodigal Superpower* (Cambridge: Cambridge University Press, 2005), 68–69.

71 Jan Strzelecki, "Painful Adaptation: The Social Consequences of the Crisis in Russia," *OSW Studies*, no. 60 (February 6, 2017), www.osw.waw.pl/en/publikacje/osw-studies/2017-02-06/painful-adaptation-social-consequences-crisis-russia.

72 In spite of the massive immigration of about five million people from neighboring former Soviet republics into Russia, the country has lost more than six million people, and the Jewish and German populations of the country have been halved. See Timothy Helenaik, "Migration and Restructuring in Post-Soviet Russia," *Demokratizatsiya* 9, no. 4 (2001), http://demokratizatsiya.pub/archives/09-4_Heleniak.PDF; Ankit Panda, "Russian Emigration Spikes in 2013–2014," *The Diplomat*, July 25, 2014, https://thediplomat.com/2014/07/russian-emigration-spikes-in-2013-2014/; "Russian Migration 2017," University, UC Davis Gifford Center for Population Studies, April 5, 2017, https://gifford.ucdavis.edu/workshop/past/2017-03-23-russian-migration-2017/; and Irina Sidorova, "Fewer Russians Want to Emigrate, Poll Shows," *Russia Beyond*, June 20, 2017, www.rbth.com/news/2017/06/20/fewer-russians-want-to-emigrate-poll-shows_786372.

73 See "Russia Military Power" (Washington, DC: US Department of Defense, June 28, 2017), www.dia.mil/Portals/27/Documents/News/Military%20Power%20Publications/Russia%20Military%20Power%20Report%202017.pdf; "2018 Russia Military Strength," *Global Firepower*, 2018, www.globalfirepower.com/country-military-strength-detail.asp?country_id=russia; Harvey Gavin, "Russia's Huge Military Arsenal REVEALED: Terrifying List of Putin's Weapons & Armed Forces," *Express.co.uk*, September 28, 2017, www.express.co.uk/news/world/859324/russia-military-strength-revealed-missile-test-north-korea-world-war-three; and Damien Sharkov, "How Big Is the Russian Army? Putin Wants a Million Troops in His Military," *Newsweek*, November 17, 2017, www.newsweek.com/how-big-russian-army-putin-wants-million-troops-his-military-715122.

74 "Russia Has 'Invincible' Nuclear Weapons," *BBC News*, March 1, 2018, sec. Europe, www.bbc.co.uk/news/world-europe-43239331.

75 Ceylan Yeginsu, "Royal Navy Escorts Russian Warship Near U.K.," *The New York Times*, December 27, 2017, sec. World, www.nytimes.com/2017/12/26/world/europe/british-navy-russia.html.

76 Shehab Khan, "Ten Deaths on British Soil That Have Been Linked to Russia," *The Independent*, March 16, 2018, www.independent.co.uk/news/uk/home-news/nikolai-glushkov-russia-linked-deaths-britain-sergei-skripal-yulia-a8260271.html.

77 Pavel Seifter, "The Real Danger Isn't Brexit. It's EU Break-Up," *The Guardian*, May 26, 2016, sec. Opinion, www.theguardian.com/commentisfree/2016/may/26/danger-brexit-break-up-eu-europe-russia.

78 Stefan Wagstyl and Henry Foy, "Angela Merkel Says Russia Damaging Europe's Security," *Financial Times*, July 7, 2016, www.ft.com/content/b2d16102-4446-11e6-9b66-0712b3873ae1.

79 See Bechev, "Russia in the Balkans."

80 "Russian Disinformation Distorts American and European Democracy," *The Economist*, February 22, 2018, www.economist.com/briefing/2018/02/22/russian-disinformation-distorts-american-and-european-democracy.

81 Ibid.

82 James Kirchick, "Russia's Plot against the West," *Politico*, March 17, 2017, www.politico.eu/article/russia-plot-against-the-west-vladimir-putin-donald-trump-europe/.

83 Alexander Nicoll and Jessica Delaney, eds., "Central Asia's Energy," *Strategic Comments* 13, no. 5 (June 1, 2007): 1–2, doi:10.1080/13567880701539952.

84 Robert Stüwe, "EU External Energy Policy in Natural Gas: A Case of Neofunctionalist Integration?" *Discussion Paper*, 2017, www.zei.uni-bonn.de/publications/zei-discussion-paper-1.

85 "Supplier Countries," European Commission, accessed August 14, 2018, https://ec.europa.eu/energy/en/topics/imports-and-secure-supplies/supplier-countries.

86 Elena Mazneva and Anna Shiryaevskaya, "Putin's Russia Seen Dominating European Gas for Two Decades," *Bloomberg.com*, March 1, 2017, www.bloomberg.com/news/articles/2017-03-01/putin-s-russia-seen-dominating-european-energy-for-two-decades.

87 Georg Zachmann, "Elements of Europe's Energy Union," *Policy Paper*, September 2014, www.bruegel.org/publications/publication-detail/publication/846-elements-of-europes-energy-union/.

88 "Electric Vehicles in Europe," *EEA Report* (Copenhagen: European Environment Agency), accessed August 14, 2018, www.eea.europa.eu/publications/electric-vehicles-in-europe.

89 "Energy Strategy and Energy Union - Energy - European Commission," European Commission, accessed August 14, 2018, /energy/en/topics/energy-strategy-and-energy-union.

90 "The Strategic Energy Technology (SET) Plan" (European Commission, 2017), https://setis.ec.europa.eu/sites/default/files/setis%20reports/2017_set_plan_progress_report_0.pdf.

91 Patryk Kugiel, "V4 Goes Global: Exploring Opportunities and Obstacles in the Visegrad Countries' Cooperation with Brazil, India, China and South Africa" (Warsaw: Polish Institute of International Affairs, March 2010), www.pism.pl/files/?id_plik=21522.

92 Jakub Jakóbowski, Konrad Popławski, and Marcin Kaczmarski, "The Silk Railroad. The EU-China Rail Connections: Background, Actors, Interests," *OSW Studies* 72 (February 2018), www.osw.waw.pl/en/publikacje/osw-studies/2018-02-28/silk-railroad-eu-china-rail-connections-background-actors.

93 Lucrezia Poggetti, "China's Charm Offensive in Eastern Europe Challenges EU Cohesion," *The Diplomat*, November 24, 2017, https://thediplomat.com/2017/11/chinas-charm-offensive-in-eastern-europe-challenges-eu-cohesion/.

94 Jens Bastian, China in the Balkans, "firmly in play in the coming years," interview by Francesco Martino, Transcript, November 28, 2017, www.balcanicaucaso.org/eng/Areas/Balkans/China-in-the-Balkans-firmly-in-play-in-the-coming-years-184178.

95 Daniel E. Franklin, "The World in 2018," *The Economist*, 2018, 67.

11

OUT FROM CRISIS OR BETWEEN CRISES? THE EU OF THE FUTURE

"After a decade of struggles," a European Union (EU) policy paper stated in February 2018, "the eurozone today is an island of relative stability in a turbulent sea."[1] Jean Monnet's famous and oft-quoted sentence from his memoirs—"I have always believed that Europe would be built through crisis, and that it would be the sum of their solutions"[2]—became common wisdom. The EU was born from Europe's most tragic and dramatic crisis: World War II. It was reborn from the crisis-ridden 1980s after two devastating oil crises and cutthroat competition in the globalizing world that shocked the Continent. These challenges led to an effective regionalization in the new frameworks of the Single Market and the common currency, which significantly pushed ahead the integration process. Did the new existential crisis of the 2010s—the strong, unprecedented discontent with the EU—became a springboard for further integration? The distant past, more recent events, and the present signal a rather mixed message about the possible answer to this question.

Steps of further integration: the road toward a fiscal and banking union

The European corporations were the prime movers of regionalization against the cutthroat competition of American and Japanese multinational companies, which conquered a huge part of the European markets in the 1970–80s when globalization gained ground. The Europe-based multinational companies significantly withdrew from the global market and turned, instead, to the integrated European markets. The unavoidable defense measures that resulted from the 2008 crisis became a new milestone on the road to further Europeanization, at least in the 19-member eurozone economy. During the early 2000s, Robert

Gilpin had already recognized that globalization was not the absolute economic apogee:

> An open and integrated global economy is neither as extensive and inexorable nor as irreversible as many assume. Global capitalism and economic globalization have rested and must continue to rest on a secure political foundation. ... The international rules (regimes) that govern international economic affairs cannot succeed unless they are supported by a strong political base.[3]

This strong base evaporated during the crisis years. The populist movements viciously attacked and successfully contributed to the erosion of the political base. The victory of Donald J. Trump in the 2016 American presidential election radically changed American policy from globalization toward economic nationalism. The "secure political foundation" of globalization was undermined. Trump's election, however, was only a new further development in globalization's decline.

The Economist published two long articles in January 2017 with the titles "The Multinational Company Is in Trouble" and "The Retreat of the Global Company." The studies looked back at the crisis years and concluded their analyses with pretty striking statements: "An increasing body of evidence suggests that [the expansion of the multinationals] has now ended"[4] and that global companies are "heading home."[5] In these two articles, the journal listed convincing facts. "Half of the big multinationals have seen their ROE [return on equity] fall in the last three years."[6] "The profits of the top 700-odd multinational firms based in the rich world have dropped by 25 percent over the past five years."[7] "In the past five years the profits of multinationals have dropped by 25 percent."[8] "Cross-border supply chains [have] stagnated since 2007."[9]

If regionalization was crucial for the European corporate world during the last decades of the twentieth century, it became even more unavoidable during the early years of the twenty-first century due to the Great Recession (2008–16). Europeanization offered a safe and secure market supported by the framework of a strongly unified legal system and product standardization. The common currency also granted the important advantage of freedom from currency value fluctuations and exchange costs.

The new required measures necessitated by the crisis led to further integration of the eurozone countries to avoid the dangerous possibility of the common currency's collapse. To save the common currency and eliminate the major weaknesses that endangered it, the EU had to take important steps toward a banking union and a quasi-fiscal union. The very first steps toward the banking union were made during the depth of the financial crisis on May 9, 2010, when a temporary measure created a safety net for three years by establishing the European Financial Stability Facility with €440 billion in funding from the Member States (this amount was enlarged to €780 billion in July 2011). This institution saved troubled banks from collapse by giving "first aid" to them. Two days later, on May 11, 2010, the European Council decided to establish a permanent institution, the European Financial Stabilization Mechanism. Funding was based on issuing bonds—at first, about €500 billion in value—with the EU budget as collateral behind it. This institution guaranteed loans for troubled banks (with an agreement with the International Monetary Fund [IMF] to double it). The permanent "European IMF," as it was called, started operating in July 2012.

A further major step was the foundation of a common regulatory framework to collectively govern the financial sector of the eurozone. In this framework, the Single Supervisory Mechanism's decision in the fall of 2013 led to the European Central Bank's (ECB's) takeover of bank supervision from national governments. The Europeanized control and assistance worked well when the major Spanish bank *Banco Popular* and two Italian banks, *Veneto Banca* and *Banca Popolare di Vicenza*, were declared bankrupt in 2014. The ECB and European control saved those banks from collapse.

The Europeanized supervision system is well functioning. As Mario Draghi, head of the ECB, stated in November 2017,

> We are now three years into the life of European banking supervision, and the track record so far is encouraging. Though the single supervisor is still a young and developing institution, it has in many ways lived up to the high expectations that accompanied its founding. … In short, European supervision and European monetary policy have proven to complement each other well. It is an approach which confirms the synergies that can be reaped when the right policies are combined at euro area level.[10]

The already existent pillars of the banking union are working and, in the long run, will have major unplanned effects on further financial integration. As the *Financial Times* reported in the summer of 2017, "The European banking union … is shaping up to be the most significant transformation brought about by the financial crisis—not just of Europe's economic structure, but of its political economy." The new system, as the journal stated, "will revolutionise European economic and political relations beyond imagination."[11] Namely, the new EU rule ended the bailout system that assisted the banks using taxpayer money. After 2008, this system became immensely unpopular with taxpayers. Instead, the new "bail-in"[12] system, as *The Economist* named it, forces the borrower's big creditors to take a huge part of the losses by writing off a part of their debt. This system forces the creditors to share not only the profits but the losses as well. Quoting again the *Financial Times*, in time this institution "creates de facto risk-sharing between countries." The transfers from creditors to debtors over time, and it

> is functionally equivalent to transfers from surplus to deficit countries, since the net savings of the former are typically lent to the latter through the banking system. … Where taxpayer-funded rescues have frequently

served to maintain existing ownership and control networks, bail-in can transfer ownership and control from previous owners to creditors who face write downs. … Given the cross-border lending from surplus to deficit economies carried out by Europe's banking system, this will over time make ownership and control more pan-European and more dominated by surplus country investors. This will gradually dissolve the tight bonds between national political and banking elites.[13]

The construction of the banking union, however, is only half-built. The European Commission has already suggested a means of creating the foundation for the missing pillar, in the form of the European Deposit Insurance Scheme. This institution, which was proposed in 2014 (EU Directive 2-14/49), would have Europeanized the protection of smaller deposits by replacing the national protection system of deposits under €100,000. Germany blocked the road toward the realization of this proposal, maintaining that it would have introduced a "transfer union." They argued that "risk-sharing" has to be preceded by "risk-reduction."[14] The latter was forced, as discussed before, upon the financially bankrupt debtor countries through the mandatory instatement of austerity policies. By 2017, the possibility of realizing the European Deposit Insurance Scheme significantly improved and the road toward compromise was paved by excluding the sharing of past losses. "With such a compromise, financial fragmentation would likely recede rapidly, leading to a larger role by private capital in cushioning real and financial idiosyncratic shocks [EU wide]."[15] The slowly emerging banking union, the EU's response to the financial crisis, pushed the integration process significantly further, at least among eurozone member countries.

The same is true regarding the quasi-accomplishment of existing monetary unification without fiscal unification. The latter was a serious mistake of the common currency's introduction. It has never happened in history that monetary unification has been introduced without fiscal unification. While fiscal unification still has not been achieved, monetary unification was introduced as a possibility in 1970 (the Warner Report); the decision to introduce the Single Market in the mid-1980s made this plan even more essential than it had been previously. Nevertheless, monetary unification was a difficult decision for member countries' governments.

In 1989, the historic political change of the year—the collapse of communism, notably in East Germany—made evident the possibility of German reunification. Chancellor Helmut Kohl skillfully worked on the project, which was more than accepted by the US. Although the British, French, Italian, and Russian governments opposed it, they were unable to stop its realization. President François Mitterrand was the first to recognize this and changed his government's policy. Instead of opposing reunification, he initiated monetary unification to bind the enlarged and strengthened Germany to the European Community more tightly. In other words, monetary unification was a political decision. However, going as far as fiscal unification was impossible. The EU member countries were more than reluctant to give up the central economic factor of their national sovereignty, fiscal policy. Governments wanted to keep the right to decide upon their budgets, spending, and borrowing, and not transfer this right to Brussels. Fiscal unification was out of the question.

The French and German leaders of the EU, however, did not hesitate to realize monetary unification without fiscal unification. Mitterrand pushed it and Kohl was ready to give up the symbol of Germany's strength, the Deutschmark, for unification. The French–German duo was the engine of the EU, and thus their agreement became decisive. Moreover, Jacques Delors, the president of the European Commission and a firm federalist, happily joined. He believed that further political integration would soon follow, and that fiscal integration would occur anyway after the introduction of the common currency. In spite of several severe warnings by various experts that it was dangerous and might lead to the collapse of the common currency, the EU leadership went ahead with monetary unification without fiscal unification. The euro was introduced at the turn of the millennium.

During the boom years after the turn of the millennium, the new currency functioned excellently. Its value equaled the dollar's at its introduction and then increased by 50 percent; the euro immediately became the second reserve currency next to the dollar. Meanwhile, this high prosperity generated a credit-fueled boom in several formerly poor member countries. People and governments recklessly spent money and accumulated huge personal and government debts. When the 2008 financial crisis hit hard, several peripheral member countries became unable to repay the debts and became bankrupt. That was the moment of truth. All of a sudden, monetary union without fiscal unification became a central crisis element, and the euro found itself on the brink of collapse.

At that instant, another weak point of monetary unification, the ambiguous status of the ECB, also became a crisis factor. This bank was established to run monetary policy (deciding the quantity of money in circulation and determining interest rates) but lacked the status of a real central bank. It was not the "bank of the banks," but instead merely the last resort for government lending, since it was not allowed to buy government bonds or control the private banks of the member countries. However, governments were still not ready to correct this mistake and introduce fiscal unification. How could they substitute another policy for fiscal unification? There was no historical example to follow. In December 2011, *The Economist* published an article with the title "The Comedy of Euros." "Once again," it stated, "Europe's leaders have failed to solve the euro crisis. ... Sooner or later, the euro will be beyond saving."[16] In April 2013, however, the ECB declared, "The euro is already 'saved.' It will survive this crisis, it will emerge from it stronger and more countries will join the euro in the future."[17] It really happened because the ECB, as its president Mario Draghi announced, was willing to "do whatever it takes"[18] to save the euro. Indeed, it started buying government bonds from member countries on the secondary market and pushed down the skyrocketing interest rates of weak member countries' government bonds. Similarly, it also initiated a quantitative easing and injected €1.1 trillion in new money into the eurozone. The Bank continued this policy for years. The crisis automatically devalued the euro (without formal devaluation) from €1.5 to €1.1 compared to the dollar. Furthermore, the EU and the IMF bailed out all of the EU's insolvent countries: Greece, Ireland, Spain, Portugal, Cyprus, Latvia, Hungary, Bulgaria, and Romania. The debt crisis was overcome. Fortunately, the congenial leadership of Mario Draghi, the president of the ECB, could cope with its institutional weakness. Fiscal unification, however, remained imperative. Germany forced a mandatory policy upon all of the crisis-ridden member countries that introduced harsh austerity measures that cut spending, eliminated current account deficits, and put countries' financial households in order. A substitute policy for fiscal unification, the compulsory austerity measures—as painful as they were—worked. Although they generated worldwide criticism and contributed to the rise of populist revolts against the EU, there were no other alternatives. Fiscal responsibility, a weak point for several peripheral countries in Europe and the EU, was established through policy measures and rules. Moreover, Germany also forced a constitutional amendment: the so-called "Fiscal Compact." This made a balanced budget mandatory and required a maximum annual budgetary deficit of no more than 0.5 percent and a debt burden of below 60 percent of the Gross Domestic Product (GDP). This substitute fiscal unification became law in the Treaty on Stability, Coordination and Governance in the Economic and Monetary Union, which was agreed upon at the EU summit of January 30, 2012. The treaty was signed on March 2 by the heads of states or governments of all EU countries, with the exception of the UK and the Czech Republic. These steps significantly strengthened and pushed forward economic integration in the eurozone. The unavoidable measures that the severe financial and economic crisis necessitated thus led to further integration. Jean Monnet's wisdom was proven true.

At the meeting of the ECB in December 2017, the bank decided to return to normalcy. This has already become possible: the ECB eliminated stimulus measures and special Bank intervention at the end of 2018, when, according to the Bank's forecast, the EU's economic growth should reach an impressive 2.3 percent.[19] On March 8, 2018, the Bank Governing Council decided to keep interest rates steady, "but dropped language from their communiqué in which they had promised to ramp up economic stimulus measures again 'if the outlook becomes less favorable.'" As that sentence had been repeated constantly by the Bank since December 2016, omitting it signaled "that the eurozone was no longer in imminent danger of going up in flames."[20] This was an expression of emerging confidence.

Saving the common currency only required the aforementioned measures of further integration to occur in the eurozone. That meant the 19 member countries of the zone became much more integrated than the eight remaining EU member countries. The long-advised "two-speed" Europe, wherein not all the member countries have to go together, was virtually realized. Some of the members went ahead with further integration, while others did not join. Although for a long time the two-speed concept was rejected on principle, opposition has gradually broken down. This became already manifest with the introduction of the common currency, which included the possibility of opting out of its introduction. These choices offer a better and easier road for countries that are ready to go further, as they do not face the risk of being blocked by the others that are not.

First steps toward a European army

Another step forward on the road toward integration is the beginning of closer cooperation on military issues, a possibility that has tremendous political significance. The plan to create a European army is as old as European integration itself. In 1950, the so-called Pleven Plan recommended the foundation of a united European army created through the complete fusion of nations' armed forces (with German participation) and a supranational command, budget, and general staff. The plan was named after French Premier René Pleven, who presented this plan to the French National Assembly for preliminary acceptance in October 1950. Although it succeeded then, it was rejected during the final debate at the French Parliament in August 1954.

Winston Churchill suggested the idea of a joint European army in the late 1940s, during the early Cold War years. In 1950, an actual plan was initiated and prepared in Washington, D.C. at the German Desk of the US Foreign Office. Henry Byroade, the author of the plan, sent it to the American representative in Germany, John McCloy, who immediately contacted his old friend Jean Monnet, and went to Monnet's country house near Paris. Based on Byroade's memorandum, Monnet drafted the European Defense Plan and presented it as his recommendation to Pleven. German rearmament, however, was not acceptable to France at that time, and the plan was shelved.[21]

Sixty-seven years passed and, although the plan sometimes resurfaced again, it was never seriously considered. This was largely due to strong and permanent British opposition. As the British newspaper *The Guardian* reported in 2016 and 2017, "In the past David Cameron, the British prime minister, has blocked moves to create EU-controlled military forces."[22] "Former defence secretary Liam Fox warned darkly that 'Europe's defence intentions are a dangerous fantasy' that risked cutting the UK off from the US."[23] A government spokeswoman said, "Our position is crystal clear that defence is a national, not an EU responsibility and that there is no prospect of that position changing and no prospect of a European army."[24]

In 2016 and 2017, however, the situation changed. Three main events should be mentioned as causes. First, the stability of the American security shield for Europe became uncertain. Europe's defense strategies, which since 1949 had traditionally been based on the NATO alliance and the American nuclear arsenal, became precarious due to the election of Donald J. Trump as President of the US in November 2016. Already during his campaign, Trump repeatedly declared that NATO was obsolete; his "America First" policy pushed Europe into the background of his agenda. President Trump's first meeting with NATO and the US's European allies in early 2017 also made clear that he did not want to repeat the basic Article 5 principle that an attack on any NATO member is an attack against all the members. Although members of his cabinet, namely the Defense Secretary James Mattis and Vice President Mike Pence, sent different messages, it became crystal clear that Europe could not rely solely on the American alliance and NATO for its defense any longer. European leaders, as Angela Merkel summed up, recognized that "The era in which we could fully rely on others is over to some extent. ... We Europeans truly have to take our fate into our own hands."[25]

A second factor of nearly equal importance was the 2016 British referendum to leave the EU. Britain's status as a permanent obstruction toward further integration, including the foundation of a joint army, disappeared. The third factor to be added to all these important changes was the newly endangered security of the EU and the emergence of a hostile Russia under President Vladimir V. Putin. His Ukrainian adventure and the border change that resulted from Russia's occupation of the Crimean Peninsula served as severe warnings. Putin started flexing his muscles by investing a huge part of his budget in developing Russia's army and nuclear arsenal. He started provoking the EU with major army movements at its border and semi-regular air and sea provocations in EU member countries' water and airspace by the Russian Navy and Air Force (discussed in Chapter 9). Europe's neighborhood also changed. The EU had to deal with a hostile—although a fellow NATO member—Turkey, an extremely unstable Middle East, and the destabilizing permanent migration crisis, as mass immigration from the Middle East, Africa, and even Asia became a major new factor in the existential crisis of 2015 and 2016.

All these changes required the reconsideration of the foundation of an independent defense force: a European army. In November 2014, the EU elected Jean-Claude Juncker, former prime minister of Luxembourg, as the new President of the European Commission. He belongs to the old federalist guard, and immediately suggested several further integration steps, among them the formation of a joint European army: "If we need to do more with less money, gradually increased defence integration is our best—and only—option."[26] During the European election campaign, President Jean-Claude Juncker had urged for a strengthening of Europe's security and defense institutions. In July 2014 at the European Parliament, he presented political guidelines that pointed out that "even the strongest soft powers cannot make do in the long run without at least some integrated defence capabilities."[27] He mentioned the integration of military capabilities, more synergies in the procurement of defense industry products, and permanent structured cooperation as next steps. His emphatic plea for a European army as a long-term project for the Member States that are ready for it has sparked a much-needed debate. Juncker has strongly articulated the many reasons for creating a joint army. As *The Guardian* put it, Juncker has argued that

The European Union needs its own army to help address the problem that it is not 'taken entirely seriously' as an international force. ... Europe's image has suffered dramatically and also in terms of foreign policy, we don't seem to be taken entirely seriously. ... Such a move would help the EU to persuade Russia that it was serious about defending its values in the face of the threat posed by Moscow.

He also argued that combining militarily "would make spending more efficient and would encourage further European integration." [28] Although at that time this idea was immediately rejected by Britain, it remained on the table, and Juncker met with supporters in Germany and other countries.

Indeed, *Deutsche Welle* reported in June 2016 that a "Weissbuch," or a German defense White Paper, was prepared that argued strongly for an EU army (although Angela Merkel ordered it to be kept under wraps until after the British referendum vote). This reflected a radical change in Germany's view on the topic. John R. Deni, an expert from the US Army War College's Strategic Studies Institute, stated that the *defense White Paper*

represents a paradigm shift in two important respects. ... What is perhaps most significant is the declaration that Germany will be willing to not simply participate in but also to initiate such coalitions. This is a major departure from the past, in which Germany consistently sought to exercise hard power solely through established multilateral institutions.[29]

Meanwhile, Germany soon made some initial steps. Even as the debate about a common EU army continued in Brussels, *Foreign Policy* reported on May 22, 2017, that "Germany and two of its European allies, the Czech Republic and Romania, quietly took a radical step down a path toward something that looks like an EU army" by announcing "the integration of their armed forces."[30] After the change in the international situation that revoked Britain's power to oppose a joint army, Germany and France are pressing ahead with the creation of an EU army. In November 2017, *Reuters* reported that "European defense planning, operations and weapons development now stands its best chance in years as London steps aside."[31] In response to Britain's exit from the EU, Germany and France promoted cooperation in the field of defense between the remaining 27 EU Member States.[32] Substantial synergies in member countries' national budgets intimate the further concentration of forces.[33] France and Germany's defense ministries both proclaimed their eagerness to galvanize the creation of a common EU defense policy. In a September 2016 "policy document seen by Reuters, Germany and France, the EU's two remaining military powers ... made a detailed list of proposals, including a joint and permanent EU command headquarters for its civilian and military mission."[34]

At last in November 2017, the joint army project had a breakthrough at the EU Summit in Bratislava. A few days before the meeting, the *Financial Times* forecasted that about one-third of the member countries would join the agreement.[35] It turned out that the forecast was overly pessimistic. Of the 27 EU member countries, 23 accepted the joint French-German recommendation. (Denmark, Ireland, Portugal, and Malta did not join; Ireland left open the possibility of joining later.) The Permanent Structured Cooperation on Security and Defense (PESCO) was established. In a joint statement, the two ministers of defense, France's Jean-Yves Le Drian and Germany's Ursula von der Leyen, stressed that it was "high time to strengthen our solidarity and European capacities in defence, to more effectively protect our borders and EU citizens, and to contribute to peace and stability in our neighbourhood."[36] The German Minister of Defense made it crystal clear that Germany wants "to remain trans-Atlantic but also more European."[37] The international media was full of news about the integration of military funding, weapons development, and deployment of European defenses to "help reinforce the EU's strategic autonomy to act alone when necessary, and with partners whenever possible."[38] They triumphantly welcomed the agreement. The

> European Union countries have officially launched a new era in defense cooperation Monday with a program of joint military investment and project development to help the EU confront its security challenges after Brexit and as Russia flex its muscles to the east.

Countries

> signed up to the program, known as … PESCO… to improve EU coordination on defense and weapons systems development. It is part of efforts led by Germany and France to reboot the European Union after Britain's shock decision to quit and follows the announcement in June of a 5.5-billion euro ($6.4 billion) European Defense Fund.[39]

"Twenty three out of 28 EU states … have agreed to create … the nucleus of a joint army."[40] The agreement supports the development of rapid reaction forces and an updated military with high tech weaponry and armaments. This "milestone in European development,"[41] as Germany's Foreign Minister Sigmar Gabriel put it, includes "binding national plans to increase defense spending and military R&D."[42] What some are calling "a small step toward a European army"[43] is nonetheless a step toward military unity that many see as a catalyst for further European integration.

Two days later, the EU's High Representative for Foreign Affairs and Security Policy, Federica Mogherini, spoke of a "historical breakthrough":

> This is a historic achievement, but it is not only a day for celebration. It is also the start of a journey on which we will embark together. This is the beginning of a new story, and not the closing of a page.[44]

At the annual conference of the European Defense Agency she announced that

> the EU was currently working on over 50 projects to follow up the deci-
> sion by 23 EU members to create a common defence fund. ... The new
> capability development plan will point at the main gaps we need to fill
> and the sector we should invest in. We will have at least three new tools to
> develop these capabilities. ... First the newly established Permanent Struc-
> ture Cooperation (PESCO). The first projects that have been presented
> already—there are more or less 50—show the great potential of the Per-
> manent Structure Cooperation.[45]

The European Commission reflection paper that was added to a document on
the future of the EU in the summer of 2017 also presented a concept about the
future of European defense.[46] This paper presented, among others, a comparison
between the European and American defense forces that documented the weakness and fragmentation of Europe's weaponry. While the American army has 1
type of battle tank, the EU countries together have 17 types. Europe has 29 kinds
of destroyer frigates compared to the US's four kinds. The US uses eight types of
fighter planes, while the EU member countries have 20 types. Altogether, compared to the Americans' 30 types of weaponry, the EU uses 178 types. Overall,
the Commission's report recommends the joint standardization and unification
of the weaponry.

The paper also compares the defense expenditures, which clearly show that
the European Community of nearly 500 million people spends €227 billion
on defense—less than half of the US's €545 billion (in the country of roughly
330 million citizens). Said another way, the defense investment per soldier in
Europe (€27,639) is only roughly one-quarter of the US's (€108,322). These
facts themselves may lead to clear conclusions about the necessary steps Europe
should take to strengthen the Union's defense. What is even more alarming
is that the EU member countries are spending four times more on defense
than Russia, but militarily the EU as a whole is much weaker than frightening
Russia at its borders. Furthermore, combining the EU's defense market would
make European defense cheaper; the countries together could save about €26
billion per year.

In a somewhat surprising way, after President Trump's clear announcement
of the US's protectionist turn and rejection of NATO and Europe in early 2018,
the leaders of the American defense establishment expressed their dissatisfaction
with the European military plans and PESCO. "American officials have raised
new questions and doubts about these European plans, expressing concerns that
they could weaken the NATO alliance and cut out US military manufactur-
ers from bidding on certain European projects." The American ambassador to
NATO clearly added, "Washington did not want PESCO or a new European
Defense Fund 'to be a protectionist vehicle for E.U.'" As Katie Wheelbarger,

deputy assistant secretary for international security affairs at the US Department of Defense, explained:

> We're going to watch carefully, because ... it could splinter the strong security alliance that we have. ... We are supportive of it, as long as it is complementary to and not distracting from NATO's activities and requirements. We don't want to see E.U. efforts pulling requirements of forces away from NATO and into the E.U.

As former American ambassador to NATO Ivo Daalder noted,

> the failure to deliver a clear American message of support for Europe was a mistake. ... But President Trump and his administration have made it clear that they see a world of competitors, not allies. They had made it clear they don't want a strong Europe, but see Europe as a competitor.[47]

Upon closer look, however, the PESCO agreement does not look like a historical breakthrough and exhibits severe shortcomings. As an EU analysis underlined,

> a significant gap between political rhetoric and military reality is apparent, and often ignored in discussions in Western Europe. ... For some countries, the discussions about strengthening European security and defence policy are becoming a substitute for taking meaningful action in this regard ... [The] agreement on PESCO in this format marked a victory for an inclusive political approach towards strengthening military cooperation in the EU over the idea of creating an exclusive European military vanguard.[48]

In December 2017, the Member States participating in PESCO submitted a list of the first narrowly defined 17 projects which they will jointly implement. Each of those projects has a different set of participants. PESCO is focused on crisis response in the southern neighborhood of Europe; this is reflected in the heightened involvement of Italy, Spain, Portugal, and Greece's involvement (between 9 and 16 projects). On the other hand, the Central European Member States are involved in an average of 1–4 projects and are hesitant participants who do not want PESCO to reproduce NATO in the sense of potentially serving most of the West European military industry (as they expressed it). The Nordic states were also reluctant. The countries that feel threatened by Russian aggression and are members of NATO, especially Poland, regard PESCO with skepticism and would prefer collective defense through a reformed NATO. In other words, the PESCO agreement showcased major differences among the member countries and uncovered significant potential weaknesses for the future of military cooperation.[49]

Nevertheless, in June 2018, nine countries, including Britain (which is leaving the EU), agreed upon a new "European Intervention Initiative." This entity will operate independently from PESCO. It was initiated by French President Emmanuel Macron as part of plans for an autonomous European defense force that was outlined in September 2017. According to the new agreement, this joint force "will be tasked with quickly deploying troops in crisis scenarios near Europe's borders." As the French Defense Minister Florence Parly stated:

> The goal: that our armed forces learn get to know each other and act together. ... Thanks to exchanges between staff and joint exercises, we will create a European strategic culture. We will be ready to anticipate crises and respond quickly and effectively.[50]

The European military integration is inching forward.

Alternatives for further integration

While quite a few important steps were made in the further economic integration of the eurozone and the military area, the institutional framework, decision-making procedures, and several other sources of the EU crisis remained unchanged. Further reforms and a renewal of the EU are definitely needed. But several member countries do not want major changes or even a reform of the existing system of cooperation. The 2010s became an interesting and important period for rethinking the EU. Indeed, there is no shortage of plans about how to eliminate the danger of collapse by further integrating the EU or at least the eurozone. The newly elected and pro-EU French president Emmanuel Macron has an ambitious plan to renew the EU. "Mr. Macron has laid out an ambitious set of reforms," the *New York Times* reported, "for the eurozone and the bloc itself, pushing for more centralization ... both in economics and defense."[51] Among other suggestions, he has proposed harmonizing taxes and the minimum wage to stay globally relevant. He wants a common European asylum agency and border police. His most sensational plan is to create a eurozone finance minister that will be in charge of the eurozone budget and responsible to the European Parliament. This would push fiscal unification a giant step forward. He also proposed establishing a European Monetary Fund to aid Member States in budget trouble.[52]

These ambitious plans, however, were presented when Germany was paralyzed by the lack of a majority party and was thus unable to form a strong new government. Coalition negotiations required roughly half a year before a new coalition government formed in the spring of 2018. During the elections in Germany in the fall of 2017, Angela Merkel led the Christian Democratic Union, which gained only 34 percent of the votes and looked to form a majority coalition. The second-strongest Social Democratic Party (with a 20 percent share) at first rejected the offer to join a new grand coalition. During the first negotiations with a few small parties, the Free Democrats also refused to join, and the formation of a multiparty coalition collapsed. After the caretaker government of Angela Merkel, however, a new coalition agreement was formed with the Social Democratic Party. At last in the spring of 2018, a new grand coalition was established. Nevertheless, the coalition is fragile and there are major conflicts even between Merkel and her Bavarian sister party. Merkel's position is rather weak, and the Franco-German alliance is unable to act as before.

Meanwhile, the political atmosphere regarding the EU has been growing more positive again. Eurobarometer surveys in the summer of 2017 and November 2017 reflected the growing optimism of the people.[53] The majority of the Europeans—56 percent—are optimistic about the future of the EU. This percentage is six points higher than a few months before in the fall of 2016. Optimism impressively increased in France (by 14 percent), Denmark (13 percent), and Portugal (10 percent). In November 2017, 80 percent of the Irish people were optimistic about the EU. Trust in the EU has improved from 36 to 42 percent. At the end of 2017, the poll reflected that, as an average, trust in the EU was higher than in national governments: trust in national governments was only at 36 percent, and at 35 percent for national parliaments. Trust in the EU gained ground in ten countries and was the highest in Lithuania (64 percent) and Bulgaria (57 percent); 68 percent of the people considered themselves to be EU citizens, and at the end of the year 71 percent believed that the EU is "a place of stability in a troubled world." In the eurozone, almost three-quarters of the people support the common currency. Support for the free movement of people (against closed borders) was 81 percent. A significant majority supported the energy union (72 percent), the migration policy (69 percent), and the economic and monetary union (61 percent).[54]

The improving position of the EU is also reflected in the very positive views that citizens of several key countries in the world have on the EU: in China, 84 percent of the people have a positive conception of the EU; in India, 83 percent; and in Japan, 79 percent. Interestingly, note that in the US, three-quarters of the population (in contrast to the Trump administration itself) have a positive opinion of the EU. (In Russia, despite the official propaganda, still 43–45 percent of the people view the EU positively.)[55]

In the stabilizing Europe, the population—in spite of the cracks caused by the crisis and the confrontation between creditor and debtor member countries—still has quite high levels of solidarity and a strong moral standard about assisting those who remain behind. In the Eurobarometer poll of November–December 2016 (during the darkest period of the immigration crisis of Europe, when more than a million Middle Eastern, African, and Asian migrants chaotically flooded Europe), 78 percent of the people who were asked maintained that the EU has a moral obligation to help people in poverty. An overwhelming 89 percent felt that it is important to help people in the so-called developing countries, and 68 percent considered it one of the main priorities of the EU. (Only in some peripheral member countries like Croatia and Greece did most people share the uncharacteristic view that it was not their business and that they did not care: only 31 and 38 percent felt that the EU had a moral obligation to help.)[56]

Has the Pandora's box of discontents that was opened in the early 2010s finally been closed? Optimism has not really reemerged. Several member countries in Southern and Central Europe are extremely critical and are challenging integration in various ways. The time has arrived to discuss the future, to make new plans, and to emerge on new roads. In 2017–18, there were, indeed, already several plans for the future on the table. *Quo vadis Europa?*

Plans for the future of Europe

In March 2017, the European Commission presented a "White Paper on the Future of Europe." The Commission offered five scenarios, including one without any changes, wherein the EU would remain as it currently is. Another scenario was to concentrate solely on free trade within the Single Market, with "no shared resolve to work more together" on various other issues. [57] But among the possibilities for future progress, there is also a scenario for further integration in an à la carte form: "those who want more [could] do more." If "certain Member States want to do more in common, one or several 'coalitions of the willing' may emerge to work together in specific policy areas. These may cover policies such as defence, internal security, taxation or social matters." That was also an explicit scenario for creating a "several-speed" Europe. A group of countries could go ahead with integrating their defense; and others their security, police force, and intelligence. Under this plan, some member countries would establish "a joint public prosecutor's office" to

> collectively investigate fraud, money laundering and the trafficking of drugs and weapons. They decide to go further in creating a common justice area in civil matters. A group of countries, including the euro area and possibly a few others, chooses to work much closer notably on taxation and social matters. Greater harmonisation of tax rules and rates reduces compliance costs and limits tax evasion. Agreed social standards provide certainty for business and contribute to improved working conditions. Industrial cooperation is strengthened in a number of cutting edge technologies, products and services, and rules on their usage are developed collectively.[58]

A more radical scenario suggests further common integration between all member countries in certain limited fields:

> The EU27 steps up its work in fields such as innovation, trade, security, migration, the management of borders and defence. It develops new rules and enforcement tools to deepen the single market in key new areas. ... Typical examples include further cooperation on space, high-tech clusters and the completion of regional energy hubs. ... The European Border and Coast Guard fully take over the management of external borders. All asylum claims are processed by a single European Asylum Agency. Joint defence capacities are established.[59]

Lastly, the Commission described a scenario for radical further integration that would create a near-federal state with a Defense Union, an Energy Union, and a Capital Union:

> On the international scene, Europe speaks and acts as one in trade and is represented by one seat in most international fora. The European Parliament has the final say on international trade agreements. ... In full complementarity with NATO, a European Defence Union is created. ... Within the EU27, there is a strong focus and ambition to complete the single market in the field of energy, digital and services. Thanks to joint investment in innovation and research, several European 'Silicon Valleys' emerge to host clusters of venture capitalists, start-ups, large companies and research centers. Fully integrated capital markets help mobilise finance for Small and medium-sized enterprises (SMEs) and major infrastructure projects across the EU. Within the euro area, but also for those Member States wishing to join, there is much greater coordination on fiscal, social and taxation matters, as well as European supervision of financial services.[60]

The European Commission, without explicitly recommending any of the possible scenarios, called attention to Europe's decreasing strength and, implicitly, the need to stop this trend through further integration. In its introductory part of the White Paper, the Commission presented frightening facts: Europe's share in the world population was 25 percent in 1900, 11 percent in 1960, and only 6 percent in 2015. If the trend continues, by 2060, it will be only 4 percent. The Continent is also aging. Its average median age is the highest in the world (45 years), while the world average is 33 years. Europe's share of the global GDP is also declining. At the turn of the twentieth century, Europe produced nearly half of the world's GDP; a century later in 2004, only 26 percent of it. Moreover, even between 2004 and 2015, it dropped from 26 to 22 percent. By uniting the European forces, the Commission implicitly said that Europe's standing would be stronger. Only a cooperating and further integrating Europe has the possibility of keeping the Continent in the top tier among all countries in the world.

Unlike in the past, however, the EU, the Commission, the Council, and the Parliament do not want to make central decisions from above for the Community. To avoid central bureaucratic decision-making and to cope with the often criticized "democratic deficit" in EU governance, the Commission suggests

> wide-ranging debate with citizens on how Europe should evolve in the years to come. Every voice should be heard. The European Commission, together with the European Parliament and interested Member States, will host a series of 'Future of Europe Debates' across Europe's national parliaments, cities and regions. The ideas and determination of the hundreds of millions of Europeans will be the catalyst of our progress.[61]

The Commission's White Paper was followed by various Reflection Papers on special topics. One of them was the Reflection Paper on the European Defense Union.[62] Another Reflection Paper presented plans for deepening the economic and monetary union, and describes an ambitious plan from now until 2025.[63] "This will involve completing the Banking Union and making progress on reducing and sharing risks in the banking sector." A

> Capital Markets Union is also paramount. … Further political integration could involve a rethinking of the balance between the Commission and the Eurogroup and could justify the appointment of a full-time permanent Eurogroup chair, as well as unifying the euro area's external representation. The idea of a euro area Treasury—possibly with a euro area budget—as well as a European Monetary Fund are also discussed in the public debate, and could be considered at a later stage.[64]

The flexible plans—which range broadly between keeping the present state of affairs to establishing the fiscal, military, industrial, and political union of all the member countries—opened several avenues leading toward the prospect of "an ever closer union," as the preamble to the 1957 Treaty of Rome stated. Further plans are emerging from other circles as well and may continue to materialize. In February 2017, for example, the Brussels think tank Centre for European Policy Studies (CEPS) organized a major "Ideas Lab," with various panels and hundreds of experts, about the future requirements of "reconstructing the European Union."[65] As an example, let's recall the several important ideas for change presented by the ambitious new French President Emmanuel Macron. He recommended establishing a new key position, Minister of Finance, for the eurozone. That would radically push forward the fiscal union of the eurozone countries. He also suggested the creation of a new system for the election of the President of the European Commission. An old complaint is that the current election system, which uses a closed decision-making procedure for this key position, contributes to the Union's "democratic deficit." The existing *Spitzenkandidaten* (or top candidate) system is opaque. The so-called party family groups of the European Parliament—such as the European People's Party and the Party of European Socialists—each select one candidate. After the parliamentary elections, the party family candidate who receives the most votes is the new President of the Commission. A major shortcoming of the system, however, is that the party families are extremely heterogenic groupings. The People's Party family, for example, includes Angela Merkel's Christian Democratic Union (CDU), Silvio Berlusconi's Forza Italia, and Viktor Orbán's Fiatal Demokraták Szövetsége (FIDESz). Macron decided that his new party, La République en Marche, will not join any of the existing heterogeneous party families and suggested that the Union replace the top candidate system with direct elections.

It also pays to quote from the recommendations of a group that includes the former EU Commissionaire and 14 French and German economists.[66] They suggested strengthening the eurozone's architecture. This suggestion is related to Emmanuel Macron's idea but goes even further than that. They called attention to the deep institutional, political, and democratic underpinnings of the euro-crisis. That means that political reforms are also unavoidable. Without it, the monetary union will become politically unsustainable. They maintained that while the creation of a banking union extended by a capital markets union would provide enough risk sharing to act as an insurance system to stabilize the currency union—and thus might convincingly redress the worst flaws of the initial architecture—it is ultimately not enough to ensure its success. Institutional and political issues, rather than economic solutions, should be at the heart of the reform debate. The last few years have shown that the institutions governing the eurozone are not fit for the purpose of preventing crises, and even less so for managing them. Economic policy orchestrated by an ineffective combination of complex rules, erratic market discipline, and loose intergovernmental cooperation arrangements cannot continue to be the way forward for the eurozone. Instead, the Union needs a new political approach, led by a real European executive power that is democratically accountable to a eurozone parliament and enacts economic policies with political autonomy. A mere credit line from the EU budget or rainy day fund for difficult times would be far from adequate to fund such an adjustment mechanism. It would be only possible with a real and sizable eurozone budget, which would perform various critical functions.

All these functions would require new revenues, which could be raised from a portion of value added tax, corporate tax, or even a new carbon tax. The budget of the eurozone could start at a modest size of at least one percent of the eurozone GDP and should exist outside of the EU budget to provide the eurozone with enough financial and institutional independence and flexibility. A European commissioner (finance minister) should be in charge of the monetary and fiscal affairs of the eurozone. He or she would chair the Eurogroup, make executive decisions on its behalf, and be democratically accountable to a eurozone parliament formed by a subset of the European Parliament.[67]

To regain popular support Europe-wide, major structural reforms are also needed to cope with the "democratic deficit" that characterizes the EU's activities as a whole. I summarize an EU document from 2018 that presents the historical context behind one of the new recommendations: popular dissatisfaction with the functioning of the EU is not a new phenomenon. It first manifested in the Danish rejection of the Maastricht Treaty in 1992; similar sentiments were repeated a few times after that and were also expressed through the gradual rise in Eurosceptic and nationalistic political options. National referenda opposed European decisions in Greece, the Netherlands, and Hungary (let alone in Britain with the Brexit referendum). Democratic legitimacy has acute political consequences at all levels, and so far it has undermined the integration process. It is impossible to further integrate in the absence of public consent.

Former institutional reforms aiming at increasing the democratic nature of the EU—such as the introduction of direct elections for the EU Parliament and the gradual increase in its role after 1979 as well as the 2009 "European Citizens' initiative," which enabled one million citizens from at least seven Member States to bring legislative proposals before the EU Commission—did not change the situation. This is clearly documented in the perpetually dropping voter turnout in EU Parliamentary elections, which declined to 42.5 percent in 2014.[68]

Ideas were born from the French experience, especially after the tremendous electoral success of Emmanuel Macron's *En Marche* movement. His pioneering strategy organized a grassroots movement, activating a network of more than 3,000 local committees that were open to join or organize. Their discussions were forwarded to the *En Marche* leadership and included in Macron's electoral platform. This method could be adopted in Europe to "give the people a voice" through the creation of citizens' conventions all over Europe. The ideas of local organizations would be synthesized on a national level through a "European committee of wise persons" from representatives of the national committees. Democratic conventions could become a fixture of decision-making in Europe, increasing democratic legitimacy as a permanent structure of EU decision-making.[69]

In 2018, however, it was not foreseeable what kinds of new and newer reform ideas would emerge and even less so which ones would be realized. On April 20, 2018, a report from Brussels that noted the outcome of the Italian elections and Angela Merkel's weakened position pessimistically concluded, "After all the hoopla, Mr. Macron's proposed overhaul has been gutted. If not 'as dead as a dormouse,' as the German weekly Der Spiegel opined, his European initiatives have been heavily watered down."[70] The question is still open as to whether the EU can further integrate. The EU's institutional and procedural systems, however, definitely need—and are waiting urgently for—reforms. What is more than certain: the EU will change, and it will be different from how we now know it. The most foreseeable change might be the further integration of the eurozone, which is absolutely necessary to stabilize and save the common currency. If this happens, it might create an outer zone of member countries that do not use the euro, especially in Scandinavia, Central Europe, and the Balkans. This is a kind of realization of the "two-speed Europe" idea. A more-closely integrated core that lacks the burden of hesitant or even anti-EU members (which would remain in the outer zone or leave), would make the EU much stronger.

On the other hand, if no important monetary crises happen that demand immediate reform, the severely anti-EU governments currently in power in several member countries may endanger the entire achievement. Populist-nationalist attacks may paralyze any further actions and any further steps toward integration. Stagnation and endless inside opposition may lead to new crises and new actions that seek to undermine the existing integration of the member countries.

In light of the current situation, a common decision and decisive agreement is less foreseeable than before. Even the proposed "two-speed" EU does not offer a full solution. It is strongly opposed by several countries. As Barry Eichengreen phrased it, neither the "one-size-fits-all" nor the "two-size-fits-all" structures are working.[71] Without any doubt, some basic reforms are needed to further strengthen the European Parliament and make it a real legislative body. Other democratizing steps, probably even as drastic as the creation of a direct election for the Commission's President, are crucial. The EU can act together in commonly accepted issues such as the institutional defense of the common currency in the eurozone, the joint defense of the EU's borders, and further development of military unification plans. Considering the strong populist challenge and the weakened German leadership, the most foreseeable and possible option would be an à la carte EU where, through a highly flexible framework, member countries may participate with others in certain projects but choose not to for others. In many ways, this is already the reality. At the moment, the federalist dreams are dead, but they may become resurrected through a future crisis. The EU, such as it is, must be saved not only because of the present advantages it affords to the countries on the Continent but also because of the paramount future possibilities.

Notes

1 Daniel Gros, "The Eurozone as an Island of Stability," *Centre for European Policy Studies*, February 19, 2018, www.ceps.eu/publications/eurozone-island-stability.

2 Jean Monnet, *Memoirs*, trans. Richard Mayne (Garden City, NY: Doubleday & Company, 1978).

3 Robert Gilpin, *The Challenge of Global Capitalism: The World Economy in the 21st Century* (Princeton, NJ: Princeton University Press, 2018), 13.

4 "The Retreat of the Global Company," *The Economist*, January 28, 2017, sec. Briefing, www.economist.com/briefing/2017/01/28/the-retreat-of-the-global-company.

5 "The Multinational Company Is in Trouble," *The Economist*, January 28, 2017, sec. Leaders, www.economist.com/leaders/2017/01/28/the-multinational-company-is-in-trouble.

6 "The Retreat of the Global Company."

7 Ibid.

8 "The Multinational Company Is in Trouble."

9 "The Retreat of the Global Company."

10 Mario Draghi, "European Banking Supervision Three Years On" (Second ECB Forum on Banking Supervision Welcome Address, November 7, 2017), www.bis.org/review/r171107g.htm.

11 Martin Sandbu, "Banking Union Will Transform Europe's Politics," *Financial Times*, July 25, 2017, Digital edition, sec. Opinion, www.ft.com/content/984da184–711c-11e7-aca6-c6bd07df1a3c.

12 "From Bail-out to Bail-In," *The Economist*, January 28, 2010, sec. Finance and Economics, www.economist.com/finance-and-economics/2010/01/28/from-bail-out-to-bail-in.

13 Sandbu, "Banking Union Will Transform Europe's Politics."

14 Tobias Tesche, "Europe's Banking Union: What Progress Has Been Made?" University, *London School of Economics* (blog), November 3, 2017, http://blogs.lse.ac.uk/europpblog/2017/11/03/europes-banking-union-what-progress-has-been-made/.

15 Stefano Micossi, "A Blueprint for Completing the Banking Union," *CEPS Policy Insights*, no. 42 (November 2017), https://papers.ssrn.com/abstract=3078577.

16 "A Comedy of Euros," *The Economist*, December 17, 2011, sec. Leaders, www.economist.com/leaders/2011/12/17/a-comedy-of-euros.

17 Jörg Asmussen, "Saving the Euro" (April 25, 2013), www.ecb.europa.eu/press/key/date/2013/html/sp130425.en.html.

18 Mario Draghi, "Global Investment Conference Speech" (Conference Speech, July 26, 2012), www.ecb.europa.eu/press/key/date/2012/html/sp120726.en.html.

19 Jack Ewing, "Europe's Central Bank, Lagging Behind Counterparts, Faces Eventful 2018," *The New York Times*, December 15, 2017, Digital edition, sec. Business Day, www.nytimes.com/2017/12/13/business/economy/ecb-draghi-rates.html.

20 Jack Ewing, "Europe's Central Bank Is Keeping Its Cool Despite Uncertainty over Tariffs," *The New York Times*, March 8, 2018, Print edition, sec. Business Day, www.nytimes.com/2018/03/07/business/economy/ecb-euro-italy.html.

21 Ivan T. Berend, *The History of European Integration: A New Perspective* (London: Routledge, 2016), 82–83.

22 Andrew Sparrow, "Jean-Claude Juncker Calls for EU Army," *The Guardian*, March 8, 2015, sec. World news, www.theguardian.com/world/2015/mar/08/jean-claude-juncker-calls-for-eu-army-european-commission-miltary.

23 Jennifer Rankin, "Is There a Secret Plan to Create an EU Army?" *The Guardian*, May 27, 2016, sec. Politics, www.theguardian.com/politics/2016/may/27/is-there-a-secret-plan-to-create-an-eu-army.

24 Duncan Robinson and James Shotter, "Jean-Claude Juncker Calls for Creation of EU Army," *Financial Times*, March 8, 2015, www.ft.com/content/1141286a-c588-11e4-bd6b-00144feab7de.

25 Steven Erlanger, "E.U. Moves Closer to a Joint Military Force," *The New York Times*, November 14, 2017, sec. World, www.nytimes.com/2017/11/13/world/europe/eu-military-force.html.

26 See: www.theguardian.com/.../jean-claude-juncker-calls-for-eu-army-european-com... March 8, 2015.

27 Jean-Claude Juncker, "Political Guidelines for the Next European Commission" (European Commission, 2014), https://ec.europa.eu/commission/sites/beta-political/files/juncker-political-guidelines-speech_en.pdf.

28 Sparrow, "Jean-Claude Juncker Calls for EU Army."

29 John R. Deni, "Germany Embraces Realpolitik Once More," War on the Rocks, September 19, 2016, https://warontherocks.com/2016/09/germany-embraces-real politik-once-more/.

30 Elisabeth Braw, "Germany Is Quietly Building a European Army under Its Command," *Foreign Policy*, accessed August 21, 2018, https://foreignpolicy.com/2017/05/22/germany-is-quietly-building-a-european-army-under-its-command/.

31 Robin Emmott, "EU Signs Defense Pact in Decades-Long Quest," *Reuters*, November 13, 2017, www.reuters.com/article/us-eu-defence/eu-to-sign-defense-pact-may-allow-limited-british-role-idUSKBN1DD0PX.

32 Ibid.

33 "Press Release: The European Defence Fund: Questions and Answers" (European Commission, June 7, 2017), http://europa.eu/rapid/press-release_MEMO-17-1476_en.htm.

34 Robin Emmott and Gabriela Baczynska, "Germany, France Seek Stronger EU Defense after Brexit: Document," *Reuters*, September 12, 2016, www.reuters.com/article/us-europe-defence/germany-france-seek-stronger-eu-defense-after-brexit-document-idUSKCN11I1XU.

35 Michael Peel, "EU States Poised to Agree Joint Defence Pact," *Financial Times*, November 7, 2017, www.ft.com/content/29f6fe76-c2eb-11e7-a1d2-6786f39ef675.

36 Alex Barker, "Paris and Berlin Push for Tighter Defence Co-Operation," *Financial Times*, September 12, 2016, www.ft.com/content/fd637b0e-7913-11e6-97ae-647294649b28.

37 Steven Erlanger, "U.S. Revives Concerns about European Defense Plans, Rattling NATO Allies," *The New York Times*, June 8, 2018, sec. World, www.nytimes.com/2018/02/18/world/europe/nato-europe-us-.html.

38 "Permanent Structured Cooperation (PESCO) - Factsheet," European Commission, accessed August 23, 2018, https://eeas.europa.eu/headquarters/headquarters-Homepage_en/34226/Permanent Structured Cooperation (PESCO) - Factsheet.

39 "EU States Ink Landmark Defense Agreement," *Daily Sabah*, November 13, 2017, www.dailysabah.com/europe/2017/11/13/eu-states-ink-landmark-defense-agreement.

40 Andrew Reittman and Caterina Tani, "EU Takes Step toward Joint Army," *EU Observer*, November 13, 2017, https://euobserver.com/foreign/139854.

41 Emmott, "EU Signs Defense Pact in Decades-Long Quest."

42 Reittman and Tani, "EU Takes Step toward Joint Army."

43 Bernd Riegert, "A Small Step toward a European Army," *Deutsche Welle*, November 13, 2017, sec. Opinion, www.dw.com/en/opinion-a-small-step-toward-a-european-army/a-41366311.

44 "Foreign Affairs Council Meeting Minutes, 13/11/2017- Consilium" (European Council, November 13, 2017), www.consilium.europa.eu/en/meetings/fac/2017/11/13/.

45 Aurora Bosotti, "Dawn of the EU Army? 'FULL SPEED Ahead' with Defence Plans, EU Foreign Affairs Chief Warns," *Express*, November 25, 2017, www.express.co.uk/news/world/884091/European-Union-army-military-news-EU-foreign-minister-Brussels-defence-security-video.

46 "Reflection Paper on the Future of European Defence" (European Commission, June 7, 2017), https://ec.europa.eu/commission/sites/beta-political/files/reflection-paper-defence_en.pdf.

47 Steven Erlanger, "U.S. Revives Concerns about European Defense Plans, Rattling NATO Allies," *The New York Times*, June 8, 2018, sec. World, www.nytimes.com/2018/02/18/world/europe/nato-europe-us-.html.

48 Justyna Gotkowska, "The Trouble with PESCO," *OSW Point of View*, no. 69 (February 2018), http://aei.pitt.edu/93565/1/pw_69_pesco_ang_net.pdf. 6,16, 18.

49 Gotkowska, "The Trouble with PESCO."

50 Judy Dempsey, "Trump May Be Doing the European Union and NATO a Big Favor," *The Washington Post*, July 6, 2018, sec. Global Opinions, www.washingtonpost.com/.

51 Steven Erlanger, "At E.U. Meeting, a Hobbled Merkel and a Stalled Agenda," *The New York Times*, December 16, 2017, sec. World, www.nytimes.com/2017/12/15/world/europe/eu-angela-merkel-emmanuel-macron.html.

52 Steven Erlanger, "Emmanuel Macron's Lofty Vision for Europe Gets Mixed Reviews," *The New York Times*, December 22, 2017, sec. World, www.nytimes.com/2017/09/28/world/europe/france-macron-european-union-reforms.html.

53 The Eurobarometer started regular polls in 1974, asking 1,000 people from each member countries questions in face-to face interviews.

54 "Press Release - Autumn 2017 Standard Eurobarometer: Fixing the Roof While the Sun Is Shining" (European Commission, December 19, 2017), http://europa.eu/rapid/press-release_IP-17-5312_en.htm.

55 "Standard Eurobarometer 87" (Brussels: European Commission, August 2, 2017), http://data.europa.eu/euodp/en/data/dataset/S2142_87_3_STD87_ENG.

56 "EU Citizens' Views on Development, Cooperation and Aid" (Brussels: European Commission, April 2017), https://ec.europa.eu/europeaid/sites/devco/files/sp455-development-aid-final_en.pdf.

57 "White Paper on the Future of Europe," White Paper (Brussels: European Commission, March 1, 2017), https://ec.europa.eu/commission/sites/beta-political/files/white_paper_on_the_future_of_europe_en.pdf, 18.

58 Ibid., 20.

59 Ibid., 22.

60 Ibid., 24.

61 "White Paper on the Future of Europe," 17.

62 "Reflection Paper on the Future of European Defence."

63 "Reflection Paper on the Deepening of the Economic and Monetary Union" (European Commission, May 31, 2017), https://ec.europa.eu/commission/publications/reflection-paper-deepening-economic-and-monetary-union_en.

64 Ibid.

65 "Reconstructing the Union - Report of the 2017 CEPS Ideas Lab," *Policy Paper*, May 12, 2017, www.ceps.eu/publications/reconstructing-union-report-2017-ceps-ideas-lab.

66 Signed by *László Andor, Pervenche Berès, Lorenzo Bini Smaghi, Laurence Boone, Sebastian Dullien, Guillaume Duval, Luis Garicano, Michael A. Landesmann, George Papaconstantinou, Antonio Roldan, Gerhard Schick, Xavier Timbeau, Achim Truger,* and *Shahin Vallée.*

67 László Andor et al., "Blueprint for a Democratic Renewal of the Eurozone," *Politico,* February 28, 2018, sec. Opinion, www.politico.eu/article/opinion-blueprint-for-a-democratic-renewal-of-the-eurozone/.

68 "It's Official: Last EU Election Had Lowest-Ever Turnout," *Euractiv,* August 7, 2014, www.euractiv.com/section/eu-elections-2014/news/it-s-official-last-eu-election-had-lowest-ever-turnout/.

69 Corina Stratulat, Yann-Sven Rittelmeyer, and Paul Butcher, "Discussion Paper: En Marche l'Europe?" (European Policy Centre, January 11, 2018), www.epc.eu/documents/uploads/pub_8198_emeurope.pdf.

70 Erlanger, "Macron Had a Big Plan for Europe. It's Now Falling Apart."

71 Barry Eichengreen, *The Populist Temptation* (Oxford: Oxford University Press, 2018), 176.

INDEX